Breaking Through
2nd Edition

Implementing Disruptive Customer Centricity

Sandra Vandermerwe

First published 2014 by
PALGRAVE MACMILLAN

Palgrave Macmillan in the UK is an imprint of Macmillan Publishers Limited, registered in England, company number 785998, of Houndmills, Basingstoke, Hampshire RG21 6XS.

Palgrave Macmillan in the US is a division of St Martin's Press LLC, 175 Fifth Avenue, New York, NY 10010.

Palgrave Macmillan is the global academic imprint of the above companies and has companies and representatives throughout the world.

Palgrave® and Macmillan® are registered trademarks in the United States, the United Kingdom, Europe and other countries.

ISBN 978-1-349-48419-5   ISBN 978-1-137-39551-1 (eBook)
DOI 10.1057/9781137395511

A catalogue record for this book is available from the British Library.

A catalog record for this book is available from the Library of Congress.

Typeset by MPS Limited, Chennai, India.

Breaking Through

Regards

For the six men in my life:
Heath, Mac, Hopefield, Jimmy-Heaven, Nelson and
Vuvuzela

CONTENTS

Contents

LIST OF EXHIBITS

LIST OF TABLES

LIST OF BOXES

DEFINITIONS FOR THIS BOOK

DISRUPTION

A break with the conventional
Changing the status quo
Creating a new industry standard
Causing an unexpected paradigm shift
Overturning old consumer market sector industry beliefs, convictions, assumptions, habits
Uprooting displacing an existing product service or industry
Creating new social and business practices
A different way of doing things
A process of substitution that plays out over time
Breakthrough that brings something to the market that makes customers, organizations and others better off
A new business model that leads to human, organizational and societal progress

DISRUPTION IS NOT

A technology – technology is an enabler
An innovation – although disruption is by nature innovative

CUSTOMER CENTRICITY

Ability to get and stay ahead, by giving long-term value *to* and getting long-term value *from* customers, in a way that makes it difficult for others to catch up

ENDURING

Long lasting
Continuing
Sustainable
Durable
For the long term
Self-reinforcing
Perpetuating
Multigenerational

INTRODUCTION: SHIFTING THE CENTRE OF GRAVITY

Getting and staying ahead

Customer-centric enterprises consistently outpace those that are not, in good times and in bad.

And invariably they are disruptive.

Such enterprises may be traditional organizations reinventing themselves, newcomers changing the existing game or new market makers – that is, outsiders that see and make manifest what others cannot.

Although points of departure vary, these enterprises all have one thing in common. They break the mould and change the nature of the industry. Unfailingly, with enduring energy, they create new standards for customers and themselves. This is what builds them an advantage and makes it difficult for others to catch up.

Customers become the lens through which these enterprises see the world – and their compass for making decisions.

Their consequent customer power becomes their barrier to competitive entry.

How do they do it and how do they sustain this achievement in the long term? Have we learnt enough about them to enable others to follow their example?

This book is an attempt to provide answers to these questions.

What we know they know

Customer-centric organizations start with the basic premise that customer centricity is a dominant logic that should pervade the entire organization. So the challenge to transform from a product or industrial logic to become customer centric is necessarily company-wide, and not an activity to be mistakenly left to the marketing department. Customers are at the core of such firms' missions, into which a higher purpose is embedded. They have, and inspire, a set of contemporary beliefs that attract and keep the right customers, employees, partners and investors – and make them allies.

They know that customer centricity has a starting point, which is the recognition that the transformation will be a journey, a quest to future-proof the enterprise. They take that journey consciously and conscientiously in order to ensure that it succeeds and lasts.

Acknowledging that disruption is not a technology but a way of thinking about how to create growth, they use it as their enabler.

They don't expect customers to tell them what to do – they proactively stretch and foretell a future, which they themselves invent.

Because their missions have higher purpose, which include public as well as individual good, these trailblazers go from being just successful (doing well) today, to being significant (doing well and good) enduringly.

With new mindsets and mindsights they shift the thinking of enterprises to new levels of meaning, actively seeking to change and improve the lives of customers and citizens, and the environments in which they live and work.

They have heightened beliefs that transcend single individuals or enterprises. And they don't believe in trade-offs or compromise, or just making and redistributing money. They believe in creating plus sum gains – new, increased and shared wealth for all.[1] That is what ultimately fuels financial and economic growth for them, and contributes to human progress and social development, in a virtuous circle that they themselves trigger.

These disruptors know that no matter how good or innovative their products or services may be, they bring short-lived rewards that diminish in value over time – unlike customers, who increase in value over time. So they concentrate their efforts on holding on to customers, not products. Their innovations are dictated by their need to create elevated customer value propositions that overturn existing ways of doing things and, as such, are not just improvements that can be copied. They do this with value-generating networks of inside and outside partners with whom they deliver new integrated experiences for customers, which cut across products, units, divisions, companies, industry sectors and countries.

They measure, reward and report success differently from traditional product-focused firms.

And they invest to build a powerful customer base, an asset that they know how to leverage over time, constantly and consistently giving and getting customer value.

Becoming indispensable to customers

We also know that customer-centric enterprises and the champions within them seek to become indispensable to customers. They do this using multiple or omni-channel engagement, which they actively increase whenever and wherever it's possible for the brand to touch the customer. They couple this with continuously recycled and updated information and knowledge, which builds ever-heightened customer value.

It's not that products are unimportant to them or to customers. Who can deny the wonder of a tomato plant that is able to automatically change its genetic structure to fight off an infection? Or a printer that can make a three-dimensional object? Or a car that can drive itself? Or a computer that can be worn like a piece of clothing?

But the point is that however sophisticated these products may be, they are nonetheless easy to emulate. What traditional firms do not understand is that products are only a means to some end or, in customer-centricity speak, the desired customer outcome – what the customer either knows they want to achieve or may only come to know after the fact.

This desired customer outcome is encapsulated in a 'market space' definition that frames the new competitive arena that the customer-centric enterprise seeks to dominate. And, better than anyone else, they fill that 'market space' domain with values for customers.

The reason that becoming indispensable to attaining customer outcomes is so important is that this is the way in which customers 'lock on'. This means that customers voluntarily spend more, over longer periods of time – in the process costing the enterprise less to maintain the relationship. And through their customer advocacy and positive public sentiment, the brand is stretched – with the multiplier effect of compounding growth.

Equally important is that customer 'lock-on', and the capability to achieve it, is the best and only real barrier to competitive entry. Having more products, or more sites, or more stores, or more factories, can never achieve this.

Nonetheless, most traditional enterprises still try to grow by doing more of the same. This leaves them to deal with the whims of disenchanted customers, and the ups and downs of business cycles and share prices. Or, like any other undifferentiated vendor, they become trapped in a price treadmill.

Brains, brawn and balance

Many executives have intuitively grasped the need to reinvigorate their enterprises and the significance of customer centricity in this, and that it requires a fundamental change and commitment. What has held them back from putting customer centricity into practice has been the lack of a systematic process that gets their organization to make the leap, pull people out of their old mindset and then take them along on the journey.

Such a voyage has to do two things simultaneously: It needs to spark the creativity and imagination necessary to see and chart new ways of doing things for customers. This often must be done without the comfort of hard facts, as unnerving as that may be – 'you can't research your way into the future'. And they need to do this, often relying on intuition, foresight and imagination, along a discovery path, with the persistence and courage of only a few select people's conviction at the beginning.

At the same time, the process should also provide the structure and discipline necessary to complement creativity and intuition. Achieving the right balance is fundamental to getting customer-centricity ideas and insights understood and accepted, and making sure that people don't fall back into their old product-focused moulds. It also ensures that sufficient momentum is gathered to maintain the necessary pace and energy.

A common mistake is trying to get everyone aligned at the same time so as to move the organization in one fell swoop. This can't work. People accept change at different rates. So do customers. Part of the success of this formula is that it is a phased and managed approach, getting the right people and customers involved at the right time, moving them through a set of defined moments, which are reinforcing and cumulative so as to reach critical mass. Then ultimately, as the transformation gathers momentum, customer centricity becomes a way of life in the enterprise.

Working from strength is the key. This is not about making everyone happy or taking a vote. It's about picking the best brains and the 'points of light' who 'get it' from the very outset, and will make it happen, even against the odds.

Fusing strategy and implementation

It is ironic that while the importance of customer centricity is irrefutable, actually making it happen remains a conundrum for most executives and most implementations fail. A mere 5 per cent of all organizations implement strategies successfully, 70 per cent do not, and the remaining 25 per cent have some success but never meet the intended potential of the vision.[2]

But if enterprises and those who run them don't learn how to remake themselves, not only do they lose the upside of getting enduring increasing returns, they may risk losing their grip on the market, even becoming extinct.

Before this process can even start, however, executives must first be willing to abandon a long-standing corporate orthodoxy: the mistaken yet firmly held belief that strategy and implementation are two distinct activities, with implementation beginning only once the strategy has been formalized and finalized. This tenet inevitably leads to a disconnect, since those charged with implementing the strategy will lack the deep, rational understanding – as well as the emotional commitment – to actually drive the energy that spurs people on further. This lack is lethal for any kind of strategic initiative, but especially when disrupting an organization and market in order to tap into yet to be developed futures.

In reality, the articulation of a strategy and its implementation are part of one interconnected and reiterative transformation process, with each element reinforcing and nurturing the other. The moment that a catalyst makes the right people see the need for a new and different direction – when it has tempted them out to play and start making the vital moves – implementation has begun.

And once the new approach begins to take root in the market, more people in the enterprise become more confident. They start looking for more opportunities, start building more expertise and achieving more victories, so drawing others in and propelling the implementation further forward at an ever faster pace, as the necessary breakthroughs from one phase to the next are made.

Energizing through positivity

This raises another orthodoxy that customer-centric disruptors know how to conquer: spending too much time on resistance and resistors, an inevitable fact in any change process, since generally people don't like to go outside of their comfort zone. On top of that, customer centricity, by its very nature, raises all sorts of questions and fears – this is because people identify with product categories, are structured into product silos, refer to themselves in product terminology, and are often rewarded by product silo, even at the very highest level in organizations. In general, enterprises have more faith in product than customer longevity and feel comfortable having familiar spreadsheets with product rather than customer projections.

Customer-centric leaders move the enterprise ahead, gripped by the positive energy that builds the tempo and pace that make the journey viable and doable, especially at the outset when the enterprise may be precariously poised in its approach to the new beginning. Otherwise a stubbornly negative pattern can set in, with forces so strong they can stall and even compromise the entire endeavour. No matter how well articulated, how finely formulated, or how critical to the enterprise's future a new initiative might be, under such conditions it will be slow to take off, if it leaves the ground at all.

Working with positive energy or individuals I term 'points of light' has the reverse effect: people feel excited and enthused and so actively seek out opportunities instead of making only episodic changes when it's obvious they are in trouble. 'Points of light' are individuals who not only conceptualize a new market configuration and get it quickly, but want to be the ones to make it happen. The energy of their actions and the strength of their convictions and strong intrinsic belief in customer centricity as the route to lucrative and long-lasting growth, inspire others, 360 degrees up, down, and sideways in the organization.

The customer-centricity transformation process

Disruption is a process that happens when a market takes on a new innovation that substitutes an existing way of doing things, overtaking traditional incumbents, until finally it becomes mainstream – the new standard. But even new ways of doing things can be copied. So disruption must be continuous. Masters of disruption never stop disrupting both themselves and the marketplace.

Customer-centric disruption is different in that its central theme is to get customer lock-on. So, when an enterprise disrupts, it takes customers with it on its never-ending quest to enhance value.

The process of transformation, to get from an inward product focus to disruptive customer centricity, is a well-defined deliberate phased approach, which can be mapped into five overlapping stages. Each phase has its own time frame, marked by ten critical breakthrough points (see Exhibit 0.1). The step-by-step breakthrough moments punctuating these phases are remarkably consistent across enterprises and industries. Successful engagement means getting to and through each of the ten breakthrough points. Missing or leapfrogging the steps can seriously delay or damage the process, because each of these phases and breakthroughs are designed to work in concert in order to get the traction that propels the transformation to the next step.

Along the way, the transformation gets buy-in internally and externally in a cumulative conversion process, based on the assumption that not everyone will take on the new concept at once. Whilst some disruptions induce instant take-up, mostly adoption rates have to be managed and orchestrated. Buy-in is mobilized along the way, until finally there is a groundswell followed by critical mass, and the new way of doing things becomes *the* standard – inside the organization and out in the marketplace (see Exhibit 0.2).

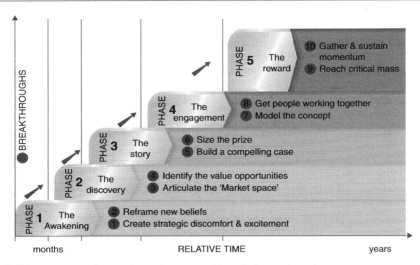

Exhibit 0.1 Transformation phases and breakthrough points

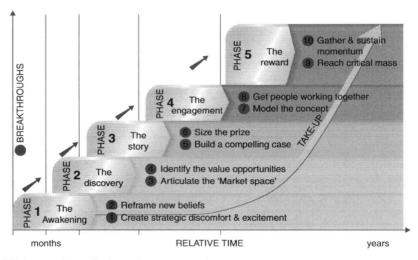

Exhibit 0.2 Cumulative take-up over time

This book will guide you through the transformation process, which usually takes from eighteen months to three years, sometimes even stretching out further, depending on the circumstances and starting point. The impetus for some could be a dire crisis; for others changing environments and pressure from deteriorating financials;

some will proactively see, sense or seek growth opportunities, which they then cannot resist, while others will be starting from scratch, taking advantage of the lacklustre approach to customers in mature industries.

Pressure due to losses does help people to see the point, but credibility often suffers as a consequence, and resources are not readily available. Moving in good times is often easier, therefore, although the sense of urgency may not be as easy to muster.

The book is organized into each of the five phases, with emphasis on the critical success factors that create the ten breakthroughs or milestones that finally propel the enterprise to full and lasting implementation. It is from managing this process that customer centricity can become imprinted into the culture of an enterprise, so that it can refresh and remake itself continuously.

Background and research

Over the past decades I have watched and been part of customer-centric transformations in my capacity as an academic lecturer, researcher and consultant in both the private and public sectors globally. And I have come to the conclusion that when customer centricity is done properly it is both strategic and disruptive.

My research began in the 1970s with my doctorate, 'The Influence of the Marketing Concept on Company Performance', which looked at how a CEO's attitude to customers and the marketplace influences enterprise success.

At IMD Switzerland from the mid-1980s I developed the term 'market spaces' to depict competitive arenas that mirror customer outcomes as the foundation for a customer-centric approach. This was followed by the development of the customer activity cycle methodology – a tool now used in organizations worldwide – to identify values for an integrated customer experience as a template for building new propositions and game changers.

It became obvious, however, that whilst customer centricity was achieving more attention from practitioners, and being acknowledged as a disruptive model, implementation was the huge challenge.

It required skills and a process that was specifically geared to guide enterprises through a blueprint that engaged, because it was structured, yet engendered creativity and inspired thought in dealing with the unexpected.

At the Management School Imperial College London from the mid-1990s into the 2000s the next research period was to gain more insight into how corporations were transforming themselves globally, from products to customers, to change business regimes. Here, I set out to model a systematic process for achieving customer centricity. The result was the identification of the specific transformation process, with breakthrough points needed for implementation.

More recently, working with the Gordon Institute of Business Studies (GIBS) (University of Pretoria's Business School) in South Africa, I have applied my work to emerging countries, or expanding economies as some people prefer to call these markets.

I have found that it's not just the vast numbers of middle- and lower-end (previously deprived customers) that make the emerging markets significant and attractive today. It's also that the principles of customer centricity are entirely applicable to these emerging countries and, in fact, that much of the leading practice in customer centricity today comes from them.

The significance of emerging markets

I have embedded examples of customer centricity in this book and, as many of these will illustrate, long-standing preconceptions about emerging markets are being utterly shattered as we learn that:

- Many unprecedented innovations and concepts are coming from enterprises in high-growth emerging markets, which are leading customer-centric thinking and practice.
- Instead of innovations emanating from rich countries and then exported to poorer countries, with some tweaks for local adaptations, new ideas developed on the ground in and for emerging markets are being exported back to the developed economies in a phenomenon known as reverse innovation.[3]

- Some of these innovations come from local enterprises, who become emerging 'powerhouses', which having succeeded at home then take their new ways of thinking and doing things into advanced countries, becoming serious contenders.
- Multinationals go into emerging markets, therefore, not only to tap the new wealth but also to protect their local markets from innovations originating in these environments and then ricocheting back into their home turf.
- Many of these customer-centric innovations are opening new ground in dealing with some of the toughest environmental and social issues of the day.
- Frugal innovation in product and service industries, intended for emerging markets, embodies offerings equally good but more affordable, using fewer resources, and is gaining popularity worldwide.
- Customers in emerging markets are not gradually catching up – they are leapfrogging, skipping over existing products or services used by more advanced markets.
- The new middle classes have expectations and aspirations (including the need for service) that make them equally as demanding and sophisticated as customers in developed countries.
- With mobile phones now a basic necessity, and a social equalizer in emerging markets, and the growth of smartphones proliferating, customers use social and online media to share their experiences, both good and bad.
- The new rising middle-class consumer in the emerging markets is well wired and digitally savvy, and is increasingly using mobile phones to make decisions and transact.
- Price is not the primary driver in purchasing decisions. Quality service, availability and assortment play equally important roles.
- Emerging market customers are equally and sometimes even more receptive to the prospect of breakthrough innovation than their developed economy counterparts.
- Many emerging countries have large numbers of millennials, many of whom are or are being educated, driving two paradoxical trends: determined to express their independence through consumption, both their own and that of their families, and collectively buying, using and consuming.

Customer centricity as multidisciplinary

This book builds on my previous works, particularly *Breaking Through: Implementing Customer Focus in Enterprises*. Like most books, it draws on research, experience, observation, history, management literature, and other hard and Internet-based published material. It brings together the overlapping and sometimes divergent theories of innovation, disruption theories, market orientation, strategy, change management, growth economics, services management, new accounting, social technologies, and reverse and frugal innovation, all of which are relevant, but none of which on its own can really supply the concepts or tools for the multidisciplinary approach needed to transform to customer centricity.

It is written for executives heading a contemporary organization or unit, who acknowledge the need for customer centricity and the role of disruption, and are looking for a blueprint to help them through the process quicker, easier and with an increased chance of success. It can be equally useful for new start-ups, business students, non-government organizations (NGOs) or investors seeking guidance on leading practice, and on how to achieve growth and enduring prosperity.

Although I have found that the ideas and template hold as a generic formula, executives will have to adapt them to their own culture and circumstances so that it works for their situation and settings. After all, that is what matters.

Acknowledgement and gratitude

To those who have supported my work, inviting me into their organizations to watch and participate, to research and record, and build this theory and framework, to those who listened when they weren't sure and trusted me – when the stakes were high – to help them with their customer-centric challenges, I am truly grateful for the learning and inspiration of nearly 40 years.

I am indebted to all of those people, for without their collaboration this book would have been impossible, and others would not have been able to benefit from their experiences. I hope I have captured the key learning – both good and bad – from their examples, and from the people who have influenced and continue to influence and invent our markets and our worlds.

Special thanks are due to Nazz Rhoda, my PA, for day-to-day help over and beyond what anyone could ever hope for, and editing work on the references.

Many of the examples are based on applied action-based research with enterprises, and observation. In this type of research, concepts and tools are developed, tested and refined to describe collective leading practice, in case studies and other works, and then articulated and made transferable and useful to others, while it is still happening. Most examples are current and I have deliberately tried to make them as diverse as possible in order to gain geographic and industry coverage, and provide a selection of business-to-consumer (B2C) and business-to-business (B2B) examples, across market spectra.

I am aware that using examples is risky because things today change as quickly as we tweet. However, I have rightly or wrongly taken the view that examples are the best way of demonstrating a point. For this reason, where older cases from previous works have become classic, I have kept them in this text.

The word 'product' or 'industrial' is used in the book to demonstrate a dominant logic that is the antithesis of customer centricity, but this is not meant to exclude enterprises that are in services.

Much of the information included in this book is now in the public domain. So if I have skipped or omitted to acknowledge anything or anyone, I apologize.

Finally, all quotations are genuine from my research and consulting work, unless otherwise stated. Some are attributed, others remain anonymous in order to protect the individuals' privacy. Either way, the responsibility for interpretation is entirely mine.

The Awakening

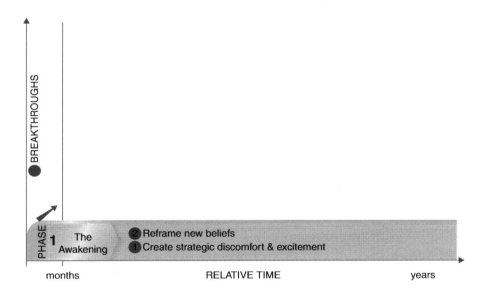

Create Strategic Discomfort & Excitement

Key idea

The customer-centric champion or catalyst needs to make sure that, initially, the right people see and feel the need for change, and to do things differently, and are able to articulate why. Dispensing with old-fashioned minds and models, seeing and sensing the future they may invent and involving 'points of light' – the positive energy forces who will give the transformation the impetus it needs.

Why the mighty fall: and then (some) rise again

How is it possible that Kodak, once one of America's most well-known brands – *the* dominating force in the photographic market for over 100 years – crippled by its staggering decade long losses, ultimately had to file for bankruptcy in 2005?

In 1900 Kodak gave the world the Brownie camera for $1 with the slogan 'You push the button, we do the rest'. The buttons changed, but Kodak did not. The corporate icon, which prided itself on innovation, missed the digital market tide and got swept under. Why?

Arguably, the digitalization of photography was a natural extension of the original Kodak owner George Eastman's goal to make the camera 'as simple for customers to use as the pencil'. But top management somehow failed to take itself into the digital era. They did not see digital as compelling enough for them to make the moves needed to enter this new disruptive frame, even though it fitted perfectly the Kodak value proposition – to provide convenient high-quality photography.

Actually, Kodak could easily have been the market leader in digital photography. Way back in 1975 Steve Sasson, a Kodak engineer, first invented the digital camera. He took it to senior management, who promptly discarded it (we will discuss several similar examples of managerial myopia throughout the chapters).

Kodak did research which established that indeed digital was inevitable and had the power to change the way photographs were taken, but it gave the company ten years before the technological transformation would have an impact. This was long enough for Kodak to do nothing. And by the time the top management made their move, smartphone cameras had taken over.

This raises the essential first phase in any customer-centric transformation: someone high up (enough) must let the organization know that something 'different' has to be done. This act of awakening may be in reaction to a market signal, change or discontinuity already manifesting in the market. Or it may be more proactive – someone senses and anticipates a shift or imagines an innovation they intend to make happen, before anyone else does. Either way, what needs to come first, in order to achieve true and deep customer centricity, is the sensitivity and awareness that something new needs to happen, which invariably means a disruption.

Yet what is amazing is that all too often this sense that the organization needs to be refreshed or transformed, if it is to continue to flourish, is starkly lacking. This is especially true when things are going well. Not hard-pressed to find and make opportunities to create new wealth, often complacent, victims to their successes, executives become strategically paralysed in their own comfortable space and are surprised when their enterprises begin to falter as others take centre stage.

If these custodians of a brand at one time or another considered *the* best are slow and wait too long to act or react, if they are too rigid to change, then the enterprises will begin to flounder. A downward spiral follows: the more customers leave, the worse the financials become and the fewer resources are available to reconfigure the business, so even more customers leave. Until a transformation takes place.

Take Burberry, the quintessential British outerwear manufacturer, which rose to fame when it was commissioned by the UK war office to design a uniform for British officers during the First World War. Its 'trench coat' was elevated to iconic status when it was adorned by the rich and famous by such Hollywood stars as Audrey Hepburn, Humphrey Bogart and Peter Sellers, who wore them in historic films such as *Casablanca*, *Breakfast at Tiffany's* and *The Pink Panther*. Then the stylish brand faded. Customers stopped buying its trench coats, and upmarket shops stopped stocking them, so customers bought ever less.

A steep downward spiral ensued, until a series of transformations culminating in the newly appointed CEO Angela Ahrendts' arrival in 2006. She was hugely uncomfortable at how the brand had been dissipated in a series of uncoordinated efforts by disparate license agreements, which had downgraded the brand around the world. So she set about globally reinstating the trench coat and the brand to billion-sterling stature.[4]

Is the enemy within?

With social media encouraging customers to share, compare, rate and rank their feelings and brand experiences, the negative vicious cycle can be exacerbated. Bad news travels faster and more furiously than ever before.

When the competition comes, especially from new players gunning to disrupt the status quo, often companies focused inwardly on products or services – and the processes and procedures to make and deliver them – don't see it coming. And even when it comes full on, they don't take it seriously enough.

This was the case in bookstore retailing when Jeff Bezos, then 30 years old and based in Seattle, decided to enter the book-retailing fray with Amazon. One of his aims was to give people unlimited access to books via the Internet. Borders in the USA, and HMV in the UK, were thriving businesses at that time. Today they are extinct. Even years after Bezos had taken customer centricity into the digital age, and proved his case, these two companies continued with their obsolescent business model.

When disruptors come into a market they redefine the strategic landscape by reframing boundaries – who is in and who is out – leaving the uninitiated vulnerable. This is what happened to IBM in the 1990s, which resulted in the biggest single loss up until then in US history. Its folly was that it refused to go outside its comfort zone, sticking to its top-of-the-range PCs and mainframes that it so proudly made and sold, instead of moving into the more lucrative service arenas. They saw no foe. And as history has taught us, anyone who sees no competition is unsafe.

With a customer-centric perspective it's obvious that no enterprise can escape competition. So if they simply compare themselves and benchmark themselves to others doing what they do, they become trapped in their own limited frame. Only when that is made clear in an organization is it possible to create the wave that will carry the momentum to get the enterprise into a new era.

Microsoft, the wealthiest corporation in the world until 2000, set the new industry standard on microprocessing and thereafter dominated the industry for decades. But it failed to sustainably hold on to its advantage, responding late to the smartphone wave. It lost out to Apple's inventiveness, which became worth many times more than Microsoft. This is ironic, since Bill Gates had helped to save Apple from ruin only 15 years before, and he himself had predicted in his famous 'Beyond Gutenberg' paper (published in *The Economist* in 1999) that the smartphone would overtake the world.

Customer-centric leaders see that competition is likely to be disruptive, and come from outside the industry.

Jorgen Vig Knudstorp, leader of Lego's renewal, admits to having competition, but he divides it into three categories. The first are those that emulate with cheaper versions and pretend to be Lego; the second are those that emulate and offer similar quality but don't have the Lego brand power; the third are those who offer children different things to play with, in different ways. The latter is what he is concerned about.[5]

The fear of obsolescence

Part of the problem that corporations have is that they don't change because they fear cannibalization and building-in their own obsolescence. Which of course means, as many writers have pointed out, that they open themselves up for someone else to do it for them.

This is what happened to Kodak, so reluctant to stop relying on the film product that had made its fame and fortune.

That is why many enterprises fail to act proactively or are even slow to react to consumer trends. As enterprises such as Apple, Google and Amazon roared ahead, Microsoft, despite having a technological lead in these areas, was late to respond and became relegated to the follower role. Even as the world watched the explosive growth in the emerging markets – leapfrogging across single traditional PCs and Microsoft's software devices and servers – from mobile phones to printers, and direct to cloud computing.

Compare this approach with that of Mark Zuckerberg, whose Facebook grew to a billion users in 2013 because, despite a strategy that relied on traditional desktop PC interface and advertising, he deftly shifted gears and direction to deliver his billion-strong customer base experiences across all digital devices, including mobile, which his enterprise was not originally designed to do.

Or Bezos who, having spent years investing in perfecting warehousing for world distribution, made the bold move into the Kindle, a mobile portal linked to an ever more economic cloud universe, which allows customers to download e-books in whole or in serial format: whatever, whenever, wherever. First in the USA, and then Europe and Japan, Kindle is now also making inroads in emerging countries such as China and Brazil, raking in the new middle-class customers. Not without its share of rivals, Amazon has consciously got its e-books and digital content to outnumber the hard-book-sales business it so carefully nurtured.

Most people would argue, as indeed some of the management at Amazon did at first, that letting customers buy second-hand is bad business, because it cannibalizes sales. However, Amazon's data intelligence told them that once customers can easily buy second-hand books and experiment with unfamiliar authors for whose works they wouldn't be willing at first to pay the full price, they go on to buy new books by that author.[6]

Neither of these two disruptors that started as dots and became phenomena was afraid to give up what it did best. Instead of just being good at doing things right, they become good at doing the right things for customers, who they don't just follow, they lead. Neither continued to be wedded to what they make or do well. As Ginni Rometty, the ninth CEO in the hundred-year history of IBM says: no one should love their product to such an extent that they cannot let go.

Ironically this phobia about cannibalization can make enterprises victims to emerging market disruptors, because reverse innovation takes frugal innovations intended for emerging market customers back to be sold in developed countries. GE Imaging, who itself cannibalized its scanners with ultrasound in the old days, under Jeffrey Immelt, developed ultrasound products and services in emerging countries such as India and China, some of which were sold back into the USA and Canada.

Previously GE, with its high-end and expensive products, practised a skimming policy in the emerging markets. Then it changed its approach to instead deliver quality offerings that were also affordable. It started this in India, which has one of the highest rates of heart disease in the world, with many young people afflicted with the disease. GE did this not only to tap new wealth and opportunities, but also to protect its markets from emerging market competitors, who might build innovations locally and then export them to the more advanced countries.[7]

Can old stay relevant?

Why do brands, even the mightiest, fall?

As the examples illustrate, the trap is not size. It's about a way of thinking, and not allowing decisions to play to existing outdated strengths, which is unfortunately what many organizations do.

If customer centricity is deeply fixed into the convictions and underlying models of enterprises, and the executives who run them, the risk and pain of not changing is often perceived to be greater than of making new moves, even if it means disrupting themselves.

Some argue that it is inevitable that heritage enterprises, especially (but not exclusively) the larger ones, merely get too fixed in old ways to re-create themselves, or the market they serve. Legacy brands and the people who are there to protect and grow them have, they say, limited life span and tenure. They cannot see or acknowledge that their core business is mature. And they don't get the younger generation customers, who need different heads and hearts.

This, they say, includes the boards, who often can't pick the right person for the right time. Take Kodak. Interestingly what perpetuated its product inward-looking logic evidently was its board's decision to deliberately choose a new CEO who embodied the old film model, instead of the other candidate who wanted to dismantle the past and push for digital.[8]

Contrast this with a statement by Virgin Group's Richard Branson: 'When we boldly venture into new businesses about which we know next to nothing, we always hire people who know the sector well, but who, like us, also understand that it is ready to be shaken up.'[9]

What many legacy enterprises lack

What holds any organization back is a lack of:

agility – it becomes rigid, not nimble enough to move quickly enough;
sensitivity – it is incapable of sensing danger, or seeing opportunities that are groundbreaking, because these are too far removed from what it does well;
flexibility – it is so big and complex that it doesn't have the wherewithal to reconfigure systems and processes, to accommodate a new approach and model;
commitment – the culture is fixated on past success and short-term operational capabilities and procedures for getting there;
cohesion – internal strife and power structures, win–lose fiefdoms and empire building prevent a fluid convergence and mobilization of thought and decision making at the top;
customer connection – reliant on old-school brand marketing and distribution, it is out of contact with its end-user market.

Nokia's decline – from the powerhouse it had been when it first announced that mobile communication was the way forward, to being a follower in handset manufacturing – is a classic example. The small and insignificant Finnish pulp and paper mill emerged out of nowhere in the late 1980s to take the centre spot. By being first, it gained the initial benefits and took the lion's share. But heart and head it remained a manufacturer, making and moving products, even when it was obvious that the action was shifting. The initial success proved fleeting: sales bobbed up and down depending on market conditions, business cycles and competitive bombardment from traditional rivals, who unveiled new handset features as quickly as Nokia did.

Despite having the technology first, reportedly seven years before the iPhone appeared, Nokia even failed to deliver on its own high-tech product potential. It couldn't muster the speed needed to move into smartphone platforms, and missed the importance to customers of applications and software, which is what they needed to use the device to pay and play, as opposed to just the hardware. When it did move, it did too little too late, in typical follower mode, without a well-entrenched customer-centric compass to guide it. Having spent a decade cutting costs and destroying its leading margin market, and bringing out product range after product range, it finally sold its handset and smartphone business to Microsoft.

Why others resurrect

IBM is a good example of a legacy giant who, having fallen and then courageously embracing customer centricity, reinvented itself several times, constantly adapting to climb to new levels. Resurrected first as a service company, and since then thriving in ever stormy markets, extending both its own boundaries and those of their customers and customers' customers into the fast smart new world.[10]

After Burberry gradually faded from the fashion limelight it was reinstated in one of the most successful fashion transformations ever, for global luxury for high-end and new generation customers of the future in hundreds of countries. This it did against other established players such as Louis Vuitton, Chanel and Gucci, to name a few, which despite huge budgets had ignored these millennials.

In both cases, in shaping their futures leaders contemporized past values, using history as a positive force. Burberry went back to its original roots – its heritage trench coat. For IBM it was building on the back of its long-standing psyche that went back to its inception – that societal progress is essential to strategy. This became the foundation for harnessing its cutting-edge technology to bring about SmartCities.

Customer centricity is a way of thinking.

In my work I have found that if the model is put centre stage and becomes ingrained into the organizational DNA, the probability is high that it can endure.

Arguably, it is easier to build customer centricity afresh than to have to reinvent a well-entrenched product-type enterprise, which is why we see so much of the customer-centric leadership coming from new entrants. And it's probably why it is so prevalent in emerging countries where enterprises don't have legacy infrastructures, systems and cultural baggage, weighing them down.

But doesn't this make the case for customer-centricity transformation even more compelling for those not yet there?

Hiding behind the numbers

Old predictors of enterprise success have changed, but ways of counting have not adapted. Finding the right data to support their convictions can help the change catalyst make the first step in any transformation to awaken the organization.

For over 100 years Marks & Spencer was as well known as the British royal family. What is more, it had spread its tentacles way beyond the British Isles to become a prominent retailer in Europe, Asia and the USA. The world's most profitable retailer for over 50 years, the Marks & Spencer brand seemed to be on its way to becoming as popular globally as it was at home, where it had supplied the UK population with one-quarter of their suits, almost all their underwear and one-third of their sandwiches. The centenarian enterprise had been voted by its peers as having the most admired management in Europe, and Harvard Business School epitomized it in a case study as one of the greatest companies ever.

Then everything came tumbling down. No one guessed that Marks & Spencer was in trouble and that new competitors were closing in. The problem was only seen clearly when the new CEO realized that although this legacy retailer was the first to make a billion pounds in profit, it was making this from investment in out-of-town shopping-centre properties instead of from superior retailing for customers in its stores.

Traditional accounting aggravates the problem of complacency. Figures easily disguise the truth about how well an enterprise is doing. Leadership boards and top management are looking for and at the wrong data and therefore continue to feel safe. Or they are kept in the dark, rather than on red-hot alert and pressured by the need for change. With conventional approaches, figures can be made to look good, even authoritative. But they may hide how far a company has moved away from its customers, and new market trends, making it easier for a new entrant to disrupt. Instead of the figures being a window to threats and opportunities and a signal or warning of risks ahead, the unsuspecting or uninitiated are left unaware and unquestioning.

Old obsessions and new role models

All sorts of accounting conventions encourage obsessions and short-term behaviour, which get in the way and block pathways to making customer centricity a reality.

Obsession with immediacy

Research and leading practice constantly remind us that the refusal to compromise long-term goals for short-term demands is what keeps the most admired enterprises ahead. Short-term focus brings short-term results and customer deficits.

Short-termism, we all regrettably know, also plays havoc with the ability to transform an organization. It has led to more destruction of wealth and brands than possibly anything else.

The problem is complex and propelled by the stock exchanges of the world, which create pressure on companies and their top executives to lift short-term stock prices and foster cultures that drive and reward them, including emphasis on earnings per share. (Some emerging market stock exchanges such as JSE South Africa, BOVESPA in Brazil and BMV Mexico, to name a few, are instead high-profiling criteria such as governance and sustainability.)

Interestingly, one of the first things that Lou Gerstner did when he took charge of IBM was to change the stock option policy for senior executives. Amazon's Jeff Bezos rewards his teams with restricted stock, which becomes valuable only over time, if and when the company succeeds – this deliberately avoids short-horizon thinking and behaviour.

Obsession with immediacy is also part of product culture and dictates that research and development (R&D) and marketing must pay their way quickly, which is transferred into reporting and performance contracts. Because costs and revenues are tightly squeezed into the same short time period, people tend to ask 'how much are we getting from the various products in their respective silos now?'

instead of 'what are we doing right with customers now, to give us an edge that is sustainable?'

Is it because most traditional types tend to overestimate in the short term, and underestimate in the long term, that makes them feel comfort with short-term projections and pictures?

Amazon could have made a profit long before it did, but Jeff Bezos, rated by *Harvard Business Review* in 2013 as the best performing living CEO (along with the late Steve Jobs), aimed at creating long-term value by sturdily building the customer platform from which to capitalize later on.

Some investors realized this, stating that the company's initial losses were a sign of health not sickness, but others didn't. At the height of the controversy and panic that Bezos would fail hugely, taking his creditors with him, he kept his cool and stood against the anti-Amazon contingent, continuing to hold on to his long-term vision.[11]

Here are some more of his classic quotes from that time, which are worth repeating:

> *We have always taken great pains to urge investors who have a short-term investment horizon not to invest in our stock.*

> *We don't focus on the optics of the next quarter we focus on what is going to be good for the customer.*

> *We want to grow seeds that grow into big trees, and that may take five to seven years.*

> *The company is not the stock ... when the stock was booming we had 14 million customers ... in 2000 when the stock was busting we had about 20 million customers.*

Today the number of active Amazon customers globally is hundreds of millions, both affluent shoppers and aspirers, coming on-stream via mobile phones in both developed and emerging economies.

When governments adopt a short-term approach the consequences can be devastating. Take Britain for example, which has one of the world's worst cancer survival rates. With cost cutting in mind, the British government recently ordered doctors in the National Health Service to ration the number of patients eligible for cancer screening.[12] This will most likely result in later diagnosis, which not only increases the risk of patients getting cancer but also adds cost to total patient care.

Another dramatic example of taking the short-term view comes from Russia. One million square metres of low-cost standardized mass-produced prefabricated micro-rayon dwellings, intended to last for 150 years, are expiring faster than other types of building, because they were manufactured to be cheap, not sustainable. Within the next 30 to 40 years up to 40 million people, 50 per cent of the population, will be affected and potentially will have to shift homes.

Poorly constructed to save cost, with technology that thwarted extension or alteration, the high cost of maintenance and energy usage has far outweighed the upfront saving. The consequence is that micro-rayons have been the draining of a whole generation, financially and emotionally. The city of Moscow is now seeking creative alternatives that not just ensure the long-term value of property and land, but also people's overall quality of life. Citizens, builders, social services, educational institutions, infrastructure and transport departments, and politicians have joined forces to influence future plans. Most importantly, as David Erixon, director of the Strelka Institute of Architecture, Design and Media points out, the customer is finally getting a voice in a market still pretty much dominated by a one-size-fits-all mentality, where in the past the individual, particularly those without economic means, has had very little say.

Obsession with market share

When the world was getting ready for the new millennium, Lego, which grew from wooden toys to make plastic bricks, was as well known globally as Disney. Described by *Fortune* in 1999 as 'the toy of the century', it had a world market share in building construction toys of over 70 per cent, and in Europe just on 90 per cent.

But due to a combination of demographics such as low birth rates, competition from China, and video games and computers, it had lost its share of kids' spare playing time. This is a showcase example of how market share may look good and create comfort amongst the uninitiated, while really saying nothing about markets and market activities, only about product categories. And saying still less about how well the company may fare in a future that has already begun to make its impact.

Market share is an anomaly. It simply measures share of product category, not share of action in which the market is playing and for which it is paying. As long as an enterprise aims at mere market share, it will simply get share of product, not share of market or share of customer. And it will not know who its competition is, and consequently it could risk falling off the competitive radar.

So even if market share is stable or increasing, it in no way relates to customer behaviour or where the market is going, or being taken. As such, it can be downright dangerous. Also, the exaggerated faith in market share is misleading because it can be bought with an accompanying loss of profit. Moreover, winning a chunk of market share could be due to the replacement of lost customers, with all the resulting real and hidden costs.

And so while the numbers in conventional reporting can make an organization seem to be moving forward, because it meets old-fashioned product/market-share targets, it may be standing still or even reversing its fortunes, because it is getting a larger chunk of a diminishing market, as was the case with Lego (let's not forget that in 1990 Kodak had 70 per cent of the film photo US market).

This insight that market share is a lag indicator, and that it limits operating spheres making goals too narrow and discrete and thus hampering growth, is probably one of the most important triggers in any awakening.

Obsession with the bottom line

Managing the bottom line is fundamental to keeping any enterprise economically viable, and many executives are trained to do this obsessively and are rewarded accordingly. However, with customer centricity as the focal point, this is a by-product not the driver.

But all too often the product culture gives this its main attention, confusing the need for operational efficiency with the need to build capabilities to excel with customers. The highly scrutinized product numbers tell no tale about impending trends that may ultimately make or break the business. And, what's worse, to get numbers up costs are cut, sometimes to the detriment of customer service, because executives believe that this will make the business more profitable.

From one executive comes this remark: 'We had someone get the president's prize for reducing the supply chain costs by x per cent of sales. Meanwhile the reduction in inventory cost us far more – it destroyed our image and relationship with customers, which took us years to recover.'

Another misguided reason to reduce cost is that the lower the price the more market share can be won. This is despite the research that over and over again reveals that price wars don't help anyone sustain success.[13] That is especially true when profits are achieved to the detriment of keeping innovation active. Time and time again we see that when customer investments are halted, organizations suffer in the long run whilst those who sustain spend on these, even in bad times, win.

If profits are not accompanied by increases in the top line, representing real market growth (as opposed to just buying more share of an existing product category), it's a clear signal that the enterprise is out of touch.

IBM's blue, so to speak, was that it failed to see that by sticking to the 'boxes' it was losing out on the new wealth, because they were getting only 10 per cent of entire networking spend, whereas 90 per cent of the new money was going to others who were helping people make the boxes connect and talk to each other.

Getting the sense of urgency

Who of us likes wake-up calls? But they must come if customer centricity is to be activated and if people are to be aligned and inspired. Waking up an enterprise so that it can become truly customer centric means that someone must be able to create strategic discomfort or strategic excitement, or both, depending on the circumstances. In my experience, rarely does a customer-centric transformation lift, unless someone either from inside or outside the enterprise is able to achieve this.

This *discomfort* may be about losing out, or not getting a share of something new and lucrative, or not behaving in a way socially appropriate for the times, with undesirable consequences. The *excitement* is about not missing out on potential that is either on the horizon or about to happen. Either way, the needs for change must be explicitly stated and felt by someone high enough in the organization. As Gerstner said, 'the right leaders need a sense of urgency in good times and bad'.[14]

Creating the crisis

Great transformations happen because someone sees and is able to articulate a crisis that others ignore, or simply cannot see. This is either a 'crisis of threat', a 'crisis of opportunity' or a 'crisis of consciousness'.

Some writers and practitioners object to the word 'crisis'. They feel that it could lead to panic and anxiety and give stakeholders the wrong impression, doing more harm than good. I have found that if the word 'crisis' is used metaphorically it can give exactly the right impression. It can provide the much needed energy to get the right people engaged at the right time.

The caveat? It must have integrity, be meaningful and compelling.

'Crisis of threat'

The object of creating a 'crisis of threat' is to deliberately cause what I call 'strategic discomfort'. A 'crisis of threat' means that unless things change the enterprise could seriously lose out, and either its product or relationship with customers, or both, can become commoditized, as we saw with Kodak in photographic film. Fujifilm of Japan undercut its prices and then proceeded to do what Kodak couldn't: reform itself, by shifting with the market into kiosk technology. Then came the onset of digital photography that eroded demand for traditional film, pushing down margins still more. Then, after Kodak finally moved into digital cameras, the digital phone camera arrived, and then the discounting of digital cameras began.

A 'crisis of threat' is often reactionary – something has already happened that prompts actions. This is what triggered the Lexis Nexis turnaround to customer centricity. Its Legal and Professional division began the transformation as a reaction to customers beginning to shave off their budgets for content publications, in protest against the plethora of information freely or cheaply available over the Internet. In any case, customers could do their own search and research, making traditional vendors less and less relevant to their lives. And this was reflected in sales.

Or it may be a response to some evolving trend that has not yet quite solidified. This was the case for the South African subsidiary of the worldwide communications group Ogilvy & Mather, led by CEO Abey Mokgwatsane, when it embarked on an ambitious attempt to redefine its business model to embrace customer centricity. Several things were happening all at once. End users were consuming and reacting to media differently, and companies were engaging more intensely with them, and in different ways, demanding two-way conversations rather than one-way monologues. The role of the marketing practitioner was radically altering, playing a more strategic role at board and CEO level, to drive sustainable growth through brand rather than just communicating how good or how different they were.

Mokgwatsane acknowledged that if Ogilvy & Mather were to really service their clients – the chief marketing officers – in this new paradigm, it would have to help them actually grow their business. This would mean having to look beyond just delivering the best creative campaign.

The numbers may not reflect a crisis that the catalyst sees. For instance, Ogilvy & Mather South Africa had enjoyed steady organic growth.

But for others, as pointed out earlier, the numbers may be subtle and slow to surface, and require interpretation in order to undercover the real picture. In Box 1.1 are financials that can be used as triggers in the awakening phase in order to provoke dialogue and get people thinking about the need for a new perspective.

Box 1.1 Financials to help trigger the awakening

- You have good company earnings, without commensurate top-line growth.
- Investments are for cost efficiencies, not for expansive customer innovation.
- Your revenues are slipping, though profits are up.
- You have a good market share, but the market is changing direction and you are getting a larger share of a shrinking pie.
- Your market share is up but your customer replacement costs are high.
- Your profits are good but competition is coming increasingly from outside the industry.
- Your profits are good but from cost cutting.
- Your revenues come mainly from price-driven deals and performance.
- You are growing by expanding into emerging markets, without a real customer edge in your home market or in the new market.
- You are using mergers and/or partnerships to grow your business, doing more of the same, unlikely to change or expand the marketplace.
- You are growing revenue without growing your customer base.
- You are selling off assets to increase revenues, which could hamper long-term prospects.

'Crisis of opportunity'

Sometimes causing discomfort can result in fear, which needs to be counterbalanced by the 'crisis of opportunity', which causes strategic excitement. Its intention is to communicate that in order to grab new wealth a new business model needs to be adopted. That if new moves are not made, something big will be missed. Again, this may not be obvious to all, so it's up to the transformation catalyst to make it understood and felt.

Per Bay Jorgensen was one such person. Though Denmark's International Health Insurance (IHI), with policyholders in over 150 countries, was doing well at the time, he believed that there was an opportunity to capitalize on the burgeoning expatriate market. But this could happen only if the company could shift from selling policies and managing claims to becoming a more important force in the lives of people who were relocating to a new country, or had ensconced themselves somewhere in the world, as expatriates, for work or retirement.

Later, sensing that the growth and wealth would be in 'unpatients' – people who were well and would be prepared to pay to stay that way, or get their organizations to do so – in early 2000 Jorgensen began to revitalize his company around the concept of helping customers – mostly high end, high value – to be well, rather than merely selling them or their employees health insurance, like everyone else was doing. He redefined the notion of being well to include being fit and feeling safe while relocating, so as to be able to get to and stay at work productively.

This new approach kept IHI growing even as others in the industry fell on hard times after the millennium, which culminated in its being sold to BUPA International, the UK corporation, in 2005. It also changed the industry perspective forever – wellness is the mantra most health insurers espouse today, though only some do the remarkable job of making it happen.

'Crisis of consciousness'

Making the case for a 'crisis of conscience' completes the trilogy, embedding the all-important new values that bring customer centricity into a contemporary era. Put simply, it involves looking for lucrative opportunities that are also socially transformative and uplifting.

When Lorenzo Zambrano, Cemex's towering CEO, changed the world's largest ready-mix concrete producer from a commodity supplier to an inspiring new world enterprise, he was responding to a price war in which the industry was embroiled, with sales of cement going down due to an economic crisis and deregulation. But instead of fighting this head on, in a market clearly deteriorating, he saw the opportunity to do something different.

Cemex was founded in Mexico in 1906 and became one of the world's largest manufacturers of cement. Zambrano realized that the next frontier was the poor, who up until then had been neglected. With 60 per cent of the Mexican population earning less than $5 per day, he knew that their spend on cement would be small. But cumulatively the amounts were quantifiably enormous, particularly since 40 per cent of this deprived population bought building materials for DIY.

But to this was added a social problem that needed resolving. Most poor Mexicans lived in small houses that many families shared. Many homes were not completed and were tiny with several families living under one roof, kids growing up on the streets, stress and crime levels high, and hygiene and esteem low.

A far cry from making and selling cement, this became the spirit of the new Cemex: to enable poor people to build, repair and upgrade their homes, thereby giving the enterprise a market, as well as a social signature.

Living like customers

Disruptive leaders don't need complicated research to drive their motives or make their moves. Though on paper things may not be perfect, or 100 per cent clear or obvious, they use whatever information they have, plus their own intuition and 'it just feels right', or 'it's so obvious, isn't it?' – a sentiment often expressed.[15]

They don't spend fortunes on analysing transactional data or on elegant mathematical formulas in the hope that that's what will reveal the big new idea. Nor do they crunch the numbers, hoping to find proof that the new market indisputably exists.

That is not to say that they don't use data, in fact the more they can substantiate their case the better. It's just that new wave makers acknowledge that what they are looking for isn't just in the figures – the uncharted territories they are about to unlock and create don't yet exist, they actually have to invent them.

It's absurd to think that the mistake is the inability to respond to customers' needs or follow shifts in customers' demands. Yes, that is probably the case in a product-oriented environment, where added features are the focal point. But customers can't have needs or demands that don't yet exist. Somewhere between sensing a need, and anticipating where the market could go, is where the disruptor finds room to magnify market opportunities. Whether it speaks to a simple need, like using soap for a market who don't know they need it, or getting people to commute in a driverless car.

Customer-centric disruptors combine a healthy respect for data, using creativity to imagine what's possible in their vision of the world – a world, say, without cameras, or physical book stores, or banking without branches, or cars that have no driver. Then they form an educated hypothesis or proposition about how that world could look – which they may see and others may not – and decide what they need to do to get there.

Ethnographic research works for disruptive customer centricity, where customers cannot be expected to visualize a future yet to be. Here you don't ask customers what they want, you watch them in order to see how they behave and live.

Ethnography, a branch of anthropology, looks at how people live *in situ*. It rests on social observation and enquiry about markets that old-type research cannot answer. Its intention is to provide an in-depth description of the everyday practices of groups of people. Teams go into the places where customers work and play – and literally become one of them. The feedback they collect is qualitative and often in the form of stories and narrative rather than reams of hard data. This is particularly relevant in the rural areas, where literacy or local language problems are an issue.

With this type of intervention, trends are allowed to emerge, and if questions are asked they are open ended to try to get a conversation going without respondents being confined to selected answers. This may be complemented by interviewing through social media and blogging, or exchanges done via virtual or physical local research centres.

The theory is that ethnographic approaches should provide insights from the insider's point of view. Executives not only live in communities they also work in communities, and often multinationals expect employees to actually do community chores in order to get a better feel for the culture, habits and people. They become part of the local scene, 'hanging out with the groups in which they are interested'.

The feedback that Cemex got from its distributors was that the only way to deal with the poor in Mexico was to pull down the price. So they produced a smaller bag of cement. Customers hated it, because the larger bags were a status symbol, and so the price-driven strategy was a dismal failure. Then came the big breakthrough. Cemex top management issued a 'Declaration of Ignorance' (metaphors like this can be very powerful to drive energy), an admission that the firm knew almost nothing about the local market's building habits.

Teams then spent six months living in shanty towns engaging with low-income customers to develop a deeper understanding of their aspirations and challenges in achieving home ownership, including what they bought to build, how they applied it, and what they did wrong that was costing them time, energy and money.[16]

Another example, Overseas Chinese Banking Corporation (OCBC Bank), trading in Singapore as a traditionalist since 1932, decided to aim at the youth Generation Y market, locally and abroad. Teams there spent 15 months with young people in malls, universities and cafés to see how they used money, how they felt about it, and how they liked to shop and interact. This all became the foundation of its customer-centric transformation.

This type of immersion research is useful to awaken the organization, because it gives credence to the new hypothesis, and adds substance to the conversion and process. But it cannot tell an organization what to do.

As Steve Jobs, who made his company a superstar customer-centric disruptor, once said when asked what research went into iPads: 'It's not the customer's job to know what they want.'[17]

Finding 'points of light'

When the pressure and vision comes from the apex of the organization, so much the better. In fact, most people who have been through a customer-centric transformation, or failed to get one off the ground, say that unless the CEO, old or newly arrived, is involved the change from the product to customer simply will never materialize.

In practical terms, this is probably true when an enterprise is in deep financial distress or forced to adapt to negative market signals that are already apparent. Here, executives say, the CEO must be visibly present, seen out front, pushing the endeavour and claiming responsibility for doing whatever is needed to change minds and behaviour.

Some executives believe that when the transformation comes directly from up high it can in fact be resented, as senior and middle management feel they are 'being forced into changes they don't necessarily understand or want to do'. And, if the transformation is being driven by the CEO, it may not be sustainable if they leave or get distracted. As one executive put it: 'it only takes the CEO to exit or an excuse, to change course and all efforts are lost'.

I have worked with transformation where change has been originated by someone other than the CEO, someone who sees the danger or discomfort and has appetite for a change that is obvious to them but not to others. This person becomes the 'moral authority' or voice for why and how customer centricity is needed, in order for the enterprise and brand to excel, rather than suffer. And it can and does work, provided whoever is driving the transformation is senior enough, has credibility and uses a well-orchestrated process.

In such cases the CEO and top management must become sponsors and allies, and be willing to allow lead players to get on and push their fresh unorthodox views, with enough time to make and prove their point so that the new way can spread.

This is a significant shift from the past, when change had to be cascaded downwards in an organization. Today, in theory, change catalysts can come from anywhere. They are now more tolerated, even appreciated and admired, rather than ignored or punished. And sufficient numbers of people and organizations have been successful for us to learn some valuable lesson from them about customer-centric transformations – what works and what doesn't.

These change catalysts typically have to be able to enthuse and mobilize people. I say enthuse *and* mobilize very specifically, because getting people afraid or excited is one thing – getting them to give up time and be part of a process that cuts into their daily routine, as well as keep the momentum going, is quite another. Most executives who have been successful at it agree that it is better to be inclusive: managers responsible for making the transformation work need to be involved in setting the direction and agenda, irrespective from whence it emanates in an organization.

The consensus myth

But we are getting ahead of ourselves. The important question that people at the forefront of making new things happen have to ask themselves is this: how many people should we involve, and who, in what order? This has to be resolved early on, if leaders are going to be able to move the process forward in a positive way with gusto and tempo – enlightening rather than just frightening, inspiring rather than just commanding.

Paradoxically, trying to involve as many people as possible is a barrier to success. High-energy, positive individuals who are likely to be inspired, and can and will influence others despite the potential problems, are the primary candidates for this first phase. Often the temptation at the start is to involve as large a group as possible, but I assure you that executives have learnt the hard way that this can be fatal. Especially if the wrong people are involved. In trying to get this consensus, executives have had to use a disproportionate amount of effort, battling with objectors and objections, instead of working with positive forces that propel a customer-centric journey forward.

Not only does not having to continually encounter and counter points of resistance save on wasted time and effort, but it speeds up the process and ensures that the energy level remains high enough to carry it forward, especially at the crucial breakthrough points. So, increasingly, enterprises are learning to avoid or ignore the inevitable 'nay sayers'.[18]

Executives still have to deal with resistance – it's a normal part of any change process. But when most of the precious time and energy goes into this resistance rather than into getting alignment and traction, it can damage, delay or permanently derail the process, particularly at the early phase.

From my work with executives who have been through this come the following remarks:

There are some people you take with you, and others you just can't, so don't try.

It could have been quicker if we hadn't spent so much time trying to convince people who were inconvincible, and just got on with it.

Some typical refrains from the resistors include:

Tell me who has done this in our industry.

We have done this before and failed miserably.

We don't have the capabilities.

The timing is all wrong.

Our business is different.

There is no burning platform.

We barely have enough resources to cope with day-to-day problems.

How does this fit in with our existing strategic plans?

Part of the problem is that in traditional organizations people with the most power and say are those managing the traditional assets (factories, stores, product units). And, unfortunately, often it is they who have the most to lose from a disruptive change.

History has taught us that seniority guarantees neither sensitivity to markets nor a willingness to change. And that only a small proportion of people really propel an enterprise forward. The remainder will wait for others to move first and will concentrate on short-term operational issues and firefighting.

Moving with positive energy

Rather than spending precious resources on breaking down resistance, customer-centric transformation champions actively look for 'points of light'. Especially at the start of the process. These people are more than just innovators who take on any new ideas first. They become the fulcrum for drawing others into the process, managing the consecutive waves so that that the transformation takes them and the rest of the organization forward, through the ten defined breakthrough points.

This means that disruptors pushing for customer centricity must find not just the influencers in their stakeholder base but the 'points of light' among them.

Here are the main differences between resistors and 'points of light':

- While resistors want to hang on to the past, 'points of light' see that to make a real difference they need to do things differently.

- While resistors tend to be negative and put emphasis on the problems, 'points of light' are positive by nature and consciously find ways to solve problems.
- While resistors can only react to tangible evidence, 'points of light' are comfortable with intuitive reasoning.
- While resistors are uncomfortable with change, 'points of light' actually enjoy change.
- While resistors conspire with others to block change, 'points of light' are energizers who are able, by example, to inspire others.
- While resistors are usually stuck in a silo mentality, concerned about protecting their own turf and position, 'points of light' see the bigger picture and constructively work for the good of the whole.
- While resistors want certainty, 'points of light' are able to adapt, improvise and experiment until they get it right.
- While resistors look for facts, 'points of light' are able to imagine what's possible (which resistors may find impossible).
- While resistors tend to play to the existing system, 'points of light' are not afraid to buck the system.
- While resistors create mistrust and division, 'points of light' foster goodwill and collaboration.
- While resistors like answers, 'points of light' can deal with ambiguity.

Distinctively, 'points of light' don't care who takes the credit, as long as things are moving in the right direction. But perhaps most importantly they are bold, not afraid to have the courageous conversations with peers and superiors. Adept at using their personal and political capital to influence others, 'points of light' expand and spread energy and can effectively influence across 360 degrees in the organization. Through their networks and tenacity (they know how the enterprise and its politics work) they propel the implementation on, with persuasion and goodwill.

That is why they are beacons, and others gravitate into their orbit and identify with their ideas. Most important, 'points of light' are equally comfortable with what can be a paradox: using creativity and imagination to find the future, while having the structure and discipline to get there, which is critical to making the process of customer centricity work.

BREAKTHROUGH 2

Reframe New Beliefs

Key idea

The leader needs to frame new beliefs about success, show how these are different from those currently held and more relevant for enduring growth. Beliefs that are strategic and contemporary, and embed higher purpose, attract the correct customers, employees and investors, and form the basis for all changed thinking, which gets the enterprise from product to customer centricity. Central to this is customer 'lock-on', where the customer voluntarily wants the enterprise as its sole or main choice permanently. How to attain this, on an ongoing basis, is at the heart of customer centricity, and its rewards are lasting.

Making beliefs strategic

An important part of the awakening stage is that once the urgency is felt and communicated, sufficient numbers of the right people are committed to making the change happen. If people with high levels of positive energy are chosen to be in the lead group, the process will be smoother and swifter.

However, once a sense of discomfort and excitement bring on urgency about the existing status quo, an emotional vacuum can easily set in, unless new beliefs are formed. Beliefs lead the organization in a particular direction, and determine what a company does in order to create value. They are firmly held sentiments and convictions about what constitutes success. Disruptors manage to change these beliefs with new assumptions, whether they are those held by customers, the industry, their company, or any combination of these.

Because beliefs are the fuel that drives decisions, participants in the transformation need to be made aware that the beliefs they currently hold stem from product logic. And then made to understand the need to change to a customer-centric perspective of the world.

Google founders crafted a document in the old days in which they outlined what they referred to as 'Ten Things We Know To Be True'. From time to time they revise them, to see if they still hold true. The point is that the ten truths is what has impelled everything they do and don't do, which they believe to be central to their success, including the belief that 'you can make money without doing evil'.

IBM distinguishes strategic from operational beliefs, because they force people to keep the long view in mind and as such they are more enduring, says Ginni Rometty, and more fitting for the contemporary world.

Cementing new beliefs while eradicating the old gives people a common understanding, not only about what customer centricity means and why it is so relevant to their enterprise, but about how far off their current belief system may be.

Beliefs need to appeal to people on three levels: 'You can't teach beliefs like you can rules'.

The three levels are:

- the cognitive – getting people to *think* a certain way;
- the emotional – getting people to *feel* a certain way;
- the social – getting people to *care* a certain way.

This is in line with the Greek philosopher Aristotle's belief that, in order to persuade, one has to appeal to people at three levels:

- Logos (logical) – reason and conclusion.
- Pathos (emotional) – feelings.
- Ethos (ethical) – character and integrity.

To make the shift from old to new beliefs takes an induction, an intervention which can last anything from one day to weeks or months, depending on the number of people and geographies involved. The object is to get the right people motivated, aligned and, literally, speaking the same language, with new beliefs and concepts firmly anchored.

Once a different lens has been presented and accepted, new horizons begin to open up, with a visible shift in energy. People see the past as different from the future, what notions should be replaced, and how the locus and focus of value must change. This allows a collective spirit to emerge, which pulls the implementation along.

At Lexis Nexis, past behaviour would have looked for more innovative content to publish as well as trying to cut the cost of doing this. During the awakening, the emphasis was on demonstrating under what circumstances customers would be willing to pay for information. Top management got people to gravitate around the idea that people who have to make a decision which carries a high degree of risk, such as law enforcement officers, patent officers, litigating lawyers or in-house scientists, would be prepared to pay for information if it was presented in a way that helped them better manage that risk in their decision making, say to track down a criminal, access a patent application, win a case, or develop a breakthrough product.

The ability to recast beliefs about what brings long-lasting success, in an inspiring and relevant way, is all part of the breakthrough agenda, which enables the business model to be recast from products to customers at this awakening phase. Without some time devoted to this, the process will lack the necessary grounding and people can so easily fall back into old thinking and behaviour patterns. And it will be difficult, if it is even possible, to re-create the initial bursts of enthusiasm and energy.

Also needed is a deep understanding of why these beliefs mean having to deal differently with customers, and the rewards that this will bring. It is only when this becomes clear that people begin to feel ready to proceed comfortably and confidently.

Turning the product corner

That wealth must come from extracting value from customers, rather than from products, is fundamental to customer-centric thinking. An essential part of the awakening, therefore, is getting people to change perceptions that value solely resides within products.

So here is the first customer centric belief:

Customer-centric belief 1
The value of customers increases over time, whereas the value of products or services, diminishes with time.

Product logic is limited mainly because advantages are short-lived. Products or services for that matter, however good or innovative, cannot in and of themselves give an enterprise a sustainable edge, because someone will always find a way to copy.

With sophisticated marketing techniques, also easy to copy, industrial types parade their product or service difference in various ways in order to obtain their share of the pie. They are only really comfortable dealing with the stuff. That's probably one of the reasons why Nokia has still not managed to pull itself out from hardware into the software-application era. First came the low-cost players, who quickly incorporated new technologies into their goods, and then the newcomers, who arrived placing the Internet into the palm of customers' hands. With its phone-first mindset, Nokia tried everything to fix and update its products with new features, none of which impressed customers or investors.

Changing the curve

When enterprises compete for products (or services) rather than customers, investments must be extracted as early on as possible, before the inevitable competitive onslaught, which erodes margins. This is old industrial product-life-cycle logic, and pressures executives to deliver quickly, often with short-lived results, because products diminish in value over time. Until the next version, which behaves in exactly the same way. (See Exhibit 2.1).

Even in very sophisticated markets, such as health care where biology and science advance daily, no product, technology, patent or scientific merit can keep a company ahead enduringly because, as history has demonstrated, the early advantage gained is easily undone.

In stark contrast, customer centricity believes that once the correct moves are made to gain a customer base, this releases possibilities to get increased value over time, even exponentially (see Exhibit 2.2). This may mean a period of negative returns, until the tipping point is

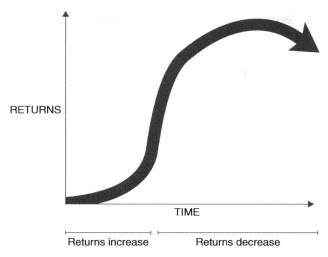

RETURNS

TIME

Returns increase | Returns decrease

Exhibit 2.1 Product curve and returns

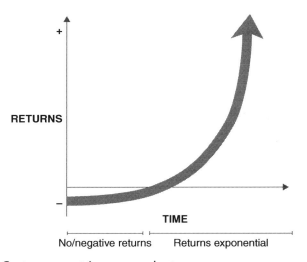

+

RETURNS

−

TIME

No/negative returns | Returns exponential

Exhibit 2.2 Customer-centric curve and returns

reached, when the company gets the benefit of longer and stronger share of customer wallet.

This brings us to the next strategic belief:

Customer-centric belief 2
Innovation means we create new ways of doing things for and with customers, not just incrementally improve our products or services.

When we are dealing with the future, innovation is not an incremental improvement to existing products or processes. Rather, it is a new way of doing things for and with customers.

Traditional pharmaceutical companies typically sell as much of their drugs to as many customers as possible, as soon as they can, in order to recoup development costs and satisfy short-term return on investment (ROI) requirements. The world continues, however, to experience high costs of wasted medicine and failure, and unnecessary administration and replacement costs.

Contrast this with a customer-centric approach, where the pharmaceutical fraternity would use new genetics and biotechnologies to create new ways of developing healthy populations, to keep them well, prolonging lives at peak performance levels. Outsiders taking that different perspective are already zooming in on the opportunities presenting themselves. With 80 per cent of all the medical data known in the world on oncology, IBM's Watson computer has the power to transform the speed and quality of care, as never before. This could radically influence how many and what type of drugs will be needed in the future.

The great customer-centric disruptors put their minds to changing social and work practice. IBM's Watson could provide hospitals with new ways for doctors, nurses and carers to make improved treatment decisions. Apple became the most valuable US company ever, by making customers communicate, play and work differently; Google made customers instant searchers and researchers and anyone an advertiser; Facebook made people share their lives and intimacies (50 per cent of all new mothers send messages or update their Facebook page while in labour); and Amazon made customers get rid of bookshelves (and books) and read differently – any place, any time.

Fact: Nokia sells more mobile phone handsets in Africa than any other supplier. But it is the service providers like MTN who are using digital to find new ways of doing things in Africa: from Masobi's market trading information for farmers and fishermen in Senegal, which can mean the difference between poverty and a good return, and the much-needed real time information that health workers in Malawi get on mobile phones in order to better diagnose patients, to systems for secure local and international remittance of precious funds for Ugandans, or, in Ghana, essential educational services for youth attending university, or citizens extracting cash from ATMs without having to use cards.

Customer-centric disruptors don't have to invent or own the technology: it becomes their enabler.

IBM no longer makes computers. It *uses* cognitive computer and data technology in order to get the end result to customers: predictive e-smart decision capability. Big data has the power to redefine most jobs, but as the amount of data grows machines will have cognitive computing ability to enable them to learn and predict, so that in all walks of life people can make better decisions.[19]

The foray made by Tesco, the world's third largest retailer, into South Korea (somewhat thwarted by the government's protection of mom and pop stores), is testament to new ways of doing things, using technology as the enabler. In Seoul, they launched virtual stores in subways, where hard-working commuters can now save time by strolling down these virtual aisles – displaying virtual merchandise – while en route to and from work, as they would in a real store, using their phone to choose their goods and then have them delivered to their doorstep. This has attracted millions of customers, and the app used in order to shop has the largest usage base in South Korea, especially with the younger market. This has prompted more virtual stores to be opened near universities and work areas in South Korea, extended to bus stops.[20]

New ways of doing things includes configuring what, and how, the vendor operates, to the benefit of customers. Sasol's Wax Division in Chile demonstrates a B2B example. Now wax is combined with water to forge an emulsion that is made in various factories, ordered by customers such as hardboard manufacturers, and then delivered and processed further to become kitchen cupboards. The emulsion is made at the customer's factory, providing product on demand at lower costs, intensifying the relationship between Sasol and their buyers.

Why customers 'lock-on'

A powerful wake-up call in any customer-centric transformation comes when key executives realize that customer 'lock-on' creates the value that brings lasting success. And that they haven't yet achieved it.

'Lock-on' means that the customer *wants* the enterprise as their sole or first choice over time, even over a lifetime.

Because it's voluntary, 'lock-on' is anchored in authentic brand value, rather than marketing hype. Customers are vastly different today. Digital has made them independent actors in a marketplace, where mutual gains and respect is what wins.[21] People including those in rural areas who have access to more (and in time all) information, able to make better choices, search, compare and share information, are joining this self-directed discerning new throng.

Customer centricity sets out to achieve 'lock-on' in order to capitalize on stronger, deeper relationships over time. They only get this if they are always in a better position than anyone else to provide customers with value.

So let's look at this in more detail:

Customer-centric belief 3
Customer 'lock-on', not lock-in brings sustainable rewards

With customer 'lock-on', a self-reinforcing loop (see Exhibit 2.3) is set up, which by its very nature is virtuous, and self-propagating.

The more the relationship grows, the more information is shared by the customer and, as we know, provided it is used to that customer's benefit it will continue to be shared. This enables the enterprise to put itself out front using this information to produce better value for individual customers, organizations and the people within them, and thereby get 'lock-on'. The relationships and association continue to deepen as the enterprise improves profiling and customer matching, turning this into enhanced value in a constant reinforcing loop of giving and getting better value.

What better way to protect an enterprise from competition?

Customer 'lock-on' is not customer lock-in...

Another awakener is the realization that customer 'lock-on' is not customer lock-in. But often lock-in is what traditional companies have been chasing. When customers are locked in, they are effectively imprisoned. They either can't get out because the enterprise has a 'monopoly', or they can't break free from some artificial hold, either legal, political, technological or financial.

Or the sheer difficulty in switching creates lock-in, as customers have experienced with banks in some countries. (The UK government

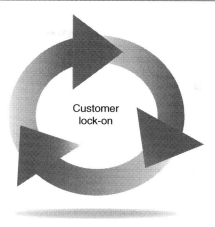

Exhibit 2.3 Customer 'lock-on' loop

has put a stop to that, with customers now able to switch providers within seven days.)

Customers also get locked in when the entire industry is underperforming. Whilst customers may be disenchanted, because everyone operates identically, they feel they have no option. Until a disruptor appears with a better proposition.

Studies repeatedly show that the primary motive for switching banks is poor service. Overall trust has diminished, and customers are increasingly showing their anti-bank sentiments to those who do not respond appropriately. In the UK less than one-third of young people believe that their banks are fair, transparent or ethical.[22]

Grabbing banking customers all over the world are newcomers, outsiders like retailers offering easy forms of credit or loans or mobile service providers offering better, quicker and cheaper offerings.

And most interesting are the new banking concepts, which provide the poorer markets with not just transaction potential, but a digital identity, enabling them to ramp up hitherto untapped credit and spend.

Take M-PESA in Kenya. Already in 2013 they had 15 million Kenyans using mobile phones to make transactions, even though 30 per cent of them were not yet on the power grid, and over 70 per cent of all households have at least one M-PESA user within it.[23]

But beware: sometimes disruptors start with an unserved market and they then advance into the more lucrative market echelons.

Consider UT Bank Ghana's indigenous disruptor that started by offering loans to locked out, unsalaried entrepreneurs, but then, having achieved broad market appeal for service and simplicity, now boasts some of the largest corporate customers in the country.

The vacuum for the underserved and unbanked market, deemed too risky and too costly in South Africa (the largest banking market in Africa) was filled by Capitec, which was founded in 2001 and named the best performer of the top 100 companies in 2012 by the Johannesburg Stock Exchange. Then, larger banks typically offered no unsecured loans, were formal, complex and inconvenient, and focused inward on administration instead of customers. At a time when, in order to save costs, banks actively discouraged customers coming into branches, Capitec built an accessible ever-growing branch network. Rather than big, intimidating complexes, it built small, convenient nifty outlet stores, strategically located for accessibility and convenience for its market, like taxi ranks, bus stops and malls. Against the industry standard, it made its relationships cardinal and its paperwork minuscule.

Nor is it conventional loyalty

The product take on customer loyalty is to achieve repeat purchasing of the same stuff, and to use loyalty schemes, often off the shelf, to incentivize sales. This has become commonplace, and customers have come to expect points as a form of discount.

No amount of money spent on these loyalty programmes, or any other transactional marketing tactic, will achieve the real 'lock-on' that brings lifetime value. It is no differentiator, particularly when every customer is treated the same way, bombarded with cards, promotional messaging and offerings irrelevant to them and, worse still, sometimes unable to spend the points they earn! On top of which the enterprise may have high loyalty in low growth market activities, which is in no way indicative of enduring success.

The customer-centric approach switches from emphasis on maximizing transaction of the stuff to maximizing interactions with customers to enhance value. Every touchpoint is used as an opportunity to obtain and use data. So that with each interaction, the enterprise gets smarter and more precise and proactive about delivering value to that person, reinforcing the 'lock-on'.

And this is why and how customers become the barrier to competitive entry.

Google has mastered this in high tech. It gets smarter about customers every time a person does a search, makes a link on the web, or clicks on an ad. And as it learns from and about its users, it acts on this, to make everyone better off, with access to information that is useful and usable, connected as they are to one aggregated mind.

Jeff Bezos pinned great hopes on his company's ability to create a 'soul mate,' a mechanism that analyses data generated by previous purchases and searches to suggest book and music titles that are likely to be interesting to visitors. The granular detail available through multichannel data and analytics is funnelled back to deliver value for that customer, by directing them to the products and services that suit them, giving Amazon the edge.

Whereas loyalty programmes are trying to pull the vendors' costs down, customer centricity is a deliberate attempt to achieve customer 'lock-on', with value-based ingredients that are used and reused, and therefore reduce costs (more about that later.)

Customers who 'lock-on' have a vested interest in the enterprise, what it does and how well it does (see Table 2.1). They are willing to share confidential information and problems, open up their books where relevant, offer new ideas, take on new innovations more quickly and, as a general rule are less price-sensitive. And the vendor gets more opportunity to engage in strategic conversations, in the higher-ground.

Furthermore, when customers 'lock-on' they become advocates, consultants, content providers, R&D advisors, designers, developers, innovators and joint venture partners. Whether joined together in customer communities, crowdsharing, or operating on their own, their growing augmented array of voices and roles are playing out daily.

'Lock-on' is more akin to advocacy than the old notion of loyalty. Customers actively build and support the brand, promote it and become active allies delivering the message in the marketplace, providing positive unsolicited opinions on the brand and the company, which they share with media and social markets. Additionally, by their association, they generate referrals and give credibility to what the company is trying to portray from the brand.

Table 2.1 Customer loyalty versus customer 'lock-on'

	Customer loyalty	Customer 'lock-on'
Enterprise Objective	Get repeat purchases of 'stuff' to meet sales quotas	Get deeper, wider, and more diverse share of spend over longer times, even lifetimes
Method	Transactions	Interactions
Relationship	Short-term, self-involved	Long-term, reciprocal
Customer Motive	Collect points, rewards	Get unique/relevant value & rewards
Economics	Cost of transactions go down	The costs of ingredients that comprise customer value, go down through use and reuse
Role Customer	Buyer	Buyer, advocate, promoter
Requires	New systems & software	Fundamental change

Beyond market segmentation to personalization

Segmentation has traditionally aimed at clustering groups with similar characteristics or needs, and then providing offerings to these collective appetites. More and more specialized knowledge of different markets or industry segments may be a starting point for engaging customers, but it certainly is not the end game.

With the Internet penetrating both affluent and aspiring middle markets at exponential rates, segmentation is becoming even less relevant. Enterprises can get to wider spreads of customers across age, gender, income and psychographic groups, anywhere. So confident is Amazon of its ability to deliver individualized offerings that executives do not even use classic segmentation groups or persona.

Personalization profiles the behaviour and changing needs of individuals, households or enterprises, and the individuals within them, and adapts to and with them, over time.

So here is the next strategic belief:

Customer-centric belief 4:
We need to personalize offerings, because individuals, not markets, 'lock-on' to a brand or enterprise.

Ancient Greek physician Hippocrates, born in 460 BC, remarked that it's more important to know what kind of person has the disease than to know what kind of disease the person has. But traditionalists go on building business models around the standardization of their products and services, to get economies of scale. They offer more of the same goods, to as many people as possible, delivered to everyone in the same way, which is the old industrial conveyor-belt mentality.

The customer-centric way is to learn how to add genuine value for individuals. That is how customer 'lock-on' and advocacy get generated, ramping up opportunities enduringly.

Google, founded in 1996, actually called itself 'googol' at first, which means the number 1 followed by 100 zeros representing infinite amounts of information. Building up a comprehensive knowledge base of what exists, it started off allowing people to fast search.

There were many other search engines at that time, but it surged ahead because, whilst the others were only providing and organizing lots of information, its founder realized that Google had to find new ways for sites to be relevant for *individuals* – that simple fact has kept it in the lead (by number of users) so far.

Making this move to personalization is a significant step towards customer centricity. It puts an entirely different lens onto the interaction an enterprise needs with a customer. Let's return to the Marks & Spencer case, with its future now more about customer lifestyle than discrete products and services. They say 'it's the difference between selling the perfect Christmas pudding, and getting to the customer everything that an individual family needs for a perfect Xmas'.

If Marks & Spencer were only selling the perfect Christmas pudding or turkey, it would use traditional marketing tools to broadcast the superiority of its turkey or puddings. With customer 'lock-on' as the goal, it offers the perfect Christmas to a family.

Be it a Google or a Marks & Spencer, personalization entails:

- Conversations with individuals, to obtain details about them.
- A customer memory bank to incorporate what is known about each customer.
- A tight relationship, with information shared back and forth, and ways to involve the vendor early on in decision making.
- A feedback mechanism for individuals to share ideas and feedback, with staff, other customers and fans.
- Participation of individual customers, in content building and co-creation.

- Interactions on options, and matching of individual profiles to offerings.
- Proactive monitoring of prices, so that individuals get the best competitive deal and option.
- Rewards and incentives for individual behaviour.
- Systems to pick up and feed back reactions to individual offerings.
- Updating and constant innovation for that customer.
- Knowledge used and reused for that customer.

Personalization is the new mass

Forget about an average view of your customers, because there is no such thing – customers are unique, and need to be treated as such.

Many vendors, such as retailers, banks, credit card companies, to name a few, have masses of information about individual customers, but they invariably aggregate this up in order to make their supply chain and merchandising more efficient as a whole. That's not the same as knowing what individuals want, and relaying that back into personalized value for them, to get customer 'lock-on' and designing systems that facilitate this.

The insurance industry is typically based on averages. There are some exceptions, though. Discovery Insure, a South African enterprise, disrupted and shifted the short-term insurance landscape when it decided to use behavioural economics to change how customers drive, and allow them to reap the rewards of this endeavour.

It treats every person as an individual, rating their driving behaviour and rewarding them accordingly. This is hugely different from most insurers who assume, for instance, that on average men are worse drivers than women, so they make all men pay higher premiums than women. Or penalizing good drivers, who are expected to cross-subsidize bad drivers by paying the same premium. Now the proposition is more fair and equitable, based on one simple idea: individuals should have more control and determine their own premiums.

Individuals 'lock-on', not markets

Personalization comes in many formats.

'Burberry Bespoke' allows customers to customize their own trench coats, and their own names can be engraved onto metal plates stitched into the garment. Lego users self-design models, load them onto its website, and order them for delivery. Additionally, customers design their own personalized Lego kits and packaging. Each model comes with instructions, but bricks can be connected in many ways and forms to suit the individual's sense of experimentation and creativity, which is part of the fun.

China has one of the highest savings rates in the world (around 30–40 per cent of annual income), so the Chinese tend to borrow from themselves. OCBC Bank, instead of ignoring these customers or forcing them to fit into the bank's mould, made all the moves to become customer centric, offering services in a totally unique way. It is branded as 'Frank', intended to convey 'speaking frankly', being honest and sincere – all of which continues to resonate with customers and increase its market potency.[24] Users have individualized cards and e-banking tools, helping them monitor their budgeting and billing. Each individual's spending is put into categories, so that they can monitor it against budget, compare this with peers and get early warnings when a bill is due. They can also have several savings jars, into which they can dip, without having to open different accounts each time they need liquidity.

The assumption that all customers are the same seeps into behaviour on the front line where and when interactions really matter. That's when employees start to hide behind rules and rituals, policies and procedures, lacking the flexibility or empowerment needed to treat customers as individuals.

Customer-centric thinking counters this, by making offerings and behaviour flexible enough to suit people. Capitec don't expect all customers to fix their accounts at the standard 30 days, six months or 12 months. Instead, customers fix the times according to their needs.

In its lifetime wellness programme, IHI's CEO Per Bay Jorgensen offered each employee a personalized health plan. It included providing intervention in each person's key concern area, from headaches to the customization of canteen food, based on their individual reactions and intolerances. From medicine to banking, education to fashion, technology has gone a long way to help enterprises move away from averages.

In education in the USA, for example, schools are blending advances in online technology with traditional classroom resources to create a whole new set of tools that can radically alter the way students learn. Each pupil can get material tailored to their own particular learning styles and pace to help them progress faster, with more proactive and timely intervention by teachers. And the numbers of teachers don't have to increase to get this private and public added value.

Technology allows the vendor to foster deep relationships with infinite numbers of customers. UK's Ocado, the online grocer, while covering two-thirds of the country treats each person as if they are dealing with a local grocery store instead of a mass retailer. A variety of customized online services from recipes to brochures are provided, goods chosen are packaged according to individual needs – for instance allowing customers to get meat as they would at a butcher's. And, if the weather is bad, alternate delivery routes are found or contingency plans made, relayed to customers via text.

The trick is to fit into the processes, customers' workflows, instead of expecting it to be the other way round. Lexis Nexis makes sure that the myriad of questions and answers that form fixed or mobile customer decision making – so they can take risk free actions – moves seamlessly into each other in order to fit into the B2B customer's daily work pattern, without them having to interrupt their routines to do that research.

Traditionalists will argue that personalization costs. Customer centricity knows that it's an investment that leads to lower costs, especially if achieved through technology.

Amazon wanted to build the right store for each person at a reduced cost. This involved recognizing customers as individuals, remembering them as individuals, learning from each single interaction, and passing that learning back to that customer, and others who matched that profile. Proof positive is that the gains in personalization have far outweighed the investment shared with customers, bringing in ever more numbers who have 'locked-on'.

Jeff Bezos had a favourite line when he (and Amazon) were still question marks in 1998:

We know 2% today of what we will know 10 years from now and most of that learning is going to revolve around personalization – the notion of making a cyber-store ideal for a particular customer. If we have 4.5 million customers, we should have 4.5 million stores.

Little did his critics know the 4.5 million customer target he set himself would grow exponentially into hundreds of millions. And his recent acquisition of the *Washington Post*, to move Amazon even deeper into customer reading, can provide people with the ability to get personalized news, without having to endure (and pay for) content they don't want.

Personalization for the poor

Contrary to what most people still believe, personalization is essential for emerging market customers, even those at the bottom of the pyramid.

Cemex found that customers want homes with unique differentiating features. It adapts its construction offerings depending on individual preferences (which are allowed to change), decided between customers and architects or technical advisors. Individuals can choose how quickly they want to build, and in what intervals they want deliveries made.

When Cemex invites the poor to join 'socio' (buying groups), not only does it provide the financing and materials to build a home, it also gives them an identity as a member of the Patrimonio Hoy, through personalized cards. This gives customers who are at the fringes of society – without birth certificates, voter registration forms, or drivers' licenses – a personal sense of identity.

UT bank in Ghana treats every small and medium enterprise (SME) customer differently. Each payment scheme is structured according to the circumstances of that vendor and the details of their cash flow, when they need money and when they expect money in. Typically, they only get money in the second or third or even the fourth month after they start trading. So UT allows for that. By the sixth month they can usually pay it all, and when that is done, there is an automatic renewal of funds, without any application or paperwork.

And India Tobacco Company in its ambitious customer centricity e-Choupal (in Hindi meaning virtual meeting place) initiative, takes all the information that diverse farmers get – which includes weather forecasts, international prices of commodities movements and forecasts, prices of raw materials, and best practice farming methods – and customizes it, both in format and content, for each individual, depending on geo-situation and language.

The value lies in the customer experience

Continuing with the customer-centric principles:

- Value is not what goes into product or services, it's what customers get out.
- Customers get this value out over time – not transactionally, at a moment in time.

In other words, success is not about how well the company makes something. Success is about how well the company manifests and lands value, at the various interactions customers have with it or its brand over time.

So anything done in an enterprise – any money, time or effort spent in any activity – that does not result in that value, either directly or indirectly, is waste.

Here is the fifth belief:

> **Customer-centric belief 5**
> *For true value to happen, it must land in the customer's space as an experience – in our space we only create costs.*

The customer-centric approach starts with the express intention of elevating the customer's experience. Then the question is: how? And then … how to resource, fund and monetize it?

Brand takes on a new meaning: instead of it being the product or service, it becomes the experience that the brand delivers.

For Amazon, the plan was never to use the Internet to sell more books, or to just discount them. It was to change the very way people found, bought and got their books – it was the new online customer experience, and that's what has dictated what Bezos did and continues to do.

Once people understand this part of the customer-centric protocol, it gets them beyond thinking *product*.

Starbucks wasn't out to sell coffee as Nestlé was (who later emulated it) and steal market share from someone else also selling coffee. It wanted to create an upmarket place – a 'third home' (now 20,000 locations in 60 countries) where people can have an experience during their breaks to work, read and … also sip cappuccinos.

In the urban landscape, including on neighbourhood street corners in tea-drinking China, Starbucks has kept on enhancing and ensconcing the coffee experience, not just the taste and variety of its coffee, which so far has kept out lower-priced coffee emulators. In India, also not a coffee culture, Starbucks has made inroads, because it is creating places where people can go to meet, chat, work and so on … as well as have something to drink.

From the start Richard Branson maintained that he was finding new ways to help people have a good time, and make Virgin a cool way to travel. His words: 'anyone can buy an airplane and we all buy planes from the same manufacturers, but there the difference stops. If you fly on a Virgin plane … you know you are going to have a completely different experience.'[25]

Customers want the same experience wherever they may be. Burberry's CEO, when she first began the customer-centric journey, found that an experience at any given Burberry store might be very different from a previous one. Different countries were all doing their own thing, including making different quality and style merchandise under the Burberry licence, and charging different prices, which became her first challenge to set right.

Customer experience may also have as much to do with what customers don't have to do, as what they do have to do. Much of what the Apple experience is about is embedded into the product. But they are all made to be as simple as possible to use, concentrating as much on what is left out, as what is put in. Which may be one of the reasons why toddlers play with iPads before they can even talk!

The 'now' customer experience

What customers also don't want is to waste time. Impatience, ever on the up, reflecting the 'now' culture permeating societies around the world, has made time *the* premium resource. This has worked to Google's advantage, which constantly designs user experience and interfaces to try to get people to automatically go to its site, and in ever-accelerated response times, push to search and research, and get results instantly, at no cost.[26]

Starbucks, knowing that many of its customers are impatient to get served and get out, has led the way in mobile payment. Customers carry a Starbucks card in their phones, and millions pay with it every week, reloading while in line, to save time. One billion dollars was loaded in 2013, effectively creating a new form of currency. And, in the future, customers will be recognized as being in the store, and they will not need to place an order if they don't want to – a knock with their card will do it for them.[27]

Maverick Michael Jordaan, CEO of First National Bank (FNB), which in 2012 topped the list at the global 'Most Innovative Bank of the Year' awards, and was named the 'coolest brand' by a local newspaper customer base, caused a revolution in the South African upper-end banking scene. One of the big four banks, none of whom has done much to innovate (despite Capitec's market intrusion), at the height of the fiscal crisis and contraction (which Jordaan believed was an advantage for him) set out in mid-2004 to migrate customers to digital channels. Jordaan was determined that FNB would radically change its dull image and appeal to the younger set by imbuing a sense of fun into the stodgy banking industry. With expectation increasingly about speed of response, this included providing immediacy to customers, epitomized in a repertoire of fast and feisty digitalized services.

This theme he permeated through the entire organization. High on the list of priorities, for instance, was that the social queries that come in were escalated from front-end media platforms to relevant departments, to make sure that response times were instant, in an uncharacteristically flattened organization, to speed up decision making.

Amazon consistently places speed as number one in the customer experience, allowing customers to download any book onto the Kindle within 60 seconds, and locating automated warehousing hubs closer to population centres so as to provide same-day delivery. It has thus managed to stay ahead of traditional retailers who have now also jumped onto the online buying bandwagon.

Don't let's underestimate the importance of time to lower income emerging customers. Brazil's Casas Bahia offers fast delivery, large assortment and convenient location, backed by long-term low-payment installation plans, thereby making possible high ticket home purchasing. This is in line with research which shows that products and services don't have to be cheap for emerging market customers, but rather affordable. In its credit granting, it deliberately concentrates on speed. Its credit system enables salespeople to apply on behalf of customers online. If an analysis is needed, credit concessions are provided immediately for the smaller amounts within ten minutes.[28]

Merging bricks and clicks

Customer experiences are multifaceted – they span time, space and distance, across numerous channels, both physical and virtual. With state-of-the-art technology as the enabler, vendors can get customers to connect to them at any time, and all the time, and engage from anywhere.

Steve Jobs was a master at user experience. In sharp contrast to Nokia, whose distribution system separated it from its customers, he extended Apple's high-tech product magic to create user experience in brick and mortar stores (which so far have proved to be highly profitable). Stores were deliberately designed not only as a place to sell merchandise – the traditional retail environment – but to mirror lifestyle and create a learning experience. And to commence a lifetime relationship with customers, not just make a sale.

Customers have been known to flock and queue around the block on opening days to get into Apple stores carefully placed in trendy districts, as happened in Hong Kong and Shanghai, with customers spending hours in the store, reluctant to go home. More like high-tech boutiques with eye-catching displays, customers are encouraged to play with machines and 'test drive' them. Products like cameras and computers are grouped, as they would be in a home in 'solution zones'. And there is 'The Genius Bar', a concierge desk for troubleshooting. Free classes in small theatres ensure customers know how to make Apple machines work for them (many computers and phones are returned, not because of a product fault but because customers have problems using them). Staff interact with customers without pressure to buy. If customers do buy, the product is personalized for them at no extra charge.[29] This kind of store experience has become a new standard for multiple touchpoint customer engagement in other industries.

Despite the techno literate nature of the young market, OCBC Bank for instance have changed the banking scene in Singapore, one of the most fast-paced Asian markets of the world, by making their branches into the kind of Apple-like retail experience their customers would understand and enjoy. Spaces are open, filled with places to sit and chat, with Apple Mac Books available to use to access information. Floors are wooden, and there are no queues. As in the Apple Stores, people called 'service ambassadors' are dressed informally and walk around casually to engage in conversations and respond quickly and, over weekends, extra staff ensure the customer receives instant service.

To be customer centric is to have multiple presence throughout the customer activity cycle, where and when the customers are either physically or virtually, instead of the other way around. This effectively merges the concept of bricks with clicks into wall-less seamless ongoing engagement.

Bricks-and-mortar Tesco, hot on its South Korean triumph, has extended virtual stores into Gatwick airport in the UK. Ocado, the online operator, in a slightly different rendering, has created branded physical presence in the high streets of London and elsewhere in the UK to be present and visible where their customers live and shop. Virtual window displays placed in shopping centres, replicating by the day, are a new mini-presence concept that can have massive consequences as increasing numbers of customers order their goods – from basics to organic specialities – with an Ocado free 'on the go' mobile app, filling their virtual baskets and then getting the goods delivered to their homes.

The social customer experience

Customer-centric enterprises work to bring customers together, and make them and the enterprise part of one interactive social community or network.

Lego builds platforms for online user communities. On these they can build their own models, upload them with drawings and instructions, make videos and share them on the Lego site or on YouTube. Each model is themed with potential for extension and longevity. Storylines have a microsite, where customers can learn about characters, play games with these characters, answer quizzes and watch mini movies.

With postmodern savvy, Burberry has used cutting-edge technology strategically, to deliver a multichannel social experience, against the established luxury sector grain, which feared digital would chase away exclusive customers. It has managed to reach and link customers across the world using the universal digital tongue of the young elite. The emphasis is to get customers to participate with the brand, face-to-face and remotely, not just to push more products.

This way, the experience is much more than just the product or service. It's the entire set of interactions the customer has with the organization or brand. Touchpoints may be deliberately embedded into the brand engagement, to purposefully engage with the customer as much as possible. 'You don't just create encounters through the existing line, you re-create and increase the line.' Completely the opposite of what old wisdom would have taught or done.

To enrich the in-store experience, and bring real time content to customers, Burberry has created retail theatre, using music and giant screens with live fashion shows. Staff carry iPads and have access to the full range of the collection to offer, not just what is in store. When there are fashions events, customers can stream the runway shows happening anywhere in real time, and order items directly, as if they are there with the crowd. When products are bought, metal tags inside coats and bags have chips that bring the products to life, triggering a mini video that tells a story about its creation and history.

The engagement doesn't end there. Burberry then continues its conversation with customers, encouraging feedback and involving them in various sites and activities. All of which has helped to make it the most pre-eminent luxury brand on Facebook with 10 million plus fans engaging, reflected in increasing revenues. For instance, its 'Art of the Trench' site invites customers to take pictures of themselves in their trench coats and post them online for the nearly 3 million viewers to see, comment upon and rate. This has got views from over 150 countries, coupled with high conversion rates and customer advocacy.[30]

Even online players are integrating social engagement into the shopping experience, to deepen their interaction with customers. Bringing food-centric content to life, Ocado has live events that they call 'hangouts' where great British chefs cook food for customers, which is then watched live by other customers on YouTube. This is combined with images of recipes in picture and video format, which is shared amongst them.[31]

With digital media being the crux of FNB's success at scooping up customers, it can provide social experiences to customers through a range of platforms and channels, so they can circumvent the corporate hierarchy. One of the distinctive features of this is that customers have direct access to Jordaan through fast short chats on Twitter, one of the many channels used, which provides him with feedback to which a CEO would not normally be privy.

He explains that through customer complaints and compliments he got to understand them and gained insight into where to improve the business. Twitter could not be used as a one-way communication channel, as customers assume that the other person is available to sort out problems and engage personally on a real-time basis. This took up a lot of his time, so much so that RB Jacobs was invented as the 'contact person', rather than just subject people to an impersonal call centre.

And at the lower end of the market spectrum, Capitec, which is still largely micro-lending in South Africa, introduced a simple but creative 'AskWhy' initiative, which invites customers onto social media open platforms such as Facebook and Twitter to share, compare and question their experiences with both Capitec and its competitors, in highly engaging digitalized ways. This is backed by a branded campaign, including on the surface of cars in campuses across the country, in order to try to attract students, including allowing them to apply to drive the cars to earn extra cash.

Moving away from the silo view

Continuing, then, with the principles of customer centricity:

- Value is holistic – customers don't care what department we belong to, who partners or owns whom, or who reports to whom.
- Value is an organization-wide effort to deliver a unified customer experience.

Experience thus means a single-minded view of the customer. That entails pulling together whatever is needed from various parts of the enterprise internally, and from external partners, to create an over-arching experience. What many companies call a 'one company' or unified experience.

Here's a B2B example to illustrate. In order to energize growth, BP UK moved away from just selling its traditional commodity products such as gas, oil, bio-thermal power, solar, wind, lubrication and so on in the mid-1990s. Each silo was operating in isolation, with its own budget business plan and set of key performance metrics (KPIs).

This derivative of product logic often means the silos compete rather than collaborate for customers and their budget. The mantra is divide and rule, symptomatic of cultures where people are encouraged to work against each other, rather than together. And the customer is subjected to different people from the same organization, an array of contracting, billing and pricing systems and, often too, variable levels of service. And it is likely that the silos each have a different way of measuring success.

What's worse in B2B situations is that the customer may also be structured in silos, with separate budgets and different people managing units or divisions, dealing with the same supplier. Not only is this inefficient in that there is a good deal of duplication and waste, but relationships become fragmented, and neither customer nor supplier benefit.

What proves astonishing to many executives trapped in silos is that actually customers don't care how an enterprise is structured, as long as they get a seamless integrated or unified experience.

In BP's case B2B customers didn't even care which commodity or combination of commodities they used to get energy. What they wanted was to keep their ships, trucks or machines moving (and therefore producing) at the lowest cost, and on budget. And since differences in energy prices could be between 10 per cent and 40 per cent of their indirect costs, they needed to keep usage, and hence costs, to a minimum, and to hedge themselves against price volatility.

A unified view of the customer requires bringing together all of the bits – product and service units, departments, companies or even industries – that are structured and kept separate (see Exhibit 2.4). The picture changes from left to right.

On the left of the diagram with product logic the vendor has various silos, each delivering separately to customers, even the same customers. On the right-hand side, the customer-centric imperative is to deliver a unified customer experience in a chosen 'market space', with internal providers (ips) and external partners (xps) brought together when, where and how needed to produce and deliver. This results in a joined-up view of the customer, with the enterprise effectively becoming the 'one company 'integrator.

The alternative to this is that customers do the integration themselves, or a newcomer takes on this role, which we are increasingly

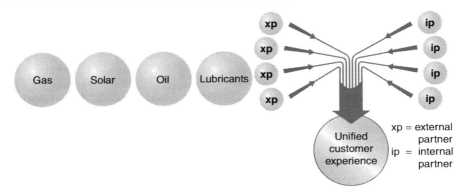

Exhibit 2.4 Product focus versus unified customer experience

seeing, with customers prepared to pay for the service if it saves them enough time, money and energy – what a customer-centric enterprise definitely wants to avoid.

What technology can and can't do

Technology is no substitute for integration, and having it – even the most advanced – doesn't mean that integration will take place. Again, technology's role is to facilitate, in this case, unification across silos for those who see the point, and make it an imperative.

Even in the public domain. This is what IBM SmartCities is all about. Gone are independent units all operating under the auspices of the city managers, without coming together to optimize decision making, and avoid delays or poor response. The first initiative was in Rio de Janeiro in Brazil, where up until then, as in most other cities of the world, departments covering energy, water, traffic, parking, public transit and crime were run as separate bits, many of whom didn't or couldn't talk to each other. Reactions to big events, like disasters or day-to-day operations such as crime or congestion, were consequently haphazard and disjointed, often to the detriment of citizens.

In a citywide system driven by the mayor, IBM integrated Rio's systems, connecting deep data pools across some 30 government departments and agencies, to enable metropolitan areas to run more effectively and efficiently, with dynamic real-time evidence-based proactive decisions, instead of the old way, which was reactive and ineffective.

With IBM as the 'master integrator', problems can now be antici- pated, responses coordinated and resources optimized, giving rise to innovative new ways of running cities that are smart and fast.

Offerings across company are clearly being fostered through data matching and advanced technology. It is, after all, what Amazon or Ocado are doing, pulling infinite things from various places, which previously customers would have had to find themselves. Ocado offers free-range organic food to some customers for some occasions and regular food for other occasions. It aggregates and compares prices for customers from various vendors, and then matches them so that customers don't have to shop around themselves to compare, which increasingly they are doing armed with shopping assist mobile apps.

Crossing through company silos has been taken to new heights in China e-tailing, where a new kind of disruption is taking place. Having leapfrogged from regional to e-market spaces in a first-of- its-kind model, Chinese consumer spending is being fuelled by the ability to choose across combinations of retailers online. These sites are more like e-marketplaces, where customers can decide what to buy and from whom, backed up by agile cross-company support services, which provide the total experience including delivery. And people in small or midsize towns and cities are using these sites as much as counterparts from larger cities.

Once the idea that integration across silos, internally and exter- nally, is fundamental to customer-centric success – because this is what facilitates the relationship and knowledge to get and give value on a sustained basis – is accepted, the more serious business of mak- ing it work for a particular enterprise can begin.

Customer centricity has higher purpose

People with higher purpose seek not just to change their organizations; they want to change humanity itself, by altering existing social and business practices. This is something Steve Jobs knew how to do. He didn't start the business to make computers. He wanted to change the way people worked and played, so as to enrich their lives, and he con- tinued to make this fundamental to Apple's beliefs, to his dying day.

Building societal significance into new beliefs is not the sole domain of a specialist type organization, today called by various names. It is a defining feature of any customer-centric organization, where brand spreads individual as well as public good. But whilst many use the buzzwords in annual reports and on websites, few deliver the promise with strategic intent.

When they do, it is a powerful binding mechanism and a way to mobilize energy during the customer-centric transformation. If it goes deep into the fabric of the organization's culture, beyond just being a promotional or PR exercise, the notion of transcendence can add an authenticity to new initiatives, which galvanizes people both internally and externally.

Today we see some people going as far as saying they would rather be seen as a cause not a company. This is completely in line with new humanistic values and rising consciousness, being expressed in various ways by consumers, employers and employees, simply put as concern for society and wider environmental issues.[32]

This takes us to the next belief:

Customer-centric belief 5
Customer centricity needs to be significant not just successful, and must have a higher purpose, contributing to human and planetary progress.

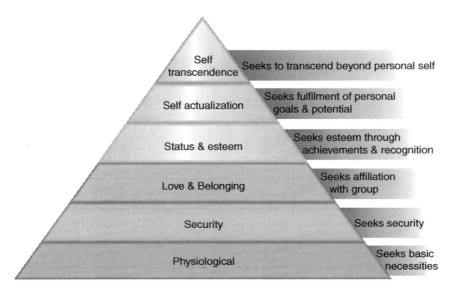

Exhibit 2.5 Maslow's updated hierarchy of needs
Source: author's interpretation of Maslow's hierarchy of needs and extra level.

Research reveals that Abraham H. Maslow, whose famed hierarchy of five progressive human needs for decades formed the basis for understanding consumer behaviour, amended his model, believing self-actualization to be insufficient as a motivational capstone, as it did not sufficiently reflect the optimally functioning human being.

He placed a sixth level, namely self-transcendence, or thinking beyond the personal self, as the motivational step beyond self-actualization, but he never published it.[33] This, plus the recent global economic traumas that have made consumers increasingly wary of the darker side of capitalism, gives a theoretical underpinning for understanding today's transcendent conscious customer, with higher order ideals and motives, mirrored increasingly in customer-centric strategies (see Exhibit 2.5).

Driving inclusivity

When beliefs implicitly embrace higher goals it enables customers who have been locked out of the system previously to get access to goods and services never before made possible. This is becoming the norm in emerging countries.

Money is not just a means of exchange it becomes the fuel for building economies and upgrading communities. In much of the deprived markets of Africa, unbanked individuals do not have regular incomes and are outside the remit of formal banking and credit sectors, so a vicious cycle has set in, whereby they continue to be locked out. Prince Kofi Amoabeng, CEO of UT Bank, had one simple desire: to provide as many underserved unsalaried entrepreneurs, unable to get loans, to realize their start-up dreams, and to make his bank an engine to boost their income and spur on Ghana's wealth-creating capabilities. He had tried himself several times to start a business, but bankers' decisions took so long that the opportunities simply slipped away.

According to Amoabeng other banks took months whereas his bank would take days. Clients hated being asked to come back again and again. UT Bank would give an answer in two days or an instant 'no' if they couldn't help. Banks consistently treated poor people poorly, whereas UT Bank would show respect. Whereas other banks wanted collateral UT Bank did not, but it would spend time getting to know the clients, under what circumstances their plans would work, and how and when they could repay the loan. UT Bank wouldn't give up on people if they had no legal address. It would go to their homes and sketch maps, with codes, for tar roads (a straight line) or for dirt roads (a broken line).

Inclusive means giving customers access. Eighty per cent of the doctors lived in cities, but 70 per cent of the people lived in rural areas and half of the drugs were counterfeit, out of stock, unlabelled, or of poor quality sold on grocery stalls, when the Kenyan micro-franchise HealthStore launched micro-pharmacy clinics to provide access to essential medicine, health education and preventative services, to underserved villages and urban areas across Kenya.[34] The object was to get medical services to the people, instead of expecting them to find their way into the towns.

Inclusive also means seeing risk differently. Product-type organizations thrive on control and controls, and therefore are concerned about minimizing their risk, and often that means leaving out customers who don't fit their paradigm. Interestingly, customer-centric thinkers approach risk differently. They mitigate risk by doing things differently.

Small entrepreneurs in Ghana regard profits and cash as identical, and seldom keep records, so UT Bank had to build the processes to manage the associated risks. Prince Amoabeng, who has since expanded operations into other parts of Africa, explains his strategy in the following way. UT Bank pay the supplier directly and once they have the payment the interest is taken off and the client is left with the profit, saving time and bureaucratic record keeping. The loan-monitoring officer is deeply involved with the customer, understands the intimacies of the customer's business and spends time with them to ensure the plan is adhered to and, if something goes wrong, will talk to the client and make adjustments, so there are no ugly surprises for anyone.

Technology makes inclusivity utterly possible.

Casas Bahia in Brazil and Cemex in Mexico both provide their customers with individual identity cards as an important tool in capturing customer data. These cards also provide the poor with a proof of existence, making it possible to be included in the financial system as cards are a tangible way to demonstrate ability to access funds and repay.

Long-term relationships with poor customers can also be built with digitally enabled data-gathering processes and technologies, which capture knowledge about the preferences and characteristics of individuals. It also enables companies to assess customer spend capacity and elevate their buying status. The customer knowledge Casas Bahia gathers in their daily interactions provides them with the confidence to extend credit to those whom most banks would traditionally shy away from. And, if the need arises, adjust repayment plans based upon changes to a customer's personal circumstances. Their result is the lowest default rates in Brazil's retail industry.

Disruption with higher purpose often means changing customer habits, and having to shape behaviour rather than just responding to it, as we see from the many examples given here. At Casas Bahia, customers are educated not to buy beyond their means, which mitigates their risk, and that of the company.

Paul Polman, CEO of Unilever, a brand that touches 2 billion people per day, embarked on a hand-washing campaign, setting in motion an exercise of monumental proportion involving millions of customers in Asia and Africa. This spoke to the much needed preventative measures against disease, not universally practised worldwide.

Unilever, whose founder first introduced soap into Victorian England to combat cholera, found that in contemporary India soap was being used for washing bodies, clothes and dishes, but not hands. Its programme, Swasthya Chetna (meaning health awakening) involved government schoolteachers and NGOs, using its Lifebuoy brand to get people to change hygiene behaviour and bring about long-lasting benefits, including for the many children who are dying young due to poor hygiene habits. This has not only contributed to its massive billion-strong brand penetration in India, but also to physical wellbeing and social uplifting.

Redefining the market of customer constituents

A customer-centric viewpoint broadens the definition of market to include consumers, citizens, communities, cities, countries and cosmos (see Exhibit 2.6). And each of these becomes part of the multiple stakeholder base, all of whom have to gain (or at the very least not suffer).

An explicit part of the IBM mandate is to work with all of these customer constituents, to help create a smarter, more connected, environmentally sensitive planet, with cleaner, safer more productive urbanization that provides better services for citizens.

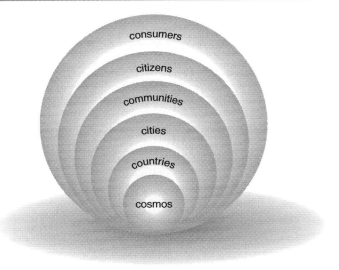

Exhibit 2.6 Multiple customer constituents

The chairman of India Tobacco Company, Y.C. Deveshaw, describes his strategy as nation-oriented, a commitment that stretches to the millions of Indian farmers who rely on its high-tech compendium of Internet-based services, which powers and empowers them to improve their crop yields. In the process it uplifts them, the communities they live in, and upgrades India's agricultural health and prosperity.

The mobile phone can significantly improve the societies and economies of Africa, in one symbiotic system, in all walks of life, real and virtual, provided the approach is customer centric. Particularly in the fields of micro business, health and education.

As its first priority MTN Ghana, led by CEO Michael Ikpoki, sought to find new ways for digital technology to help key groups of individuals vital to the development and future of the economy. The backbone of their customer-centric strategy was to identify these markets. From that came the decision to work with traders who are having a hard time growing their businesses without access to Web and mobile platforms; doctors, who desperately needed to share their knowledge and experience with each other and better communicate on mutual patients; and students, who could advance their learning and development through better use of digital.

Having a higher purpose is often linked to driving a cause and this formula works, provided it is integral to the customer-centric strategy and aims to impact over the long term.[35] This may take courage.

Fast forward the Marks & Spencer example to 2013, and it has moved to convincing customers to choose something from their closet to recycle, before they buy the latest fashion item. It now recycles 94 per cent of the waste generated by its stores, having coined the word 'shwopping' (cross between shopping and swapping). Partnering with the not-for-profit Oxfam charity outlet, customers can now drop off their old clothes before rushing to buy anew. Some people see this as suppressing demand and shortsighted: Marks & Spencer believe this is in tune with contemporary values, for more eco-friendly shopping behaviour.

When enterprises move with transcendent purpose, they not only propel customers, employees and partners to action, they can influence others vendors and legislators, which has a multiplier effect.

Marks & Spencer is hoping their core purpose will be felt by all clothing retailers and become mainstream in UK retailing in the not too distant future. Kenya's HealthStore ethos has been deliberately ramped up to decrease corruption, poor practice and dishonesty, and improve general standards in health care by forcing competitors to upgrade.

And once established as the new standard, e-books will be essential in the drive to increase literacy and education to the poor in Africa and other continents through access to mobile phones. Content can be uploaded onto a website as an e-book from and to anyone anywhere, and virtual libraries can be accessed, changing the face of education and how it is delivered.

The Discovery

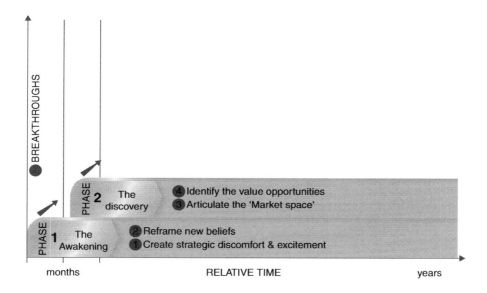

Articulate the 'Market Space'

Key idea

Together with the lead team the customer champion needs to articulate the 'market space', defined as the desired customer outcome,
from which the mission unfolds – what the enterprise has to be better
at doing than anyone else. The market space frames the competitive
arena, the domain where new wealth and opportunities will be sought
and found, which is a major step forward in the transformation process
because it provides cohesion, giving people concrete direction.

Broadening horizons and boundaries

If there is a single thing one learns about those who win with disruptive customer centricity, it's that they have a different way of seeing
the world, and framing possibilities. Customer-centric enterprises
move from thinking about how to just get market share of the stuff
producing ever diminishing returns, to how to dominate 'market
spaces', with its wealth potential.[36]

Here's the difference: **market share** *reduces* wealth – someone has
to lose for someone to gain, whereas **'market space'** *expands* wealth,
where everyone multi-sector can gain.

A 'market space' is a descriptive term to frame the desired customer
outcome – the end game if you like. In this paradigm the product or service is simply a means to some end. Whether or not customers know it
or can express it, they all want to achieve something from products and
services. This something is the desired customer outcome. The ability to
express it explicitly is a major step forward for the transformative process.

The 'market space' becomes the new competitive arena in which
the enterprise wants to operate, flourish and 'lock-on' its customer

base. Once defined and agreed, this all-important decision provides focus, and moves the implementation journey forward. Because, whilst people are bound to align around the new beliefs, at this point they are looking for application and more substance.

Finding and naming a new 'market space' provides cohesion, and is an important breakthrough point, as they start to go from the abstract to the specific. Even if the energy levels are high, and there is no 'market space' as an anchor, the process can end up as no more than a checklist of good ideas, inadequate to carry the transformation to the next step.

But it is a voyage, and as such people are learning something that was not known before, about a more promising way of looking at the market. And, in the spirit of discovery, together they start to expand their thinking and look at the possibilities.

Let's remember, too, that the more forward thinking the company wants to be, the less likely it is that conventional research or customers can express this world yet to be. So this means having to make some educated hypotheses about 'market space' – experimenting, shaping and altering ideas.

Evidently the automobile industry has been working on driverless or driver assist cars for years. And research indicates that, globally, consumers want transportation changes, and Brazil, India and China are ahead of advanced countries in terms of receptiveness to this breakthrough concept.[37] But, unlike the auto manufacturers, Google doesn't want to sell cars, it wants to tap into a 'market space' in which it has already been involved, via its geopositioning, mapping, traffic notification and social informationing. What it sees is a 'market space', call it 'enhanced commuter mobility', which it is determined to fill. This it will do partly through its driverless car, which in the first two years has ramped up hundreds of thousands of miles in the USA, without incident.

As well as capturing revenue in that space, it has higher goals to achieve, like reducing accidents (human error can in some countries account for up to 90 per cent of all accidents) and improving the commuting experience. With a conditioned mind and culture that thinks 'cars', the question is: how do we keep adding discrete features incrementally (like piloted parking, cruise control and so on)? With a disruptive mind that is customer centric, the question becomes: what needs to be done differently to produce better urban mobility for people?

Already IBM is in that space, with its predictive traffic technology analytics, which offers governments better traffic management and traffic forecasts – including in places such as China that have large volumes of bicycle traffic – with enough time for citizens to respond and choose alternative routes. As is Apple by enabling their customers, as they commute to work, to get their own favourite music through iTunes, which is poised to become the operating audio system for cars.

The implications of Google's disruption thinking are wide reaching. First it demonstrates how outsiders can get into a space like self-drive, if industries are stuck in old product or service boxes, and who are then forced to become followers. And second, it shows what associated innovation possibilities a new 'market space' and disruptive customer centricity can bring. What will people be doing with their time when autopilot cars become an extension of their work and leisure space? What opportunities lie there? And how will cities be affected? The word is, they will be congestion- and pollution-free, and that people will probably be able to live further afield because commuting won't be such a negative factor in location decisions.

'Market space' defined

In defining your 'market space' some guidelines will help. The first is to try to find a way to encapsulate the desired customer outcome, without referring to your products. The second is to make sure that it is far enough away from your existing business, pushing present boundaries outward and offering growth potential. The third thing to underscore is that a 'market space' is not product-, service- or industry-bound – it cuts across all of these.

And making sure that the 'market space' isn't simply the current offering with a fancier name, or a more advanced version of a product category. In fact, as one CEO said, as he got his executive team geared up for the exercise, 'an enterprise shouldn't have more than 5–10 per cent market share in their new 'market space'. If they do, they've defined it too narrowly, and there won't be enough room for sustained growth.'

The real take-away from this suggestion is that origin products or services are only one small part of any good 'market space' definition and potential, especially with disruption.

The other guideline, which is important, is to make sure the 'market space' reveals the competition you will have to face, who they are, or potentially will be – insiders and, more importantly, outsiders.

Box 3.1 contains the attributes of 'market spaces'.

Box 3.1 Attributes of 'market spaces'

'Market spaces':
- are an articulation of the desired customer outcome;
- provide an integrated view, linking benefits across the products, companies and industry sectors, which provide the full and integrated customer outcome;
- push the enterprise beyond existing product or service categories;
- are disruptive, because they expand thinking and change sector boundaries;
- are able to direct thinking strategy and resources;
- have potential value for customer, and for enterprise.

Let's look at Table 3.1 to see some examples, all of which will be used in the chapters that follow:

Table 3.1 Products versus market spaces

	Old approach	Customer-centric approach
Enterprise	*Seeks market share of:*	*Seeks to dominate this 'market space':*
BP	Oil, gas, solar, lubricants	Integrated energy assurance
Cemex	Cement	Sustainable home ownership
Discovery Insure	Motor insurance	Great safe driving
GE Healthcare	Medical supplies	Population health management
GE Imaging	Equipment	Personalized predictive health care
Lexis Nexis	Published content	Risk management & mitigation
Google	Search engine	Information finding
HealthStore	Drugs	Medical service accessibility
IBM	PCs, information technologies	Predictive decision support
IHI	Health insurance	Lifetime health and wellbeing management
Lego	Brick toys	Lifetime play
MTN	Service provider	Personal and professional advancement
Unilever	Disparate brands	Sustainable living
Unilever	Soap (Lifebuoy)	Personal hygiene management

A good 'market space' opens up windows for dialogue on meaning and implications, which is significant, because this engages people, and invites conversation and discussion during a transformation.

Let me give you an example. Discovery Insure defined its 'market space' as 'great safe driving' not 'driver safety'. But as the CEO Anton Ossip elucidates, safe driving is sometimes seen as slow and boring, whereas great driving doesn't have to be slow, it isn't boring, and is always safe. The Formula 1 team are the fastest, but also the safest, drivers in the world.

'Market spaces' should, however, be intuitively understood and recognized as having potential for growth and relevance for customers. It should also be imaginative, novel and forward looking.

'Market spaces' come from convergences

'Market spaces' come from convergences, not linear trends. That's why it's important to be able to project cross-sector across product industries and technologies in new and different ways, in order to come up with a range of possibilities.

One way to think of convergences is the blurring of industries, technologies, products and services. For example, M-PESA ('m' for mobile and 'pesa' meaning money in Swahili) was the result of the fusion of mobile services and financial services – a money transfer service that doesn't need an Internet hookup.[38] Apple's iTunes and automobiles are converging to create a commuter entertainment space.

Ever evolving is Lego's 'lifetime play' 'market space'. Not merely for kids, but also for people who have kids and even for 'the child within adults' it is a more complex convergence over many industries, fusing digital technology, toys, computing, games, hobbies, robotics, publishing, education, entertainment, social networking, consumer electronics, outdoor parks, virtual and augmented reality, and so on (see Exhibit 3.1).

Is a Lego robot a game or a toy? Well, it is both, and can be assembled, programmed on a PC or Mac, and controlled via applications and voice-controlled systems from any place or device and all places to join together the online and offline experience. It can be storylined and made into a serial movie and shown on YouTube or communicated to friends via a phone, or used in interactive games. But still these toys, or more accurately models, remain integral to education

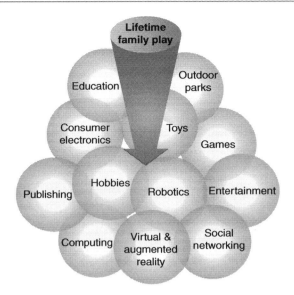

Exhibit 3.1 Converging 'market spaces' – Lego example

using both left and right brain skills, nurturing personal development and the human spirit through creativity and science.

Combine the technology with big data analytics, and products and services across industries can be integrated and knitted together into 'market spaces' in imaginative ways never before possible, to give customers outcomes that supersede anything previously experienced.

With margins deteriorating and differentiation difficult to achieve with products or services, Discovery Insure set about positioning itself as a customer-centric provider in the 'great safe driving' 'market space', rather than just selling insurance policies like everyone else. Evidently, risky driving causes 60 per cent of accidents. Through advanced and real time telematics and proprietary algorithms, Discovery can scientifically measure driver intelligence and actions, to tell customers whether or how much a car is being pushed close to the edge of its capability, risking an accident.

With its intricate design of telematics and data analytics (data is registered every two minutes), driving indicators such as speed, braking, acceleration, night driving and distance, knowledge and awareness and cornering are measured, and correlated to provide a score, which is then relayed to the customer, acknowledging that not all drivers or cars are the same.

Becoming indispensable in your 'market space'

Becoming indispensable in the 'market space' is what gets customer 'lock-on'. A good 'market space' definition shifts people's thinking from how to achieve market share in a product or service category, to how to become indispensable in a chosen 'market space'.

Imagine a world without Google in your daily 'information finding'?

No one may have to in the future, with Google's 'Project Loon', and Microsoft using so called 'white space' TV and radio bandwidth to bring affordable Internet connection and services to everyone on the planet. Including the billions of people in remote areas who have been unable to access it, due to a lack of infrastructure or resources.

The object of 'market space' is to be contained enough to provide a frame for direction and focus, but not so restrained that it prevents adaption over time to make room for growth:

Amazon started in the book-buying space and ended up as the largest e-retailer (some say not just e-retailer, biggest retailer) in the world. 'Market space' is a moving target.

IBM started its transformation from products to customers when Lou Gerstner reinvented IBM in the 1990s by moving it into services in order to help users buy, integrate and turn their computers and software into a much needed 'global networking capability'. Then, pushing still further, the new CEO Sam Palmisano rejuvenated the enterprise again, buying the management consultancy arm of PricewaterhouseCoopers, and merged IBM's hardware, software, IT consulting unit and research scientists with it, to form a global group of hundreds of thousand of business consultants and experts. The object was to take IBM into the higher ground 'growth and transformation' 'market space', extracting, extrapolating and exposing trends in order to give executives unique insights into fast-moving marketplace opportunities as well as the technological systems they needed to capture them. And then linking all of these into one system, delivered via data centres, through the Internet.

With advanced technology today, IBM is making possible interconnection and intelligence never before imagined. This nimble mammoth believes that it is destined to change the planet for the better by making it smarter. Now it globally manifests 'predictive decision support' for private homes, business practices and cities.

Anticipating that, by 2015, 75 per cent of the world's population will be urban has put strain on mayors and municipalities to make their cities smarter, safer and sustainably productive. IBM's role is to blend information and infrastructure to improve the local governments' decision making. This includes smarter governance, smarter policing, smarter crime management, smarter traffic control, smarter power and water management, smarter events and response. And the list goes on.[39]

How far do we go?

Because the 'market space' gives concrete shape and form to the otherwise conceptual idea of a unified customer concept, it is a vital part of moving people along the transformation process. It provides direction, it aligns thinking, and it stirs and excites, because people can begin to feel that they now have something tangible to say.

Once the decision on what 'market space' to choose has been taken, another important breakthrough has been made. One question that will invariably come up, though, is 'how far do we go?'

The choice of 'market space' size is based more on the spirit and sights of an enterprise than anything else. It is about foresight and the ability to see where the action is likely to be, and then taking the steps to make sure that the enterprise is in first, fast and feisty.

A bold, courageous leader or team will choose a bolder more courageous 'market space'. Even if some difficult challenges arise. Some enterprises will naturally gravitate into these more ambitious 'market spaces' 'because that's where the action is'. Others will be more cautious, playing in the smaller spaces to be closer to what they feel they know how to do.

In reality, executives tend to balance potential with passion. If the potential is there but they feel it's too big to tackle, they will scale down; if they feel strongly enough, they will find a way to make it happen, as long as it's lucrative enough.

One powerful motivator for extending boundaries outward is that, once a 'market space' has been articulated, executives are often amazed to find out how little of the wealth they currently leverage from it. For instance, pharmaceutical manufacturers are still only capturing a small portion of the total spend in the growing wellness space, of which alternative medicine (which not only treats sick people but keeps people well) is growing fast and furiously. Fuelled by herbal and nature-based products, and new medical practices, this space is exploding in many emerging countries as well.[40]

In truth there is no right or wrong decision about how large a 'market space' must be. There are some general principles, however, that are worth remembering:

- The larger the space, the larger the opportunity to get a bigger share of customer wallet.
- The larger the space the more the company and its resources need to be stretched, or redefined.
- The larger the 'market space', the more likely it is to lock out competition.
- The larger the space, the more sustainable the customer-centric initiatives are likely to be.
- The larger the space, the more partners are likely to be needed.
- The larger the 'market space', the more customer expectations will need to be shaped.

In large, highly complex organizations, such as GE or Unilever, the corporation may operate in one large space, respectively 'population health management' and 'sustainable living', but also identify smaller spaces for specific areas of the business, for example 'personalized predictive health care' (imaging) and 'personal hygiene management' (Lifebuoy soap). This works if they are aligned strategically, as these two examples clearly exemplify.

Existing, emerging and imagined 'market spaces'

The construct below, of three progressive 'market spaces', can help you to make a choice as to how far to go. These are:

existing 'market space' – (what is there, and needs to be framed);
emerging 'market space' – (what is likely to come on-stream);
imagined 'market space' – (what is possible to create the future).

Let's use a hypothetical example for a pharmaceutical company to illustrate in, say, cardiac drugs:

> *Existing 'market space'*
> Diagnose and prescribe   'cardiac disease management'.
> *Emerging 'market space'*
> Predict, reverse, prevent 'managed cardiac health care'
> *Imagined 'market space'*
> Prolong, preserve   'lifetime cardiac wellbeing'

In the existing 'market space', namely 'cardiac disease management', the assumption is that a patient already has cardiac disease and the desirable outcome would be to get it diagnosed accurately and quickly and managed with minimum pain and discomfort, maximizing and accelerating healing, and trying to hold off or reduce the risk of recurrence.

In the 'managed cardiac health care' 'market space', the assumption is that patients do not have the disease but that if they are predisposed, they would be put into a high-risk category and carefully managed. Early warning signals would be vital to spot the disease in its infancy, so as to prevent or retard its progress and reduce its side-effects, minimize damage and prevent symptom recurrence.

In the 'lifetime cardiac wellbeing' 'market space', the assumption is that the patient may never get that disease. Prenatal intervention could be used with the help of genetics to assess whether predispositions to certain diseases exist; then the necessary precautions would be taken to prevent onset, including preventative surgery, growing alternative organs, or whatever technology brings, to make sure that the disease never manifests.

Now let's look at how these constructs work for the Cemex example:

> *Existing 'market space'*
> Buy materials and build better 'building materials management'.
> *Emerging 'market space'*
> Fund, build and renovate   'lifetime home ownership'.
> *Imagined 'market space'*
> Eco-friendly, resource saving,
> well maintained, upgraded,
> multigenerational   'sustainable home ownership'

Cemex is another example of a company that has progressed from one 'market space' to another in its 'value before volume' drive. It started in 'lifetime home ownership' and then moved to 'sustainable home ownership', adding an environmental touch, outpacing analyst forecasts and competitors in the process.

Getting executives to make the connection between 'market spaces' and the future of the enterprise, and how this future will be different from the past, is probably the most significant breakthrough of all. This is because the 'market space' not only defines the competitive expanse. Importantly, it also tells people what they have to be good at doing. So from it, quite naturally, flows the mission.

For anyone driving a transformation it is also the red thread holding people and process together as the consciously managed steps of the transformation play out. Because 'market spaces' do not respect boundaries and cut across different product silos, disciplines and even industries, they are a powerful way of demonstrating to different people and units how each of them fits into a new unified customer concept. An enterprise-wide picture emerges, instead of a silo for silo plan, telling people what they need to do to succeed.

For example, people at Lexis Nexis used to consider themselves as working in one of umpteen units or databases – that is how they identified themselves. There was no market underpinning to unite them, or the offerings, to ensure customers got superior and quicker risk-free decision-making capabilities. However, when top management broadened the boundaries to reflect the 'market space', it highlighted how each played a part in risk mitigation and management, and the need for integrated content and a whole lot more. This gave clarity plus a common sense of purpose that aligned people and pushed the process along its way.

Identify the Value Opportunities

Key idea

Looking to dominate the 'market space' with values that elevate the customer experience is what the customer-centric enterprise excels at doing. And this is what keeps it sustainably ahead of rivals. To get to this point in the transformation, cross-silo team(s) need to identify value gaps or 'black holes' in the customer activity cycle, and then unlock opportunities to fill these gaps with customer-based value innovations. A value-mapping tool needs the vigour and rigour to build a strategic template and ensure that engagement and traction take place.

Value gaps and black holes

Customer-centric disruptors are always looking to create and elevate the customer experience in their chosen 'market spaces'. It is around this that they remake their organizations and industries.

Once a new 'market space' is found, they don't just improve some of the more important interactions, which is what many organizations do. Or only convert pain to passion points. They create an entirely new customer experience covering a much larger market domain.

They deliberately find opportunities by looking for the value gaps that exist in the experiences of customers, and then fill these gaps.

This is how they dominate the 'market space' and the spending – old and new – within it.

If an enterprise will not or cannot dominate its chosen 'market space', where it has made a conscious decision to play and position itself, with new customer values, it has been too ambitious and the 'market space' definition needs to be revisited.

The customer activity cycle methodology

The methodology for identifying these values is called the customer activity cycle.[41]

The customer activity cycle is a structured tool that looks at the activities that customers could/should go through in an experience to get the desired outcome. Once done, it becomes the architecture for a customer-back methodology to build the proposition, new strategy and story, in these five steps:

Step 1

Uncover the value gaps or shortfalls that currently or could exist in the customer activity cycle, either by virtue of a failure on the part of the enterprise, or the existing industry, or by virtue of a disruptive proposition, yet to manifest.

Step 2

Fill these value gaps with the missing or new value components.

Step 3

Translate these values into new innovations – products and services.

Step 4

Prioritize the new products and services.

Step 5

This finally culminates in a new strategy, told as a story with an action plan.

What differentiates this model from other approaches is that it starts with a definition of the market space, say 'lifetime health and wellness management', or 'great safe driving'. This is different from simply mapping the customer journey for buying stuff (for example, health or motor insurance), which is only one small part of the potential to deliver a desired customer outcome, and tends to result in tactical rather than strategic transformational decisions.

If the 'market space' is not first defined, the wrong questions will be asked and the wrong answers will follow. This will take the enterprise back to square one, and lead to incremental improvements rather than disruptive thinking and recommendations.

This process of value mapping will, from the customer's point of view, take the lead player and the team on a unique experience. It enables multidisciplinary groups of people in an enterprise to view the world from a common standpoint, namely that of the customer. This results in a 'one company' customer-centric value proposition.

Methodology for mapping and mining customer value

The customer activity cycle model has three generic stages, and enterprises should be in all of these stages in their chosen 'market space' arena:

Pre – when the customer is deciding what to do.
During – when the customer is doing it.
Post – when the customer is maintaining, reviewing, renewing, updating and measuring the results of what they decided to do.

You should find that the principles hold, and can be applied to B2B and B2C environments, from simpler to highly complicated settings (see Exhibit 4.1).

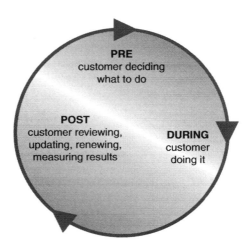

Exhibit 4.1 The customer activity cycle

The customer activity cycle methodology looks for details of the activities customers go through 'pre', 'during' and 'post' an experience in order to get a desirable outcome. It then exposes gaps, which prevents or damages the optimal result being attained at each critical point. Once these individual gaps are uncovered, it then provides the blueprint for deciding exactly what value-adds are needed to fill each of these gaps, in order to achieve the desired outcome for customers. That's how it unlocks wealth-creating new opportunities for innovation.

Imagine for a moment that Amazon did this initially for books. The questions would have been: what did customers go through to buy a book from a store 'pre' 'during' and 'post'? What are the gaps? And what can Amazon do to close these gaps, with products and services that give customers an elevated experience?

The answer is history, but if you go through this exercise in detail you will find that a very conscientious effort was made by Amazon to unlock and add value at each of these stages.

And Bezos continues to be a wizard at finding and filling gaps in the customer activity cycle, which since its inception has kept Amazon ahead. Kindle's MayDay button, for instance, connects customers over the Internet to technical support staff to help them with potential problems or frustrations once they have bought the item. Although to the uninformed this could look like just another product feature, in true Amazon style Bezos wants to eradicate a value gap, humanizing the service as close to a face-to-face intervention as possible, so that customers don't have to go to a physical store for help.

With one click, customers can talk to a real person on demand, who pops up on a side window within seconds (thousands have been trained) in order to get help in operating the Kindle, or they can do it for or with customers remotely. Special consideration has been given to security and privacy – and the image is only one way so that people don't have to worry about how they look.

Why gaps destroy customer value

Specifically, the value gaps that happen in the customer activity cycle are *points of influence* or *points of impact*, which are missed or badly executed. They could be old value gaps or new gaps that arise from an innovation or changed circumstance or trend, which could require a new customer intervention.

Specifically these gaps can be:

- Things not being done for customers during an experience in that 'market space'.
- Things being done badly by the enterprise or industry for the customer, during an experience in the 'market space'.
- Things being done by customers themselves that could be done either better or cheaper by someone else, or by some other means, in the 'market space'.
- Things that could be done differently in order to get an elevated customer outcome.

When these gaps exist, they create several disconnects in the customer engagement process, which can destroy value by:

- Preventing the customer getting a desired outcome, which can make the enterprise vulnerable to competition.
- Creating opportunities for outsiders to influence the customer's attitude and behaviour.
- Opening up opportunities for others to take customer spend.
- Commoditizing the relationship with the customer.
- Commoditizing the offering, and the margins.
- Costing more than is necessary.
- Blocking potential for advocacy.

That is when, as we have seen, companies lose their grip on the market and start to slide.

The value gaps effectively become gaping black holes, into which the enterprise gradually slides or implodes, depending on how quickly others enter to innovatively disrupt, creating new or different values and, consequently, stealing customers and revenue streams.

When value gaps happen everyone loses, including the customers, who are unable to get the results they want. The consequences can range from disenchantment to discomfort, serious loss of time, money, effort and increased costs in the short or long term. And it consequently makes the enterprise, or whole industries, vulnerable.

The loss may not be obvious and customers may not even be aware of it until a new approach is offered and its benefits are revealed.

For instance, a not-so-well-known fact is that about 40 per cent of all relocations fail, mainly due to personal rather than professional reasons. And a high proportion of executives leave a company after a relocation, even if the relocation has been successful, or return home prematurely.

Mismatching a person with a location can have a chain reaction with high consequent costs. Executives may also be late in starting their assignments in the new location/country or be unproductive once there. These are hidden costs that do not appear on any specific budget, such as the employee – or their spouse or children – being unhappy, or unsuited to the climate or culture of the country to which they have been expatriated. Research shows that these hidden costs can mount up to three times the cost of any executive's annual package.[42]

Opening up opportunities for killer entrants

Whole industries can be built up around value gaps left unfilled in 'market spaces'. We only have to think back to IBM in the old days to illustrate the point. Remembering that this was before the Internet, if one can imagine such a time, IBM was selling mainframes and PCs. But customers needed more, like:

> **'Pre'** – consulting advice, systems integration.
> **'During'** – multi-sourcing and procurement advice (as opposed to selling only IBM machines), pilot testing, training and installation, warehousing and storage.
> **'Post'** – proactive remote and preventive maintenance, early warning systems, speedy response systems that could be renewed, updated and extended.

IBM left these gaping 'pre', 'during' and 'post' holes, into which killer entrants flocked and built new industries and empires, commoditizing IBM's margins and relationship with customers. Top management made the decisions in those days, on the basis of their core business. They then learned that their core business was the customer outcome, not the boxes.

But by their moves or non-moves, new industries were born. Consultants took the gap, got into customer board rooms and other high-ground strategic places, and gave advice about how to use computers, and what computers to use for what purpose. Bill Gates evidently begged IBM to go along with him at the start, but he was rejected and so went on to build the Microsoft giant to produce the integrated systems to make PCs usable. And from every which corner small, lean and keen, small shops appeared to take the installation, training and warehousing gap left open, that heralded in the burgeoning solutions era. Even though this is now history, the IBM tale is worth repeating, because today there are still industries and companies making the same mistake on a grand scale. They allow their boxed notion of their core business, and gaps in the customer experience, to get between them and their customers and block their pathway to growth. Once disruptors see and sense these value gap windows, they become killer entrants (see Exhibit 4.2).

Stop to think for just a moment how M-PESA became a killer entrant, and made Kenya a world leader in mobile money and a cash-light society. Transferring money was complicated, unsafe and expensive. For instance, it used to take rural Kenyans trying to pay for their kids' school fees up to three days to receive the money, extra time to deposit it in the school's bank account, and then more time to take the

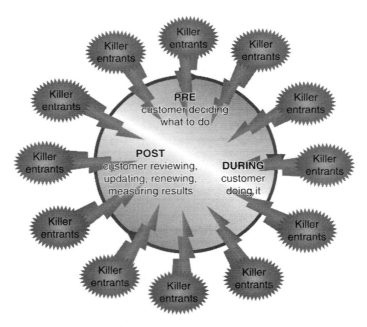

Exhibit 4.2 Killer entrants fill value gaps

receipt to the school as proof of payment. This and other value gaps – which made transferring money time-consuming if done with banks, or dangerous if done by hand – opened up the potential to disrupt.

Seeing the opportunity first, M-PESA marginalized the post office money transfer service, as well as money transfer companies and banks, as they went on to create a new way of storing money and paying for a customer base of 17 million people by 2013. Remarkably by that time, 70 per cent of Kenya's adults were active brand users, moving 20 per cent of GDP through its system at the rate of 20 million transactions per day.

Getting in sooner and staying in longer

To get customer 'lock-on' you need to get into the customer's activity cycle as early as possible, and to stay in as long as possible. This may require proactively anticipating problems early on for customers, knowing before they do what to expect. Virgin, for example, encouraged customers in African high-risk security airports to cling-wrap their luggage, financed by Virgin. The costs of this were more than offset by having eliminated the traumas and costs for customers and company alike of stolen and damaged personal belongings.

For Lexis Nexis it meant proactively thinking ahead to what would be needed by customers in order to mitigate risk. Lawyers searching for patent information, for example, were told by the enterprise about similar patents, patent holders and the legal claims that have already been made, so that when they applied for a patent they were fully equipped with everything they needed to know.

Most of the relocation decisions taken about whom to send where are based on the skills of an individual, rather than on consideration of their family profile and levels of comfort. Matching people more accurately to environments early on obviates risk, as IHI has found out. But other gaps occur once the professional is in the foreign country. For example, they may need a certain drug and not be able to find it, so a poor or no substitute is taken, or the decision about which hospital to go to in an emergency is not optimal. These can lead to costly and even devastating ramifications.

Or take a situation where an employee is not briefed about corruption and bribery in a particular country to which they have been relocated and, once ensconced there, is ordered to give business to someone against their will – with a threat that if they don't their family will suffer. The upshot is that the person is fearful and acquiesces, leading to deteriorating health and productivity. And many leave 'post' the assignment, with very few learnings shared, so as to obviate the enterprise repeating mistakes.

Most product-focused organizations find that they are present in the 'during' phase, when the customer is buying or using goods or services. But that their presence is not strong or early enough, and doesn't last long enough. The realization that this confines them to one small part of the customer's experience, limiting their points of influence, impact or revenue potential, is a powerful part of this breakthrough.

Getting in sooner...

Getting in sooner when customers are deciding what to do offers increased opportunities for stronger, hence longer, relationships. This requires having – or building – capabilities in that 'market space' to be able to:

- Move from straight selling to a more consultative and advisory role.
- Become – and be perceived as – the unrivalled expert in that 'market space', whatever it takes.
- Use data and analytics to help match customer profiles in order to correct offerings, whatever they may be.

The earlier the engagement takes place, the better.

GE prides itself on offerings that can detect a disease before the onset of the symptoms. If at-risk patients are screened early on, the chances of survival are much higher. And such is the level of detail that treatment can be applied with levels of accuracy that make the operating doctor's chances of success much greater.

Earlier also means younger. With energies and efforts directed to minimize an individual's risk of getting a disease, spot it early, manage it, get rid of it and minimize the chances of recurrence, HealthStore in Kenya provides screening services for children at school.

It also means helping people make better decisions. Once superior decisions are made about what to do, the chances of the outcome being better and consequent 'lock on' occurring are that much higher.

Lexis Nexis could simply wait for customers to ask questions and then find them the information they sought. But instead, the power of its new proposition lies in the fact that it prompts customers to ask the right question that leads to correct decisions. For example, one way that law enforcement agencies may locate criminals or drugs, or other undesirable persons or illegal items, is if they are prompted to ask: 'Who has taken out a pilot's or driver's licence in that area recently?'

Not being present early at the 'pre' stage will seriously diminish the chances an enterprise has to solidify its position and relationship with customers when it matters. This is the time, as one executive put it, 'when you show you are the expert' and become the customer's 'first port of call'.

'Pre' decisions can be made at various levels in a B2B setting, ranging from board rooms to strategic or operational planning sessions. They can be made by multinationals in their home base or in the host country. Whatever the details, it is critical to build capabilities so as to participate (provide expert objective advice), influence (not just promote) and build trust (not just hard sell).

Increasingly today, both B2C and B2B customers do their own search and research before making decisions, and whether they buy on or offline they tend to invest the same amount of time doing it. An interesting paradox in B2C purchasing habits, spurred on by the Internet and the ability to scan bar codes and make easy and speedy comparisons, is that:

• Increasing numbers of people are going online to do research before they make an important buying decision, and then find stores or service providers from whom to buy.
• Increasing numbers of people are going into stores to showcase goods or services that they will then buy later online. Before making an important buying decision they do their showrooming research in the stores – admiring, using and comparing – and then go online to buy, either from that store or another.

Combine this with various online sources from company websites, to peers on Facebook, from whom customers are gathering information, and this supports the need for solid and interactive multichannel presence early on.

... and staying in longer

In the old days, once the transaction ended and the customer paid, that was that. Until the next transaction.

Then came the services era in the mid-1980s, in which the great learning was that to maximize return on customers, relationships had to be forged, and service was the key value driver. On top of that that, a good deal of the monies spent on a product or service happened *after* the original sale. Even in recession times the after-market is considered to be the most resilient. The figures are substantial: services post-sale have the potential to exceed first-time sales by 10 to 30 times and can contribute double the profit from original sales, which is enticing if you are product focused.[43]

Customer centricity has a different goal in mind. Value provided in the 'post' phase is key to harnessing the 'lock-on' loop in the management of the customer experience. Because whatever happens at the 'post' stage influences the next cycle of the customer's decision making, when they are deciding how they have done and how *you* have done. This is the time when they evaluate and review their decisions, look at whether KPIs have been met, update their plans and decide with whom to do business next time round.

This makes it an important time to be present in the evaluation, demonstrate concrete contribution and be party to the performance loop process. Here, the ability to measure and quantify the outcome becomes part of the core capabilities of the enterprise, so that they can seamlessly move into the next cycle with the customer.

Moving around the activity cycle

Customer centricity is a high-growth logic. The question is always: how can we give more value to customers and thereby get more value from them?

Having found an entry point, killer entrants build reputation, relationships – vital links and trust with the customer base – and then move around the customer's activity cycle, broadening their reach and indispensability, absorbing more and more spend.

The incredible impetus mobilized by independent consultants in the last few decades is testament to the lack of objective advice and presence in the early stage by enterprises who focused more on the hard sell. These consultants have not only become very influential at that early stage, but increasingly they migrate around the activity cycle in search of stronger relationships and/or richer pastures.

And not just consultants. At first GE sold CAT scanners, imaging equipment and other products to hospitals, clinics and doctors. Then it began to service equipment, post sale, and manage all the medical supplies to hospitals, even operating entire radiological floors in certain hospital venues. This has escalated to helping with the efficient running of hospitals, including seminars and training to boost productivity.

How to unlock new wealth

Part of the success of this breakthrough is when the team discovers that while value gaps left in the customer activity cycle bring about damage, the value-adds can offer great opportunities for new wealth – if only they can be identified and specified.

These opportunities fall into two categories:

- *Those that put value into the customer experience*: these are activities that contribute to getting the outcome. For instance, training on corruption and bribery so the employee knows what to do if faced with that situation in a foreign country. Or helping a manufacturer to reuse or convert its energy to save on cost. Or providing a loan to an entrepreneur within days instead of months, or alerting the mayor's office to a potential flood before it happens.
- *Those that take non-value out of the customer experience*: they can be duplications, waste, added or unnecessary cost, or any activity that eats into time, energy and/or money without contributing to, or damaging or detracting from, the desired outcome. Examples could include the simplest such as eliminating waiting time at Starbucks, or the more complex elimination of duplication in a local government system, which delays a vital decision in an emergency.

Gaps can be industry wide, which is what Jeff Bezos found when Amazon disrupted the book market initially. He saw the disconnects, the innumerable opportunities to put value in, and the oh-so-many non-value-adding activities that customers were subjected to in book stores. These included a customer having to get to a bookstore (sometimes several), searching to find a book (they may not even know which one), trying to get assistance, ordering the book if it is not in stock, queuing to pay and, if they are unlucky, having to return and start the process over again.

In Bezos's unified view of the customer, he then set about providing added value at each critical point 'pre', 'during' and 'post' the customer's experience, to fill both the leisure and professional sides of people's lives, putting value in as well as taking non-value out.

Because the major thrust was to get to know who people are and what they read, do, like or find useful, insights and suggestions based on the customer's profile enabled Amazon to become a proactive force no matter how diverse customers' interests or preoccupations were, from writing their MBA thesis to becoming a star mountain climber. Since customers don't always know what kind of book they want or need, Amazon became more than an order taker: it provided lists in categories acting more like a library (now massive using cloud technology) as well as an index and summary of these books, allowing people to flip through them as they would in a book store, but much more easily.[44]

By tracking customers who read and do the same things, connections were made between unlikely topics like, say, the role of rose gardens in medieval poetry. Customers are also offered books they never knew existed, including what can be obtained on that subject in DVD, video and other formats.

After an order is placed, so intimate is Amazon's knowledge of the customer that they will alert the person to the fact that they may have ordered a duplicate book. Keeping track of what customers have purchased, Amazon also acts as a clearing house and can value the customer's collection and offer to buy back the books and turn them into cash or a credit.

Amazon Web Services also works with bricks and mortar retail merchants, large and small, helping them grow the online side of their businesses without having to start from scratch or undergo the formidable costs and hassles involved, including where they can improve performance and how they can save money. By designing the merchants' websites, and building the appropriate technology platforms, Amazon makes it easy for these merchants' customers to shop – choosing, buying, paying and getting redress when they have a problem.[45]

In addition, the smaller, niche-type publishers, music labels and studios who offer items that customers may want but could never find – either because they don't know they exist or because they can't access them, are given entry to Amazon's huge marketing and distribution machine together with one of the world's largest audiences. This is done at a nominal rate in order to create a better experience for the end user, and to give these small players capabilities they would never otherwise have. If items are sold, Amazon will process the order within 24 hours, ship it anywhere in the world, monitor inventory and automatically send an e-mail request for additional stock, based on customer demand.

Capitec penetrated the South African scene because the entire banking industry had left a serious service gap. To turn traditional banking on its head, it had to obliterate obstructions such as waiting times and complexity. All non-values were deliberately eliminated so as to enhance the customer experience. When other banks found enquiry queues getting longer, Capitec injected more face-to-face contact into the customer experience, reducing queues, frustration and wasted time, money and effort. Branches are paperless, and with the emphasis on speed they are identified biometrically with cameras and fingerprints. Where traditional banks had bundled more and more products together, making them increasingly complicated, Capitec simplified them. Whereas other customers were trying desperately to understand the fine print, and decipher what they were paying for, Capitec's customers were given transparent documentation that was easy to understand.

Capitec branches were the first to open on Sundays and they hold no cash, although customers can deposit notes and obtain cash from ATMs, or from retail stores and supermarkets from the tills. So instead of staff dealing with routine activities and paperwork, which added no real customer value, they are dedicated to their clients. The old way of handling cash was to take it from the customer to the retailer, then to the cash handler, and then take it back to the bank and to the ATM, and finally back to the customer. Capitec recycles value directly between the customer and retailer, taking out all the middle players, and relieving retailers of being laden with huge quantities of cash.[46]

A showcase customer activity cycle case

As we have said, once a company has articulated its 'market space' and scoped its competitive terrain, it can then use the customer activity cycle to find gaps in the customer's experience, and where there is opportunity to create new value. Here is an interesting example from Mexico's Cemex.

The process that customers went through to build a house, Cemex discovered, was riddled with gaps. These gaps across the customer activity cycle led to a plethora of opportunities.

At the 'pre' stage: when a person or family is planning to construct a house and raise the necessary capital, it became apparent that low-income families in Mexico followed a very different pattern of savings from that of consumers in more developed markets.

Because the poor did not have regular incomes and sometimes did not have a legal fixed address, they were outside the remit of the formal banking and credit sector. The Cemex response to this problem was the formation of *tandas* or collective saving pools within families, communities or groups of friends, to raise funds towards expenses such as education, health care and housing. But while 70 per cent of the *tanda*'s members saved, only 10 per cent actually spent money on home construction, because they ended up using the money for clothing, celebrations and emergencies.

'Patrimonio Hoy' (meaning patrimony today) became a Cemex-sponsored extension of the existing *tanda* system that offered a combination of savings and credit. Based on a micro-finance model, the Patrimonio Hoy system allowed people to build up credit to fund the materials for a home. Cemex also provided finance for the labour, which is 40 per cent of the cost.

'Promoters', primarily local women, were recruited and trained by Cemex and worked on a commission basis, to enrol groups of three customers known as 'socios' who would then embark on a savings programme to fund a housing project. At the end of an initial five-week period when the 'socio' group demonstrated an ability to save, Cemex would deliver building materials to the value of ten weeks' savings, effectively extending credit to its customers. If 'socios' remained committed to the programme beyond the first project, they could receive building materials worth ten weeks' savings after an additional two-week saving commitment – an advance of eight weeks. Deliveries were then made over a period extending between 42 and 72 weeks.

It is estimated that Mexican emigrants in America spend up to 10 per cent of their income to send money back home for the construction of the family home. Remittance has been a hindrance in the past until Cemex worked with partners to provide a way to get the funds to cement distributors, whom locals knew and trust, in the form of debit cards, in order to buy supplies.

In the 'during' phase: when construction had commenced, other gaps surfaced in the activity cycle. Distributors had no interest in delivering to remote areas, and customer stockpiling habits had led to considerable waste due to poor storage facilities.

Most low-income families either undertook building work themselves, or paid semi-skilled construction workers, who built without formal plans using methods that were sometimes unsafe. The lack of planning and building expertise, as well as predatory practices by shanty-town suppliers of raw materials, often meant that the procurement of building materials was expensive and inefficient, resulting in waste that the low-income family could ill-afford.

There was also a problem of materials storage and project planning, with lots of unused, wasted materials in front of building sites, and badly constructed, half-made rooms. To overcome these challenges, Patrimonio Hoy required each 'socio' savings group to meet with a Cemex technical advisor or architect in order to discuss the family's housing requirements and agree on a building plan, as well as future room extensions and the preferred layout of the building.

The family would be provided with not just an initial plan and materials schedule for the first one or two rooms, but an integrated plan for the sequence of rooms to be added in the future. And, as a member of Patrimonio Hoy, each 'socio' would have ongoing access to credit for future construction needs.

The family was provided with a fixed-price materials agreement and a timeline for delivery of the correct quantities of materials. Cemex also provides the services of an associated pool of skilled construction workers, all qualified by a company-approved school of masonry.

To address the problem of on-site storage of materials, Cemex offered customers a choice between immediate delivery or delayed delivery via a credit voucher. If the 'socio' decided on immediate delivery, Cemex would coordinate with its suppliers to arrange punctual delivery within a guaranteed window of a half-day. If the customer chose to have later delivery, the materials would be stored at the supplier's distribution facility.

The 'post' phase: this began at the pre-phase, because every part of the building plan was meticulously calculated with longevity in mind. Unlike families in the developed world, poor Mexicans did not necessarily build a house as an integrated project. Construction might start with a single room, with others added as the family raised additional funds. House owners might have an idea of the priority for rooms to be added in the future, but there was little formalized planning for layout and the most cost-effective and efficient utilization of space and materials.

The involvement of the Cemex technical advisor or architect during the 'pre' phase, contributed significantly to resolving this common 'post' phase problem. Future room extensions, and the preferred layout of the building, was part of the initial plan with a sequence of rooms to be added in the future, which could kick into action in the 'post' phase.

And through the Patrimonio Hoy initiative, the company maintained contact with its customers over the duration of a construction project that could stretch for years. If a customer returned to Cemex for a future project, the company was equipped with a full record of previous interactions, which eased the approval processes and referral.

Maintenance was included in the post-plan financial package. And once 'socios' had a good credit track record they could get a letter of recommendation from Cemex to present to other vendors for maintenance and extra goods and care. Through the various value-adds that were translated into new products and services, the emphasis went from being the price of cement to building better homes quicker.

'Socios' pay a weekly fee that is considered reasonable rather than focusing on the price of a bag of cement, and brand 'lock-on' has been accomplished, leaving competitors peddling product and fighting over price.

Using the customer activity cycle tool

The object of the customer activity cycle is to get executives to unlock the value components that will form the basis of the new innovative

Table 4.1 Tips on using the customer activity cycle

Don't ...	Do ...
work haphazardly	work through 'pre', then 'during', then 'post'
fill in value-adds at random as people get ideas	first go through the customer activity cycle, look for gaps, and then fill in the value components
get sidetracked by what you currently do	concentrate on what you don't do: otherwise there is no added value
allow individuals to use their own versions of the methodology	keep the method consistent, so the experience is transferable to others across the enterprise
use paper, notebooks, laptops	use post-its, and get people actively engaged or work with technology to allow for instant alterations and constant updates
try to prove anything with data	use people who know the customer, or have an educated, intuitive feel

customer approach. Here is a summary of the questions to go through during an exercise:

1. What are the critical activities customers go through or could/should go through to get the outcome as defined by the 'market space'?
2. What are the existing or potential value gaps?
3. What are the opportunities for adding value, filing these gaps by: a) putting value in? b) taking non-value out?

Table 4.1 lists some 'dos' and 'don'ts' when using the methodology.

Finding the hidden gold

International Health Insurance (IHI) had two major segments: individuals mostly living abroad for work or retirement, and corporations with employees at home, travelling or living in foreign countries. The intriguing challenge in Per Bay Jorgensen's revitalization of the Danish enterprise was to discover what value-adds would turn the growing awareness that wellness pays – not merely because people feel better, but because it costs less overall. Exhibit 4.3 illustrates the simplified IHI customer activity cycle, showing what customers do or could/should do to get a health and personal safety outcome.

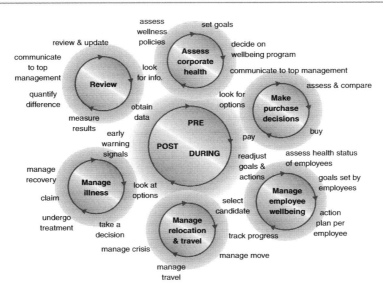

Exhibit 4.3 IHI corporate customer activity cycle (simplified) 'market space': lifetime health and personal safety management

IHI is a classic example of how a string of value-adds can be unpacked and put into the customer activity cycle at each critical point in the experience. When these are connected they attain the desired outcome, in this case 'lifetime health and personal safety management' for relocating expats (see Exhibit 4.4).

Drilling down for opportunities

The 'pre', 'during' and 'post' stages of the customer activity cycle kick into subcycles.

To illustrate: through Discovery Insure's telematics system it knows at the 'during' part of the customer's experience if they are in trouble. When this happens, a whole accident activity subcycle kicks in, which they fill by proactively going to the scene and providing medical assistance.

Very often it is down in the subcycles that the real value for customer or company is to be found. For example, providing integrated energy to hauliers involved a complex set of activities in the customer activity cycle, 'pre', 'during' and 'post' journey in order to keep trucks at peak

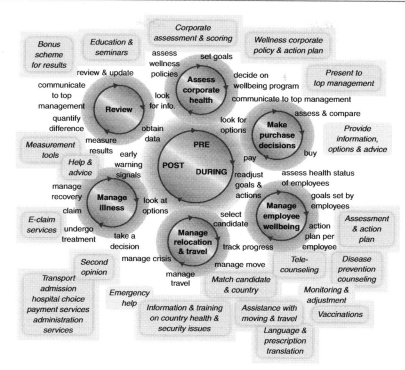

Exhibit 4.4 IHI corporate customer activity cycle and value-adds (simplified) 'market space':'lifetime health and personal safety management'

capacity at the lowest cost, minimizing wear and tear and damage to the environment:

- **'pre' journey**: is from the time the order is received, for example, planning, truck preparation, route maximization, driver selection and briefing.
- **'during' journey**: includes, for example, navigation, refuelling, breakdowns, rest, getting to destination and delivery.
- **'post' journey**: includes administration, review of performance, truck maintenance and repair, getting paid.

BP's commercial transport division dug deep into the customer activity cycle for its haulier customers in its market space, drilling (so to speak) down into the main cycle and subcycles (see Exhibit 4.5).

One small value-add uncovered came from the cabin comfort sub-sub-subcycle in the 'during' phase. BP found that while drivers

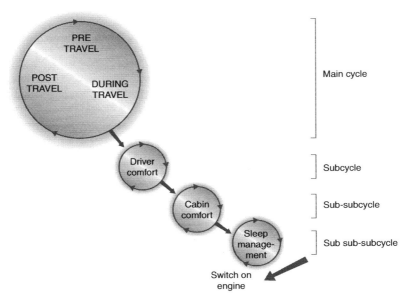

Exhibit 4.5 BP haulier segment subcycles (simplified)

slept they kept the engines running for warmth. They also learnt that this idling amounted to 5 per cent of fuel costs, accounting for 20 per cent of nitrogen oxide and other noxious emissions, which inevitably exacerbated overall wear and tear on the vehicle and engine – costs that equalled 10 per cent of overall fuel expenditure. This was an amount considerable enough to turn this vendor on to the need to get hauliers' engines turned off, and to think about ways to ensure driver comfort during sleep, without all the added costs.

The point about the various driver comfort mini-cycles shown in Exhibit 4.5 is that truck drivers must be kept in top condition and trained to perform. What's the use of fighting over a quarter per cent discount on the fuel if the driver puts his foot down too hard because he is sitting badly or not sleeping well and so is over-revving and uses five times as much fuel? In addition, if the journey is made comfortable, a better calibre of person may be attracted to the job, itself a significant challenge for the industry.

New business opportunities lie in the detail. Inside this sub-sub-subspace of the haulier customer activity cycle, not only was a value component found to enrich the customer's and employee's experience, but a whole new business opportunity was opened up for BP, together with partners.

Getting traction

Fundamental to success is making sure that the breakthrough moments are met and managed in order to get the traction that leads to an eventual compounding effect. By this stage, a small team or teams will have been formed, with their carefully chosen representatives. Use 'the best brains you've got, not the people you can spare', executives warn over and over again.

Without a team, or teams, purposefully constructed with the clearly defined mission embedded and fully legitimized, the risk can be miserable failure. This applies especially (but not only) in complex organizations, because people will invariably drift back into their own parts of the organization and start working on various disparate projects and plans in silos, losing connection with the unified customer theme and thus the momentum gained will be compromised.

People will probably have been working part-time in the workshops so far, but once the customer activity cycle takes off, it is necessary for a specific small core team – around two to five people, again depending on circumstances – to be formed to do the detailed analysis and be involved, with time out, if possible. As one executive said, 'It's only when the work changed to a day, rather than a night job that we began to really make things happen.'

If this is asking too much, getting the team together on a regular basis with set roles, clear objectives and deadlines is a good compromise. This requires strong leadership with time dedicated to the project, matched to KPIs and performance contracts. If there is no recognition or rewards for work done, or KPI alignment or pressure, it will never remain a high priority (more about this later). Even worse can be situations where the KPIs work against what the transformation is trying to achieve. Meetings in small groups will mushroom as this core group scatters to find the collective knowledge they have inside and outside the organization, do the supplementary work and test their ideas, bringing people in when and where needed. This work will then need to be communicated to the wider sponsoring group and audience in order to pull the process along and draw in others.

Sharpening sponsorship

Teams should be made up of executives from all silos in the organization, a micro representation of the functions from members of the initial intervention workshop. Ideally one person should be assigned full-time to the job of leading and coordinating the team. 'These leaders must be given high-level status in the organization to ensure that they have the clout to make things happen.' Or, 'be linked or sponsored by a senior executive or high-ranking team or committee, so as to make sure they get the support needed to pull things through the system.'

I have seen several formulae work here. The first is to have some senior person, preferably the CEO, visible and present during the sessions, driving the team(s). Alternatively, a guiding coalition which is either formed for this purpose, or already exists to ensure continuity. This team ideally will be reporting directly to or led by the CEO, or a sponsoring senior executive.

Either way, the object is to ensure funding and, when applicable, allocation of time and resources and the support of top management and the board. It also entails high-profiling findings and recommendations, getting them heard in the correct channels, formally and informally.

If the team or teams can be ring-fenced, kept away from the day-to-day operations, the process will be accelerated. The object is to shelter them from the restrictions that normally hamper progress, 'like convoluted procedures or needing consensus to make a decision', or 'loads of gates, when go or no-go decisions are made'.

One of the success factors for Ghana MTN was that the CEO appointed an existing team to drive the process. Formerly this group had spent 70 per cent of its time on day-to-day operating matters, and 30 per cent on new initiatives. Now the CEO was adamant that they had to change that ratio to 30 per cent on business as usual, and 70 per cent on the new customer-centric initiatives. His uncompromising approach to this evidently helped the team achieve timelines, which contributed to both success and speed.

Being ring-fenced also entails guaranteed access to the correct people in the organization and the ability to improvise, pulling people in, when and if needed, to supply specialized knowledge. And being given a set of customers to deal with, to whom the team has access for a period for advice, and to bounce off ideas and validate recommendations on work in progress. These customers need to be invited, in the spirit of collaborative research in which they are asked to participate. Resist the temptation to have the largest customer in on this, if they are not like-minded and open. What is needed now are leading lights, likely to support, encourage and help move the process forward.

The best results will come from some great ideas, not from consensus or compromise, and from the flow of the correct energies and synergies. Needless to say, affirmative feedback from customers at this point will build confidence among the team(s) and its sponsors, and so create positive reinforcement.

Once the customer activity cycles have been validated, the next step for the team is to use them as the strategic architecture around which to build the new story, and make it actionable.

Using the customer activity cycle to get traction

Because the value components become the future opportunities that create new wealth for the transforming organization, it is not unusual for this part of the change process to be very motivating. And this step in the discovery phase can take anywhere from two weeks to three months depending on the number of markets that the enterprise decides to work in initially, and the amount of time and resources allocated to the exercise. Now executives report feeling the breakthrough and enthusiasm most strongly, with the customer-centric vision, ethos and concepts seriously beginning to take grip.

Unless the customer-centricity process gets this traction, from the key executives who take the lead, and then from a broader population, folded in if and when necessary – an enterprise will be stalled in its tracks, frozen, unable to execute. It will constantly be battling with pushback, which will dissipate rather than ignite the energy needed to move forward.

The discovery period plays an important part in getting this anchored. First, it allows people to make the all-important decisions about where the enterprise is to play, and to frame this in a way that can be inspiring as well as concrete. This brings the customer approach into sharper focus.

Then, according to executives familiar with the methodology, the customer activity cycle gets this traction for other important reasons (see Box 4.1).

Box 4.1 Why the customer activity cycle gets traction

Cementing a common customer theme
We all felt like we were describing the same thing for the very first time.

Engaging people
People can contribute, even if they are not in contact with customers on a daily basis.

Using it as an organizing tool
It provides a template for a unified view of the customer.

Providing a company-wide view
We saw it bind people from different parts of the company, because they can now see how, and where, they fit.

Presents a single united vision
Everyone has the same view of where the enterprise is going and why.

Helping people express conceptual ideas in a tangible way
It allows executives to verbalize what they may have felt, but couldn't easily express without a framework.

Being neutral and non-threatening
It enables people who have different and sometimes opposing agendas to work positively together and jointly explore common ground.

As a powerful communication device
The image is vivid, so it makes it compelling and easy to communicate, inside and outside the organization.

Being robust *and structured*
It raises people's confidence.

Humanizes
People tend to become more involved because they can project into it.

Then, because the customer activity cycle tool is a structured methodology, it provides the discipline to keep executives on the customer track. There is also sufficient rigour in the model to instil in them the confidence to come up with very clear tangible suggestions on how gaps in the customer's experience can be translated into specific customer values. And it is by definition an inter-functional tool, with which people find they are at ease and can align.

This becomes all-important, given that the new vision that disrupts may be quite vague, and thus difficult for most to grasp at the outset.

The structured approach is also balanced by an equal dose of creative thinking. This invigorates and stimulates people's imagination so they can look for, and find, the not-so-obvious gaps and more spectacular opportunities. They are also able to explore and uncover collectively with colleagues 'what they know, or don't even know they know' and, equally important, discover 'what they don't know about customers and didn't know they didn't know, and need to find out'.

The Story

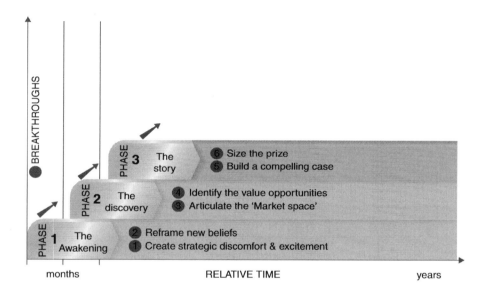

Build a Compelling Case

Key idea

Customer-centric leaders know how to discard traditional business plans, and how to tell and sell a 'one company' story, which communicates the customer-centric vision, and directs the actors and actions so that the new ways of doing things become compelling enough to get high levels of engagement and conversion, inside the company and out. In a reverse logic, flowing from the customer activity cycle, the strategy is told as a story, followed by an action plan.

The new narrative

Storytelling is a vital tool for serious transformations, whether the reconstruction is a gradual reshaping or a revved-up revival; whether it comes in response to an institutional decline, or as part of a continuous attempt to harness new opportunities through disruption, as some of the examples have and will continue to demonstrate.

Imbued with much more vim and vigour than conventional business plans, stories – the oldest and most powerful form of influence – are built for engagement and conversion. It helps the change leader and 'points of light' to build a compelling case, so that they can move up and along the change process, ultimately making customer centricity a reality.

Why stories are better

There are many good reasons why stories are better than business plans (see Table 5.1). Business plans are not conducive to change. People invariably react negatively to them, finding them rigid, deadly

Table 5.1 Business plans versus stories

Traditional business plans describe:	Stories describe:
How to improve what exists and how we will gain	What is going to be done differently, and who will gain
The series of tasks that have to be undertaken	The flow of critical events that have to be accomplished, to get a desired reaction
An inalterable fixed contract, cast in concrete	How the growth and development will take place
In one-dimensional terms what each silo is contracted to deliver	A multidimensional view of what's to be achieved, embracing the whole enterprise
Separate agendas from different parts of the organization	A unified theme, and who fits where
Comparisons between different competing parts of the business	Collaborative opportunities for working together
Hoped-for projections	The possibilities, and challenges needed to attain success

boring and generally unwelcome: 'an annual chore, more a control mechanism than a motivator'.

By contrast, stories are narratives and, if well told and credible, can present an exciting picture that people can identify with and respond to positively. An old proverb goes, 'Give people a fact or idea and you enlighten their minds: tell them a story and you touch their souls'.[47]

Research confirms this ancient wisdom: people actually think in stories. Whilst traditional business plans instruct people, a story engages them emotionally and involves them, as these remarks from my work with executives illustrate:

It's the connection between what we have now, and the future.

You identify with it personally, and you feel implicated.

You want to know how it will progress.

It compares what you have got to what's possible to get, and that makes you think about what's got to be done, and what you have to do.

People believe in stories – they are ingrained in us from birth.

Traditional business plans, written with the existing scripted framework in mind, are by their very nature product plans. So people continue to be mentally programmed to think, talk and behave in this mould, and so perpetuate it.

Business plans are built to get people to conform, restricting rather than stretching the imagination. And since they invariably hold people back, what comes out is 'the same-old same-old, year in and year out and, before long, it's too late'.

And business plans demand numbers and facts that are often extrapolated from the past and are based on assumptions such as 'we may over or under budget depending on the incentives' (see Table 5.1).

Customer-centric executives realize the limitations of business plans, and the need to develop storytelling skills to move a transformation forward:

Business plans tend to be repetitious from one year to the next – in fact, top management often insists upon that, and the only real change is in the figures.

They don't make a lasting impact therefore, whereas stories can, and do.

People dread them.

People will invariably overbudget or underbudget in a business plan, when they feel insecure.

Business plans can say anything you want them to say.

They are mindless exercises, which have no emotion in them.

In business plans people write what is predictable and is expected of them, usually the good news, the 'hoped-for projections', instead of looking for what is unpredictable, disruptive and unexpected, and the challenges associated with getting there, which is what customer-centric disruption wants. So the enterprise stays in its product mental model, instead of breaking out into uncharted territory and looking for something unique.

Traditional business plans are a snapshot of what is to be achieved in a very short space of time in the year ahead. They are static. In contrast, there is a natural flow to a story: it emerges as the milestones pass by, which happens over time, with a degree of improvisation and experimentation allowed, in order to get to the innovative end state and build a platform for continued success. Business plans make people do the same things better. Stories get people to doing different things. Stories about the past are about facts. Stories about a future yet to unfold take people on a journey, in this case a customer-centric journey.

I often ask people to imagine what story they would want to tell a major magazine and have as the headline on the cover. On the basis of some agreed upon mission, to dominate a 'market space' of choice over time, a creative combination of tools can be used in this story. These range from evocative data, customer interviews and remarks, competitive behaviour, memorable words, phrases and concepts, and/or meaningful metaphors.

Stories well told are also engaging. They make people curious, invite questions and give opportunities for answers.

Why business plans are (only) budgets

A good many companies talk about a 'one company' strategy. Yet they continue to have each section of the business produce a separate business plan, and then try and aggregate this into one overarching strategy. But in the end all they have is a disparate collection of business plans, each with their own agenda.

Perhaps the biggest handicap to using traditional business plans is that they are more akin to budgets than to elaborations of how a company is going to reconstruct or refresh itself. Executives create goals and then mechanistically try to control them, whereas stories can be modified and unfold, depending on actions and reactions, insights and learnings. Two quotes from my research: 'Business plans are more like a contract to produce the financials, which we all know we may never achieve in any case', and 'They just show the numbers; it's the columns with the figures and the calculations that people want to see, not what we want to do.'

The numbers in a business plan may also not be feasible, so any unexpected change can render them instantly null and void. Forecasts not met then have an impact on share prices, morale and credibility, with all the ripple effects. So the most important problem is that business plans reinforce silo mentalities, preventing any unified view of the customer from emerging.

When and how budgets and financial goals are going to be achieved is a part of the organization's story, but only a part: 'You never get rid of the figures. But if new initiatives end up just as business plans which are nothing more than contracts or budgets, based on products or services to make and get rid of, customer centricity will never happen.'

Stories must be told and sold

What is patently clear from those who have undergone this sort of transformation is that 'selling your ideas, and persuading people is a critical success factor in getting the buy-in'.[48] This is because 'the only thing that really works, is being able to influence, rather than command', with balanced communication that emphasizes the rational, emotional and social, in equal measure.

Stories that we are interested in (not fiction) explain a problem, and then show that there is a solution. And that is what most people respond to. To make a case powerfully, so that people react and act accordingly, the story must be communicated in a compelling way, either face to face or using social media, and preferably both. Its structure and presentation are as important as its content or message.

Using the crisis of threat, opportunity and consciousness helps frame the problem. The mission and strategy, told as a narrative, makes the connections between this problem and what is going to be done about it. Business plans fail to do this. 'You *tell* a story – it's a description of something that can happen if actions are taken' and as such they have enormous transformative power.

Increasingly, executives are being encouraged to build storyboards for presentations. When Gerstner arrived at IBM as the new CEO he found that the company was being 'managed by foils'. An executive would come to a meeting, present overhead slide presentations, then ask for funds and either get them or not, depending on how the numbers looked. Although the newly appointed CEO did ask for written proposals in advance, the time he spent with executives went into discussing and interrogating … 'tell me the story'. It is said that on at least one occasion he walked into a conference room and ripped out the projector's power cord![49]

Stories get people's attention and make them interested often because the storyteller is clearly deeply involved. Says one expert commentator on the subject: 'At the most basic level, storytelling can help a manager gain and hold his audience's attention. But if the story is good enough, it can also lift individuals and organizations to take the risks that make life an adventure.'[50]

People do not respond to data dumps. Through crafted storytelling, if it has emotional power leaders can persuade and motivate people because this is what arouses the listeners' imagination and energy, and makes it memorable.

The point is that if people want to excite and enthuse others to make fundamental changes that become a way of life, embedded into the corporate fabric for all time, they have to get them to feel and care about something rather than just *tell* them. Especially if higher purpose and compassion for others are integral to the story.

Business plans don't do that. 'You show the plan, in the hope that someone will read it and study it, and you pray that it happens as you said it would.' 'Instead, the passion must come through, and that can never happen in the kinds of documents and modus operandi that have been used in the past.'

What is to be avoided is constructing a story and then presenting it in conventional corporate speak and format. The old formula and new ideas and concepts won't fit together and executives won't get the reactions that matter from people. In addition, too much data can be a disadvantage initially. As one executive said: 'If you get swamped down in too much detail at the beginning you just can't move; the object should be to give as much as is necessary, but use it to show that it must work.'

But perhaps what is most relevant about stories is that because they engage people, they facilitate the cumulative buy-in needed in an implementation process. Because if they are compelling and told well, they are easy to remember, and repeat over and over again.

And, paradoxically, they can change and they last.

Building the story around customers

All the activities that have gone before are preludes in a defined set of managed activities to get to this next breakthrough, putting the new strategy together like a story. Building a narrative about how the company sees the future and its role in it.

What is required is a story told internally built around customer value, and how that brings value *back* to the enterprise. That is what intrigues and ignites people to want to participate, and thus pushes the process forward to that next crucial step.

But the story has to lead to action and be lived. At this time people who want more substance begin to get involved and, in so doing, start to amass the interest of their peers.

Told externally when the time comes, the story is a narrative about what the enterprise is now about (that is different and relevant), and why people should identify with it and be part of it, whether they are investors, analysts, potential employees, partners or the customer public.

Reversing the logic

Most industrial-type firms start with their economic goals and then figure out how to get the financial rewards, doing the same thing better or more of it. Customer centricity demands a reverse logic. It works backwards to find the correct pieces for the strategic puzzle, by asking and answering these questions in this order:

1. What is our chosen 'market space'?
2. What are the current value gaps in the customer activity cycle, in that 'market space'?
3. What do we need in order to fill those value gaps – putting value in and taking non-value out – so we can become indispensable to customers to that 'market space'?
4. How do we monetize this?

The customer activity cycle becomes the architecture around which the strategy, told as a story, is built.

'Market spaces' lead to purpose – the mission

Generally, when a conventional approach is used, the organization has a mission statement or purpose that often says little that is very different from what others are saying. The concept of 'market space' has three specific advantages:

- First, it encapsulates the new broadened boundary and aspiration for the enterprise compared to the status quo, reflecting or mirroring the desired customer outcome;
- Second, it becomes the new core business of the enterprise;
- Third, it quite naturally translates into a mission – the purpose and function of the enterprise, or what it has to do, in order to achieve success.

The mission becomes the glue binding the enterprise and its employees to new ways of doing things for customers. For a transforming enterprise this mission needs to be packaged and consistently communicated in a compelling way. Executives continuously emphasize that it must be *both* compelling *and* consistent. Some quotes from my work with them are:

> *We may get tired of hearing the same thing over and over again, but sticking to the same message is a major success factor.*

> *When imparted, the new mission needs to resonate and be exciting enough to get relevant employees and other stakeholders to buy-in and want to be involved, especially early on.*

> *You have to constantly and ruthlessly reaffirm the customer-centric intent, and how you are going to get there – it's the leader's role, no one else's.*

As we see from the examples already discussed, this can be a big ask for a company which has prided itself on making and moving the items, and has solidified its culture around a business model embracing product or service factories and assembly lines, capacity, stores, patents and so on, rather than on customers.

At Lego, for instance, the biggest problem in the 1980s was managing demand for its colourful bricks and controlling growth. Then in the 1990s growth slowed as its toys were no longer resonating with kids, who had more interesting ways to spend their time. The most daunting challenge in the 2000s was to get the people in the enterprise to see that while the growth potential for their toy bricks was limited, the opportunities to enhance the quality of customers' play experiences were limitless. So rather than Lego simply continuing to perfect its physical bricks to make more and more versions of the old notion of the toy, as it did in the past, the company resuscitated itself by changing its mission from building world-class toy bricks to enabling kids (and adults) to foster their creativity, conceptual thinking and interactive learning while at play (the Danish words '*leg godt*', after which the company was named, mean play well).

Embedding higher purpose into the mission

Higher purpose needs to be integrated into the mission, embedding social as well as financial goals into the new business model. These should be intrinsic to what the enterprise stands for and does.

This is not what most social responsibility programmes currently do. This is because they tend to be about subsidization – donation giving or sponsorships – often made in order to associate the brand with some perceived or subjective 'socially good' activity.

Whilst having transcendency of purpose is making sure that the strategy is having the desired impact on the people, communities and societies in which an enterprise operates. Unilever's move into promoting hand-washing in India, for instance, has said to have decreased millions of deaths due to diarrhoea, but as well had a direct and indirect socio-economic impact on Indian welfare and livelihood.

The higher purpose is that part of a stated mission that is related to what the enterprise is to accomplish other than for its own self-interest. The enterprise and the people within it don't only do things because they *can*, but also because they *care*. They go for the big ideal not just the big idea.

GE now supports and upgrades diagnostic capability by bringing affordable value propositions to rural doctors and clinics, which cater to the poor; Discovery Insure want the world to have great drivers, so as to reduce accidents and lost lives; IBM want a smarter planet for the wellbeing of citizenry; Marks & Spencer want to reduce waste. Lego's big ideal has been to try to find uses for its bricks that will inspire people to invent for future generations to come: they work with architects to build tomorrow's buildings; and NASA wants to inspire aerospace engineers to build the air and space crafts of the future, or futuristic cars that will increase fuel efficiency and reduce harmful emissions and noise. Lego has worked with 50,000 schools in 15 languages, using bricks to help kids learn how to frame a problem and imagine and experiment with possible solutions, and with universities to inspire students to design and innovate creatively.

The fight for good used to be seen as the sole domain of the so-called non-governmental organization (NGO) and charities.

No more. Today the boundaries are blurring with missions merging and converging, as enterprises take on much more of these transcendent challenges, and more NGOs behave like customer-centric companies in a private/public hybrid-type organization or network.

Here is an example from HealthStore, the pioneering disruptor from Kenya. First an NGO, then a fully fledged franchising company, it filled customer value gaps in the government's health delivery system, providing medical services in rural areas to underserved villages. Half the drugs that customers received were counterfeit or out of stock, unlabelled or of poor quality, and sold on grocery stalls and pharmacies that were impossible to get to, resulting in the death and destruction of families and communities. This led to HealthStore's mission – preventing illness and death by giving impoverished people access to basic medicine and medical services. And whilst the number of patients could have been much higher, if that had been their goal and it had gone to areas where the population and demand was greater, instead it chose to be in agricultural areas where help was needed most.

Getting from 'market space' to mission

'Market space' and mission are two sides of the same coin. Words do matter in the 'market space' definition. Because however the 'market space' is articulated to capture the desired customer outcome, becomes quite literally what the enterprise has to be better at doing than anyone else – its new core purpose or business.

Imagine you have been selling short-term insurance and now you are delivering driver safety. What does that take? Or you were making and selling cement, and now you are providing 'lifetime home ownership'. Realizing the difference shocks the organization into reality. And it leads them to a new mission.

A good way to get from 'market space' to mission, is to get people to list the words used in the 'market space' definition and really figure out and agree on what they mean.

Doing this gets behind the words to the intention. The new mission may be succinct, but it will be one that people really understand and intend to honour, in everything that follows.

To demonstrate, here is the Danish International Health Insurance exercise:

Lifetime:
- Helping people take decisions on prevention and intervention, which can have a significant impact on their lifelong wellbeing, not simply pay claims when they fall ill.
- Including post retirement, a time when health insurance becomes imperative, but also exceedingly expensive, and people often find they have no protection because enterprises generally only cover them for as long as they remain on the payroll.

Health:
- Maximizing the individual's chances of staying well and in top form ('healthier people are more productive, happier, and less costly'), by working closely with partners using advanced technology and analytics in order to understand the health-risk factors.
- Doing what is needed to assist in preserving the health of individuals or employees.

Personal safety:
- Including the personal safety of independent customers or employees travelling or living in foreign lands.
- Avoiding the many minor and major things that could go wrong, with all the ensuing problems and costs.

Management:
- Being there for customers (virtually and physically), getting them to the best service and treatment available for their specific needs, irrespective of their location or their provider's location.
- Assisting them through the various systems or procedures to save time and hassles. And measuring results, to further foster and nurture relationships for life.

From that analysis a short mission can be written such as: *To help make and keep people well and safe throughout their lives, wherever they may be, reducing costs to them, and to their company and country.*

Opportunity scanning for new products and services

The values that connect to form the outcome that emerges from the customer activity cycle echo the mission, and become the building blocks of the storyline. They are also the backbone of the new set of product and service offerings.

Going back to IHI: its customer value repertoire was built into a story developed by a small innovation team appointed to work with the CEO, based on values uncovered, which translated into a new portfolio of services. This was justified by the fact that diseases and disorders can be prevented 70 per cent of the time, lowering health care costs for both corporations – the supplier and customer – by as much as 50 per cent.[51]

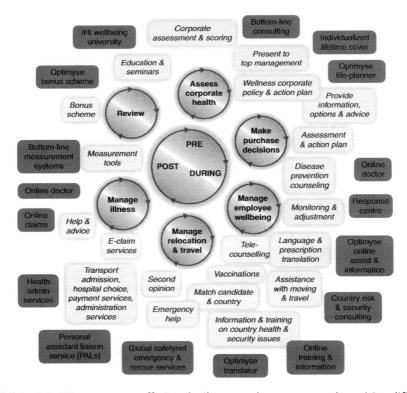

Exhibit 5.1 IHI corporate offering built around customer values (simplified) 'market space': lifetime health and personal safety management

The main set of offerings in Exhibit 5.1 are briefly explained here:

IHI Wellbeing University
The Wellbeing University was formed to influence and educate independent buyers and executives who were still in the old paradigm of only buying health insurance and looking for the best deal. A global network of leading corporations was brought together to encourage dialogue and share experiences on wellbeing and productivity, do empirical research, produce white papers and cases, and conduct public and private seminars.

Bottom-line consulting
Consulting is offered to assess corporate health policies and provide action plans, including a score against a peer benchmark. This is followed by a report and presentation to top management, showing the effects of new propositions on productivity, motivation, employee retention and cost savings, together with the ultimate positive impacts on the value of human capital.

Individualized lifetime cover
Guaranteed lifetime cover is available for the whole family, including post-retirement. This is individualized insurance that encompasses alternative remedies and a host of other benefits, particularly regular check-ups, in line with the emphasis and ethos that prevention is better than cure.

Optimyse life planner
When people are managing their health, a planning and monitoring tool branded 'optimyse' begins with a voluntary health assessment, as well as a diagnosis of predisposition to risk, followed by advice and tests when needed, culminating in a personalized health plan, with specific targets in line with each individual's personal goals.

Online doctor
There is access to online or teleconsulting, as well as second opinions. Records are kept confidential, separated from the insurance files and business.

Optimyse online assist and information
Advice and feedback are provided 24 hours per day online, with interventions suggested when appropriate and necessary. In the event of a problem, people are matched and delivered to the correct hospitals and doctors, wherever in the world they and the providers happen to be.

Country risk and security consulting
To reduce the expensive failure rates of overseas assignments, also included is matching people to countries; as well as educating and supporting individuals on health and personal safety issues (from jet lag to allergies, floods to terrorism).

Optimyse translator
This incorporates personalized patient records; kits for travelling while relocating or home use, including prescription and precautionary drugs; translations per country; alternatives and where to find them.

Global safety net emergency and rescue services
These services range from accidents and loss of baggage, to sudden illness or death in a foreign land. It also covers personal security and rescue services, including assistance with all crises and catastrophes, from emergency admission through counselling, advice and information on what to do, where to go, and whom to contact, and emergency evacuation.

Personal assistant liaison service (PALs)
On-site or remotely, help, advice, liaison and support are given by a personal assistant when people are in trouble.

Health administrative services
Employees are navigated through the labyrinth of administrative, procedural and medical issues, related to finding the correct hospital, surgeon or doctor, and dealing with hospital admission procedures, payment and reimbursement.

Bottom-line measurement systems
Reduced absenteeism and stress levels, higher productivity, lower health costs and overall increases in productivity, punctuality, morale and quality of performance are just some of the areas that can be measured with customized tools and techniques, which show the impact of the investment on bottom-line returns.

Optimyse bonus scheme
Finally, improvements are rewarded in various ways. Here, customers get to accumulate bonus points for various behaviours, for which they can either receive rebates, or benefits will be allocated to special events such as a new baby or retirement, where they can get reduced premiums or added services and cover.

No singular product or service can get the desired customer experience or outcome. The combination of all these value-add products and services is what produces the outcome and makes the offering potentially disruptive, opening up the opportunities for growth. Preferably, these value-adds should be branded, as you see in the IHI example.

Choosing lead customers

Decisions on which customer(s) or segment to choose to do the customer activity cycle exercises is very significant. To get the optimum and most innovative results, the best advice is to work on customers or segments that:

- are receptive to new ideas;
- are key opinion leaders, likely to be responsive to new ways of doing things;
- have strategic significance;
- have potential to demonstrate how cross-silo delivery and synergy could work;
- are likely to be ongoing collaborators.

The second important decision you will have to make is how many customer activity cycles to realistically do. This depends on how many segments the company serves. As a general rule, more than four activity cycle exercises become too difficult to manage, particularly if it involves people working in different venues or countries.

If groups have chosen to do customer activity cycles for several lead markets, there will be similarities between the value-adds uncovered. Some of the recommendations will therefore be generic, whilst others will be specific to particular segments and/or particular individual customers. Three categories should emerge from the analysis:

- A *generic* set of value-adds, which can be applied across all markets and customers.

- *Specific* value-adds, which can be applied to different market segments.
- *Flexible* value-adds, which are for particular individuals or corporations.

If there are several customer activity cycle exercises being done simultaneously, the pace is likely to differ from group to group. Groups should liaise from time to time in order to learn from each other and cross-fertilize ideas. This could require coordination from some appointed person, preferably with project management skills.

Choosing the hot spots

Because in a phased approach not everything is done at once, a good principle is always to work from strength, building testimony as you go along in order to create more action and traction, in a positive reinforcing loop.

You will find that once executives realize that all the value-adds don't all have to be executed at once, there is a good deal of relief. The 'big picture' – literally the totally integrated experience 'pre', 'during' and 'post' – should nonetheless be kept paramount in people's minds, anchored as the ultimate goal.

Some form of prioritizing the value-add is needed, and there are two tools for doing this: time prioritize and impact prioritize.

Tool 1: time prioritize

Time prioritization is done by dividing the new recommended products and services into different categories, according to lead times required, in the following way:

- **Fast tracks:** value-adds that can be done *immediately*.
- **Fix-its:** value-adds that *must* be done, within the next six months, currently being done badly. These are usually quite easy to identify and can come from any part of the organization, including operations, who should be part of the cross-silo teams.

- **Nexts:** value-adds that *should* be done soon, within the next budget year to 18 months. These products and services are already emerging. Nexts could also be a product or service that is a more sophisticated version of a fix-it. For instance, 'cross-silo planning' could be a fix-it value-add, which could be advanced into a next value-add, for example, 'integrated planning tool'.
- **Game changers**: value-adds that *could* be done, have never been done before, and will create a new standard, likely to take longer to execute, although work may commence on them immediately. Game changers may even lead to a completely different activity cycle.

Tool 2: impact prioritize

If this is too complex, the value-add products and services that come out of the activity cycle can be prioritized based on a combination of seven criteria, listed below. 'Hot spots' are chosen in order to get concrete wins as soon as possible, and get the organization mobilized around successes. These criteria are:

- **Do ablity** – capability to generate early wins.
- **Scalability** – ability to ramp up.
- **Replicability** – ability to repeat at low cost, quickly.
- **Importance** – how much the customer wants/is likely to want it.
- **Measurability** – ability to quantify tangible results for the customer.
- **Visibility** – ability to high profile, as well as use in internal and external promotion.
- **Referral** – ability to use as reference site, project, or case study for know-how management or promotion.

The action checklist

The customer activity cycle can be used as the overarching tool to build and communicate stories. Not only is it visually compelling, it also gets intellectual communion. It is often the best way to package the message, and get people to see what needs to be done and how, by whom.

An action plan will flow quite easily in the customer activity cycle exercise(s):

1. What do we have to be best at? – Purpose or mission, mirroring the 'market space' definition.
2. What does the new offering consist of? – Portfolio of product and service innovations.
3. Who will do what (including suppliers or distributors)? What internal and external resources and skills do we require/have to find/fund/build? – People, skills and partners.
4. How do we deliver the new offering? – Processes, platforms, tools and technology.
5. Where will the customer interact with the brand? – Multichannels, touchpoints, social networks and media.
6. Which creative messaging and media will be used internally and externally? – Brand profiling, communication and promotion.
7. How well can we expect to do, and how will we share the gains and measure success, including wider impacts? – Pricing and performance metrics and measures, incentives and rewards.
8. When do we need to activate and execute what? – Projects in what order (including folding in relevant existing initiatives)?

Size the Prize

Key idea

Part of the compelling story is making an estimate of how big the new opportunity is likely to be. Customer centricity uses a different formula. Revenues go up due to deepening, lengthening and more diverse customer spend, and costs go down thanks to new economies and other savings, including customer involvement and advocacy, all of which have the potential for disproportionate and increasing returns. The story, powerfully told and sold, elevates interest and increases conviction and conversion.

Adding numbers to narratives

When a good story is compiled that makes the case compellingly for viewing customers as the fundamental source of enterprise value, and it presents a picture about what this will take and how it will unfold, another breakthrough will have been made.

The object is to bolster confidence and enthusiasm amongst people. And also get and give clarity on the direction emanating from the beliefs, and substance needed to fulfil the mission.

Once people begin to understand, repeat and talk about the customer-centric narrative, the process will be driven outward and onward into a wider group.

There is also another part to making the case compelling, and that's when the numbers begin to look good, showing how the investment will pay off and how it will lead to greater prosperity.

This is another juncture to be managed, often the most interesting for executives.

Out of the box and onto the top line

First, the arithmetic and some key assumptions have to be altered. Or, at the very least, top management needs to be made aware of the less than perfect decisions that they could make, unless they factor in the flaws of old conventions and outdated views.

There may be a period of transition and, if there is, the enterprises can run parallel systems, using both the new and old metrics.

Here are the more important views on finance that need to be adjusted:

> **Old product view 1** – growth comes from selling unconnected items to as many customers as possible.
>
> **New customer-centric view 1** – growth comes from deeper involvement in the customer experience, constantly layered with innovation to obtain longer and stronger customer engagement and spend.

Part of the product regime is vertical integration. This looks at how much *products* go through as they are transformed and converted, and how much of this the enterprise can get involved in to maximize control of the ***supply chain***, and so grow the business.

The unified customer approach is to grow by becoming involved in as much as possible of the *customer* outcome experience. The customer-centric enterprise asks itself: how do we layer our offering with innovations, to become more involved in the ***market chain*** of activities that customers go through in order to get their 'lock-on'? Therein lies the key to customer centricity.

Take a moment to think about Starbucks. In its quest for growth, it is not only increasing its penetration of existing and new emerging markets for coffee, pulling in local urban customers. It is moving into the customer's home experience through its home-brewing systems, with high-quality-tasting coffee that is convenient for single serves. It also captures grocery-store customer spend, with rewards linked interchangeably to both its own locations and other channels offering its brand.

But, to increase its footprint in the beverage-drinking experience of its customers, Starbucks has to acknowledge that part and parcel of the customer's experience are other drinks, of which coffee is only one part. Additionally it had to speak to the seismic health and wellness trend pervading the globe. Getting beyond coffee into tea, second to water in consumption, and juice, it acquired the premium tea brand Teavana, and Evolution Juice. (The American consumer considers coffee 'busy and rapid, and skewed towards morning drinking', whereas tea is more for winding down and 'Zen-like, for afternoons, evenings and weekends'.)[52]

Additionally, since two-thirds of its existing base of 60 million customers coming into its stores every week buy food, it is upgrading and extending its food offering through the acquisition of La Boulange, a bakery of French origin.

Which brings us to:

> **Old product view 2** – competitiveness comes from making more of the same, in order to get unit cost down.
> **New customer-centric view 2** – competitiveness comes from delivering superior experiences for individual customers, which also lowers their cost(s).

One unfortunate piece of product logic is its use of head-on product-for-product or service-for-service price as its competitive tool. Customer-centric logic takes a total price performance view, which means that *price includes the hidden costs of wasted money, time, and effort.*

For instance, M-PESA is easier, quicker, safer and more convenient than any other form of sending money, but it is also more cost-effective for customers. Not because of the price, but because of better security, time gained to do and honour the transaction, and so on.

Price is the cost over time

Price is not only the cost of acquiring the items, but the cost of getting the outcomes.

The approach in Russia to low-cost housing, as mentioned earlier, is a radical departure from the old days. First, the sustainability of the actual constructions is being dramatically improved, not just to increase the life of a building, but also to decrease the cost of maintenance over time. New materials are being explored and applied, in order to also decrease environmental and energy costs as well, and projections on total savings are calculated well into the future, in order to decide what investments are warranted upfront.

In a B2B situation, reducing the customer's total cost of doing business is fundamental to developing long-term bonding, as opposed to just pricing the stuff. So instead of putting effort into reducing the cost, to make and deliver units of product or service, the customer-centric enterprise builds skills and setups, which drive down the customer's total cost.

The benefit of the new ways of doing things for Sasol Wax Chile's customers, and customers' customers, is not based on the price of the wax. It is related to the total price performance of its integrated proposition. The cost of transporting is lower, because wax is transported to customers without water: Sasol uses the customer's recycled water to make the emulsion on their site, which brings the cost down still further. Customers pay as they use, saving on procurement, administrative and operational costs. Additionally, production is easier and reduces costs, because less water is used in the process.

An example of how Sasol Wax Chile benefits its customers' customers is, for example, kitchen cupboard manufacturers. Because wax makes the construction boards lighter, it takes up less room and therefore decreases the cost of storage and transportation for the kitchen manufacturers. End users have benefits as well – cupboards are easier to open, clean and maintain, last longer, can be recycled more easily, and are lighter and more water resistant.

Even in emerging markets and in B2C settings, customer-centric companies are at the forefront of total price performance. Cemex customers used to build homes with cheaper sandstone and limestone to save money, but this made them unsafe, unsustainable and more costly to maintain. Cement costs more, but is stronger and more permanent, so over time it pays.

Price is the cost of use

Today, with the emphasis on minimizing waste, the object is to help customers to buy or use less.

A large part of the BP drive was not only to provide the correct energy solutions to customers when, where and how they were needed, but also to find ways to reduce their total energy costs, by re-engineering processes so that they could reuse energy and heat.

In B2B settings, where there is a preponderance of product logic for tendering, and contracting, procurement is often programmed (and even incentivized) to try to get the cheapest price for the stuff.

This leaves the transforming enterprise pushing for a new way of doing things, with two options – influence in the higher ground, or work more closely with procurement to alter minds and models:

Here is the next difference:

Old product view 3 – each product or service has to make a profit in its own right.

New view customer-centric view 3 – the justification for products or services is customer 'lock-on' and customer profitability over time.

Traditional accounting is very adept when it comes to figuring out the cost and profit of products or services. What it is less good at is quantifying the profitability of customers, or the cost of losing a customer, or the opportunity cost of getting only one small part of customer spend, because of what the enterprise *doesn't* do or *doesn't* do well.

To see how much damage this view can cause, one only has to look at Marks & Spencer's yesteryear decision not to accept credit cards, because an accounting piece of data told top management that it would cost the company around 5 per cent of its revenues. In fact, it cost Marks & Spencer much more, because the gaping hole left in the customer activity cycle meant that customers bought less per visit and migrated to other stores where they could use their credit cards, which helped accelerate Marks & Spencer's downward spiral. It wasn't until its recovery period in the early 2000s that Marks & Spencer lifted its ban on credit cards.

There were no exceptions at Marks & Spencer in the old days. If a product or silo wasn't making a profit, the store manager would simply remove it from the shelves (and the spreadsheet columns). Now, as a matter of principle, a range of profits and margins is accepted if a product or service is integral to the cohesiveness of the customer offering.

And yet another difference is:

Old product view 4 – monies spent on customers are expensed and expected to show a return quickly.

New customer-centric view 4 – monies spent to 'lock-on' customers are investments in future revenue streams, and should be treated as such.

This brings us to the all-important point on customer-centric investments. Invariably this is bound up with the controversy around what should be deemed an expense, and what should be regarded as an investment. To complicate matters, all sorts of legal implications surround what is and what is not allowed to be capitalized as an investment, all of which can significantly change the financial picture and, with that, investment decisions. In other words, bad arithmetic, a relic of industrial convention, can make it very difficult to make effective investment decisions about what to do, and what to keep.

If expenses are made with the express intention of getting customer 'lock-on' and leveraging this later on, these expenses become assets. What else can make sense, since *they* are the value creators?

The opposite point of view is to regard these as costs, to be expensed and recovered quickly, or drop them if that is not possible. But this effectively says that there are no future benefits to be had from building the customer base, however that is achieved, say with knowledge, expertise, software or crowd sourcing, whereas we know that is what gets customer 'lock-on' and competitor lock-out.

Who can argue that Apple's investment in its iTune customer base, all of whom have accounts – which make it the largest holder of credit card data in the world – is not an asset to be leveraged?

Leading proponents of a new accounting metrics, which we will come to in a future chapter in more depth, say that the distinction is clear. If there are no future benefits, it is not an asset: it is an expense.[53]

As the enterprise tries to find its way towards customer centricity, being able to make and appreciate the distinction between what does and doesn't make customers long-term assets that exude long-term value potential is essential on a practical level, if nothing else. The difference between the old and the new view allows executives and investors to start thinking and talking on a more profound customer-centric level. They can thus steer conversations to the important issues, such as:

- What investments are needed to make customers into future growth prospects?
- How can we make the necessary funding easier to obtain for this?
- How can initiatives be given more time, so that short-term goals don't wreck long-term potential?

Most significant for the customer transforming company, is that if the arithmetic is changed, however that is expressed, it allows people the freedom and confidence to behave with more innovation-generating gusto, making the correct investments, unencumbered by artificial number restraints.

When Jeff Bezos was asked by his finance people how much they could allow the R&D people to spend to master what they needed in order to get the Kindle project off the ground, he reportedly answered: 'How much do we have?'[54]

Unlocking new customer currency

Once horizons are opened and the opportunities for adding customer value are uncovered through the customer activity cycle, the potential for revenue quickly becomes evident. Is there ever a better motivator?

All of this needs to be built into a financial algorithm, using new arithmetic, if the numbers are to help make a compelling case and speed up acceptance of the customer-centric model (see Table 6.1).

On the one hand, revenues go up because, once customers are locked on, there is infinite possibility for longevity, depth, breadth and diversity of customer spend. On the other hand, as customers 'lock-on', enterprise costs go down, because of the new economies of skill, sweep, stretch and spread.[55]

How revenues go up

Longevity of spend

The object with customer 'lock-on' is to make relationships stronger in order to get longer customer value. As the duration of the

Table 6.1 The customer-centric financial algorithm

Revenues go up due to:	Costs go down due to:
Longevity of spend	Economies of skill
Depth of spend	Economies of sweep
Breadth of spend	Economies of stretch
Diversity of spend	Economies of spread

relationship between the enterprise and the customer grows, more steady revenue streams come from a customer, be it an individual, household or corporate, farther into the future.

Though realistically the grand ambition is to translate this into lifelong spend, this is obviously a metaphor. Theoretically there is no reason why lifelong relationships are not possible – they are, and that is where we aim. But for the purposes of making a realistically compelling case, sometimes making an estimate on five or ten years is enough to show the magnitude of the gains that can be expected.

In addition to all the 'lock-on' benefits with longevity, costs are saved because new customers don't have to be acquired to replace those who are lost, which is what happens when the formula centres squarely on market share. As long as market share is okay, many firms don't try to figure out who stayed for how long, and who exited, why, and at what cost.

And expenses in managing those customers go down, because set-up and ongoing costs associated with having to get to know them are eliminated or diminish.

Contracts in perpetuity are what B2Bs often aim for, and with good reason. BP, for instance, calculated that a one-year, say US$1.5 million fuel deal for a particular customer, had a net present value of between $36,000 and $126,000, depending on the start-up costs. A ten-year deal could boost that same customer currency up to $8.6 million.

Additionally, a lot of wasted time, money and effort goes into the retendering or renewing of contracts. All of this should be factored against the cost of getting the 'lock-on', over whatever time frame the enterprise decides is practical.

Depth of spend

When customers 'lock-on', increased spend doesn't just come from longer revenue streams. As well as buying what they always bought for elongated periods, customers who 'lock-on' also buy more from that supplier. In other words, they give the enterprise more share of their wallet in the origin items: more BP sites to fill with fuel; more employees to cover with IHI health policies; more books from Amazon online, more share of M-PESA banking transaction spend; more coffee spend with Starbucks.

In the past, buyers (especially from the corporate and public sectors) sought out more than one supplier, ostensibly to play them off against each other on price, or spread their risk lest one failed to deliver. Now, regulations aside, the tendency is to have fewer suppliers, or even one trusted partner, who can produce an outcome that saves the customer time, energy and costs associated with running around, coordinating, recontracting, tendering and so forth.

Breadth of spend

The moment the core product is expanded into a 'market space', customer activity cycles can herald a myriad of opportunities for breadth of spend. Define the business as health insurance for expats or cement for DIY homeowners and that is what you will sell. Define the 'market space' as 'lifetime health and personal safety management' or 'sustainable home ownership', and the possibilities for adding revenue for customers through new products and services are multiplied.

Anything that delivers value components that are needed to obtain the outcome is a potential revenue generator. For instance, Marks & Spencer went from selling the perfect Christmas turkey to any customer to providing the perfect Christmas dinner to individual families, which includes an infinite variety of products and services from food to decoration, wine to gifts.

It is this breadth of spend that probably energizes executives most, because here they see the potential to build new sources of revenue. For example, the publication of decisions made by the US officials on patent applications in Lexis Nexis's traditional core business was only worth 12 per cent of the wider 'market space' in one particular division. Because answers to questions about patents could be built into customer workflow applications and routines, which are constantly updated and maintained, hundreds of million of additional dollars could be brought in.

Cemex works on breadth of spend in emerging markets. For example, domestic expansion for self-construction is driven by 'socios', who begin by buying cement, but then buy other Cemex products like paint, building tools, and materials for finishing and decoration.

At first M-PESA customers used a payment system for getting and sending money. Now the mobile payment disruptor, having got customer 'lock-on', armed with information about them, is able to get into other aspects of the customers' financial dealings such as savings, micro-payments of bills such as utilities, transport, and various micro transactions from buying goods to paying for drinks in local restaurants, ATM withdrawals, micro loans, donations, disbursement of salaries. And next could easily be pension funds or insurance.

Less intuitive is that existing mobile services providers, having crossed boundaries and expanded 'market space', are getting into these financial transactions through mobile wallets. Take MTN Ghana. It enables customers to pay utility electricity and TV bills, and is poised to spill over even further into banking territory.

The more ambitious the 'market space', the more opportunity there is to expand revenue through breadth of spend. For example, when Cemex expanded to 'sustainable home ownership' it began to include eco-friendly appliances, and water and waste systems in its portfolio of offerings.

The extra revenue from breadth of spend may come from existing or new skills developed, bought or brought in. BP uses its own in-house finance skills to help customers hedge their pricing. IHI uses its outside expert doctors to help individuals build, monitor and update their health plans in order to achieve wellbeing.

Starbucks acquisition of Teavana brought together the complementary skills of the tea company's deep capability in tea sourcing and blending, with its innovative skills in store and beverage innovation. The intention was not just to add another company to the Starbucks empire, or diversify its risk. But rather to enhance the customer's beverage experience, and so generate breadth of spend from its already considerable customer base. Especially people who are concerned about drinking too much caffeine, or who may gravitate back to the store in the afternoons or weekend, preferring a less stimulating drink.

Breadth of spend may also come from a new offering the enterprise introduces to deliberately disrupt its own product range. Amazon's Kindle is classic example of this. Alternatively, extra revenue breadth may come from partners in the form of commissions or fees received. A deep knowledge of customers' individual circumstances, credit assessment, and purchasing behaviour and records has enabled Magazine Luiza to partner with Cardif, the life insurer in Brazil, and provide life insurance, disability and unemployment protection, and extended guarantee products, a first for a consumer goods retailer in that country.

Diversity of spend

In the old days, in order to grow, companies diversified – often to their peril – because they found themselves in unknown territory, difficult to manage, without any particular theme or unified underpinning to ground them. Significantly, one of the first things the Cemex CEO did, when he arrived anew, was to dispose of all the company's sidelines, so it could focus on its new mission.

This diversification is quite different from the diversity of customer spend we speak of here, where, if the brand is trusted by a customer base, the enterprise can take customers into other 'market spaces', producing a totally new revenue stream, at no acquisition cost.

There was a time, when a brand that was strong in one area, did not dare to move into another, for fear of diluting image and causing brand schizophrenia. That was when brand was associated with a product, instead of a company. Even today, some more traditional firms still prefer to use new names for a new venture, in case it fails, and their key brand becomes contaminated.

However, as we see today, with emphasis on trust, once brands have been accepted and respected, they can be stretched to grow the business. Unencumbered by product thinking and the weight of the mental baggage accompanying it, this has been the stamp of many customer-centric disruptors making their mark.

In theory, there are limits to this brand stretch. Or are there? The likes of Amazon, Starbucks, Virgin and others, are beginning to show that brands can be much more elastic than anyone could ever have dreamed possible. As the brand gets better known and trusted, the creations that spring from this can cross industries and geographies to absorb more and more diversity of customer spend. Amazon seems to be on a never-ending path to offer its customer base anything and everything, from movie streaming to couture fashion. And Starbucks is now taking its customers into the health and wellness space by offering juices and an exclusive range of nutritious yogurt offerings. Virgin has been at it for years and now is a billion-dollar conglomerate with companies in more sectors than anyone else.

But that's not the point. This is: one-quarter of Virgin's consumers strongly agreed when asked if Virgin would be the best candidate to run the state pension scheme, compared with only 13 per cent who strongly supported the government in this role.[56]

Virgin may have started life as a music retailer, but it has become a brand that can be transferred to common customers across seemingly unrelated categories, from airlines to active health and leisure, bikes to brides, mobile phones to money, trains to travel agencies, stem cell banks to space travel, with Virgin Galactic expected to launch cosmos tourism with paying customers by the end of 2014.

The theory here is that once a brand has established itself, it can go into other 'market spaces' and take existing and new customers with it. Whilst for the uninitiated the Virgin Group looks like a whole lot of disparate businesses, it is actually a carefully crafted set of companies, all with customer centricity as the common denominator, what Branson calls connecting the dots. 'We now have brand loyalists who fly with us, work out with us, use our mobile phones, and broadband services, take our trains, drink our wine, watch our films, and now can even bank with us.'

Once they get customers to 'lock-on' the enterprise can take them into other 'market spaces' at very low or no cost. Which is why, as we see, mobile service providers are in financial transactions, including insurance, and will increasingly prove to be hefty competition for banks. As will Facebook, Amazon and Google, as they create competing value propositions and new forms of currency for customers with which to trade. With currency an abstraction today, and data received and paid out on a phone, and through digital wallets, the possibilities for leveraging customer spend is endless and lasting, if done correctly.

We should remember that getting diversity of customer spend is a second-round opportunity. It can only happen after the enterprise has truly entrenched itself in its market space and achieved customer trust, advocacy and 'lock-on'.

Lego's full-length American Australian animated adventure comedy film is a case in point. Based on Lego characters, this venture and its move into making its smart brick characters into a TV series, has enabled the company to leverage its locked-on fan base across the age spectrum, with a completely new set of revenues.

How costs go down

As distinct from the mass-oriented product-focused enterprise, chasing economies of scale from products, the customer-centric organization benefits measurably from new economies that come from its customer engagement and 'lock-on'.

These are generated from the new value creators, namely knowledge, information and expertise, technology and customer advocacy. These economies I have called economies of skill, sweep, spread and stretch. Combined with increasing revenues, it is how customer centricity produces the potential for exponential returns. Here is how it works.

Economies of skill

Much of the value that goes into creating customer-centric outcomes is infused with information, knowledge and expertise. As intangibles, they have characteristics that change the economics.

Intangibles have two distinct benefits that customer-centric enterprises put to self-sustaining use. One, it costs almost nothing to reuse the knowledge; in fact it grows as it is used, so it augments in value. And two, the customer gets the benefit of multiple and collective intelligence and expertise, because this knowledge (which can also be turned into tangible content) can be captured, aggregated, transformed, disaggregated, and accessed by individuals from any device – any place, any time.

It is in this way that IBM stretches its intelligence across the world, as each and every consultant takes the knowledge of all of them with them, whenever they encounter and work with customers, accessing this intelligence with one click. Effectively, customer-centric engagements are looped back into the enterprise, when and if needed to create advantages than can accumulate and multiply.

With cloud technology, scale and economies are taken to a whole new level. Without hardware or software or employees, an enterprise large *or* small can effectively scale up and compete when information is its key ingredient for success. This is as important for the collection and dissemination of data critical in the public sphere as it is for an enterprise. It also allows for flexibility in up- or down-scaling, when and if the occasion arises, without an investment.

Combine high intangible component offerings (low manufacturing and distribution costs), with cloudsourcing (no need for large upfront investment), and the competitive dynamics change: small organizations or not-for-profits can more easily compete with large enterprises for customer currency. And intangibles, being abundant, grow and become more valuable as they are shared, used and reused, and made tangible exponentially with help from advances in technology. Therefore, with better and more knowledge and information at the forefront of offerings, the cost of serving customers gets lower.

Customers also bring economies of skill to the party, if a vehicle exists for capturing their know-how. If what they know is known, and collected, it can be recycled and constantly improved.

In an example of a synergistic sharing of information and know-how, as farmers in the e-Choupal programme discover a new farming practice method or technique to improve crop quality, they are trained and incentivized to share their experiences with other farmers from other villages in India, which increases the total knowledge base and, additionally, makes training and up-skilling costs negligible.

Economies of sweep

As the role of technology gets stronger in delivering customer-centric value and 'lock-on', so we see the cost of attachment and engagement dropping. This also has quite a dramatic impact on the economics.

Economies come about because the enterprise, both large *and* small, can sweep up large numbers of customers simultaneously, at very low additional marginal costs, compared to other forms of engagement. Between the economies of the Internet, and social media take-up with countless avenues for web engagement, enterprises can effectively transact and communicate with one or millions of customers within seconds, days, weeks or months, at low or zero extra cost.

Through its in-house applications, FNB is sweeping in customers and non-customers across all age groups, lowering banking costs for them and itself. Geopay, for instance, is a carefully crafted person-to-person mobile payment system, which helps the customers find other users in the vicinity and allows customers to pay them, even non FNB customers (who can upload the app). Funds are instantly transmitted for a purchase, without having to know the receivers' banking details.

Interaction can take place with customers over multiple channels simultaneously. One only has to look at the banking innovations in Turkey to understand how far this can go. Denizbank became the first bank in the world to allow customers to access their financial details and send money to friends as well as purchase through Facebook with credit cards, which is now becoming commonplace. Turk Ekonomi Bankas (TEB) gives customers cards with built-in high-end authentication technology, complete with keyboards and tiny screens. From these, customers can punch in a password, do online banking and validate purchases. Ziraat Bank has a network of unstaffed video kiosks that enable customers to connect to branches and staff via teleconferencing.[57]

Plus, we need to factor in the fact that customers can spend as much time as they want, at no added cost, in order to be able to make a good decision when they communicate with the enterprise via technology. What is more, having customers who stay connected longer can save them and the enterprise expenses later on, because better decisions are taken.

This is pretty obvious in developed country markets, but the model is as significant in emerging countries, where take-up of mobile technology accelerates daily, and there are moves afoot to make smartphones the norm.

Take India Tobacco Company, which gathers millions of small farmers, at low cost, providing customized value that is individual farmer-specific. Each farmer gets real-time information and know-how, which makes a direct contribution to each farm's productivity, increasing that customer's ability to demand and buy better and more products from the enterprise.

Economies of spread

With initial investments (as opposed to expenses) in customer 'lock-on' used over and over again, the set-up costs can be spread over longer periods of time, rather than have only short-term transactional value. This can make pricing much more competitive, and market take-up more rapid. Primarily this is because, increasingly, set-up costs contain resources like data, know-how that are abundant rather than scarce, and investment in systems, which once made can be updated at very low cost, and used over and over again on infinite numbers of customers.

The first corporate assessment done by IHI took a good deal of time, money and resources. Nevertheless, once that methodology had been perfected and the before and after data gathered, against which to benchmark the customer's 'corporate health', new individuals coming on-stream could be served at a much lower cost.

HealthStore's health screenings of children in schools provides a unique opportunity for franchise owners to build the systems, to assess the health of individuals within the local community, and then to reuse this foundation knowledge to very quickly build systems for both preventative action and future treatment. This is done at low marginal cost for them and the increasing numbers that come on-stream.

Thanks to intangibles, investments can also be spread into other faster-growing countries, quickly and economically. GE's development costs for China and India were easily spread into areas such as Asia, South America and Africa (more on this point later).

Economies of stretch

When customers 'lock-on' they can stretch both the customer base, by viralizing the new ways of doing things, and the brand. These economies of stretch are due to the proliferation and use of new social digital media by increasing numbers of customers to link, communicate, share and influence each other. They converse and create content, and spread it, as well as their opinions and recommendations, by word of mouth, using a massive interactive real-time network, which costs next to nothing.

If well managed and positive, this has the ability to stretch the brand through referrals and advocacy, at little or no cost. This pushes the cost of customer acquisition down, even to zero, while the ability to use and reuse social networks goes up.

Jeff Bezos was probably the first person to invite customers to influence others via the Internet, when he asked them to post their opinions and review the books they read, which Amazon then passed on to other customers with similar profiles, at no cost to them. It now promotes the top reviewers as rated by customers, in its 'Hall of Fame', and allows them their own pages, making some of them powerful, with even more clout and influence than professional book critics.

Probably one should factor in the cost of getting to these influencers and advocates in quantifying economies of spread. But note that any investment in systems developed to facilitate these platforms and networks multiplies in value at very low cost.

A last word on this subject: if the enterprise passes on its economies to customers, it can reinforce the 'lock-on' loop. Customers get the benefit of the enterprise's scale, and this weds them still further to the brand.

Consider FNB: All the economies of skill, sweep and spread it has created in the digital sphere, it gives back to customers, like for instance unmetered access to data and social networks such as Facebook, YouTube and Twitter and any of its own websites. This kicks in economies of stretch (advocacy and social endorsement), so extending the market for digital banking, and its portion of it.

The total value equation

The value of customer centricity can only realistically be sized if enterprises consider customers, and all that goes into making them long-term prospects, as assets that will bring rewards to the enterprise well into the future.

The uninitiated are still perfectly willing to project returns from products and services years ahead, because they consider these to be predictable and reliable, even though first-mover advantages – the time lag between launch and being copied – is getting ominously shorter. (Witness for instance the loss pharmaceutical companies have experienced due to inroads made by generics.)

However, in reality, enterprises are still reluctant to project into the future when it comes to customers. The most common argument against lifetime value, they say, is that customers are simply too volatile: they're always on the lookout for the cheapest or best deal; they have no real loyalty; and they are just plain risky.

Of course, if we're only talking about products and services, 'branded commodities' that can be easily compared, then customers *will* look for the best buy; they *will* shop around and be looking at alternatives; and they *do* have more and more access to information, which makes flitting around even easier to do than it was in the past. But that's a symptom of a much bigger problem.

With a customer-centric approach, the cost to *customers* of switching shoots up – not because the enterprise has made it difficult for them to leave, but because it has made it easy for them to stay. It has become indispensable to them, setting up the reinforcing 'lock-on' loop, with all the two-way benefits.

So built into making that next breakthrough in the transformation process is a statement of the contemplated prize, from lifetime customer value. This isn't a linear trajectory, in that executives simply project a figure with a built-in factor for economic growth, based on repeat business, with customers buying what they have always bought before.

The object is to connect so closely with customers, and so early, that as they progress – get older, develop or whatever – the enterprise moves with them, or may even instigate their change or the headway they make. The deeper and stronger the bond gets early on in the customer activity cycle or their lives, the more information, knowledge, time and ideas that are shared, so the greater becomes the possibility of affiliation and bonding and the benefits arising from that. It is then that the magnitude of the value which the enterprise can produce for and from that customer escalates.

UT Bank started to offer basic loans to unsalaried entrepreneurs, but never left it at that. Once they had helped their furtherance, they then set about actively assisting them to assess what they then needed to grow business even more, and then offered it to them. For example, the entire gamut of exporting services such as foreign exchange, trade lines, insurance or letters of credit.

MTN Ghana, having deliberately chosen students as one of their prime lead markets, and through its MTN Social Club they call Y-Cliq on eight campuses nationwide, with tens of thousands of students and numbers ramping up every day, are in constant communication, helping in campus life and career-making moves. The newly formed 'Kuul Peeps', an online portal with academic content is made available through streaming, and is deeply woven into campus culture, the first point of call for breaking news, social events and career counselling. In addition to this, students get free invitations to youth programmes, special discounts on MTN services, free subscriptions to MTN radio, and opportunities to work for and with MTN during vacations.

The point is that these are not promotional campaigns that expect immediate returns. They are deep investments, intended to connect with students, add value to their professional lives and lifestyles, and make them lifelong advocates for the MTN brand.

Doing the sums

In trying to assess what customers could be worth in the future, certain assumptions must obviously be made about gains to be had, and costs to be saved that result from these long-term relationships.

Clearly these relationships are not guaranteed, but what the enterprise must to do, and do well, is motivated by a desire to maximize the chance of sustaining customers as allies. There will always be some fall-off rate. So once estimates of customer worth become specific, they can always be tempered by a risk or loss or hedging factor, or some other weighting measure.

Using probabilities or scenarios helps executives navigate the figures to make the case for a financial projection into the future that does not yet exist. A simple 'best case', 'most realistic case', 'worst case' classification makes the task a lot more credible.

Material benefits gained and cost saved from customer 'lock-on' that need to be quantified and factored into the equation are very specific to industry settings, but here are some of the more frequently encountered and cited possibilities:

Potential benefits gained

- predictable cash flows;
- less price sensitivity;
- advocacy, word of mouth, and potential for positive viralization;
- easier to sell to, by about 50 per cent;[58]
- increased share of wallet;
- barriers to reaching influencers shrink, giving access to higher levels;
- selling high-level high-margin new services;
- increased and quicker take-up of new innovations and extensions;
- ability to improve forecasting, through information sharing;
- joint risk taking, with a vested interest in the outcome, by all parties;
- opportunities for joint ventures and collaboration;
- retention of good employees.

Potential costs saved

- expertise, knowledge and information reused;
- expertise, know-how and information turned into tangible even saleable content;
- eliminating waste and duplications;
- eliminating protracted expensive renewal, tendering and bidding negotiations;
- lowering cost of capital;
- lowering cost to serve and transact with customers;
- decreased costs of engagement, as familiarity and trust set in;
- sharing of resources;
- benefits from customers' ideas, design and R&D;
- other free work done by customers, such as help desks.

Back from the future

The total customer value approach calculates the net present value of future customer worth, over the customer's life expectancy, given what the enterprise is able to do for them better than anyone else.

How much share of this lifelong value an enterprise can extract is regarded as the true sign and only real measure of customer competitiveness. That becomes the aspiration and target.

Lifetime net present value calculations can be very sophisticated and complex, and the literature abounds in different versions.[59] Box 6.1 contains a useful guideline for calculating total customer value.

Box 6.1 Total customer value equation

Revenues over a meaningful period from longevity, depth, breadth and diversity of spend – calculated with a built-in risk factor for customer loss.

Minus costs of initial acquisition – when there is such a cost.

Plus decreased costs listed where relevant (including new economies).

Plus extra gains listed where relevant.

Minus cost to serve.

Equals net present value using discounted cash flow, at cost of capital or any other acceptable metric.

The most important part of making the case financially, as far into the future as executives dare and the organization will permit, is that it will influence decisions on investment. For some, making the financial case rigorously granular, with statistics down to the last decimal point, will be necessary to justify these investments. They want the certainty and security they find in the details, which they believe minimizes their chances of making a mistake.

Others will accept looser approximations, knowing that the powers that be will spend time thinking about what the numbers tell them, about how big the opportunity could be – and what they have to do to capture it and make it last. They focus on finding big ideas and ideals that lead to big results.

The Engagement

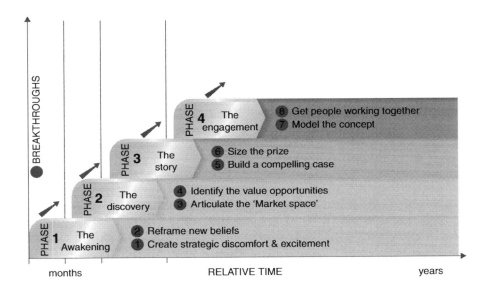

Model the Concept

Key idea

Customer engagement begins by getting carefully selected like-minded customers to model the new ways of doing things. Getting beyond pilot testing to just incrementally improve products and services, disruptive customer centricity needs to change social and business practice, with a different approach. Once customers have helped provide proof of concept, demonstrated early wins and take-up, credibility and confidence both inside the organization and outside heighten, with predictable adoption rates deliberately orchestrated to spur on the transformation process.

Choosing where to aim

This is the phase of the transformation at which engagement needs to take place, with more people from inside and outside the enterprise drawn in. Not only to be enthused and motivated by the new core purpose and the rewards down the road, but demonstrably involved because what they do fits, or soon will fit into the design, delivery and support of the new proposition.

Up until now the catalyst and lead players with their chosen representatives will have been driving the efforts, tapping into the positive energies within the organization. Either they will have been deliberately placed in teams, or they will have gravitated to them of their own accord. But now commitment will have started to multiply, and engagement is needed from a broader spectrum of the population if the momentum is to keep going, and the new ways of doing things become codified and institutionalized.

It is at this point that customer involvement begins and, as a consequence, the harder core component of the organization who, up until now, may have been reticent, begins to buy-in and amass.

What we know about buy-in

Ever since the work of Rogers, we have known that people take on innovation at different rates, and times.[60] If the enterprise is to move systematically through the step-for-step process that will get it to where it needs to go, the right people must be taken through the five phases at the right time.

Enterprises still talk about driving a transformation vertically down the organization, whereas in fact, it diffuses vertically or horizontally through one population to another, depending on the risk profile and people's willingness to accept new ideas and change, irrespective of where these individuals are layered in the organization.

What we also know is that there will always be resistance to change and a portfolio of reactions. People will ask: 'Why do we need to do this at all?' 'Why now?' 'Why this way?' 'Let's wait until the time is right.'

Furthermore, we also know that for the most part these people have an uncanny capacity to resist change, especially (but not exclusively) if they are in traditional settings or large complex environments – be they private or public. What may be blindingly obvious, even exciting to some people, may bring out negative feelings and behaviours in others, such as fear of the unknown, failure or loss, disbelief or cynicism, lack of loyalty, even sabotage, or token gestures without real commitment. All of these are to be expected, but can and need to be managed and minimized.

Categorizing people

People tend to fall into different categories, depending on their risk profile and ability to take on new ways of doing things. Part of avoiding the resistance, and minimizing delays and disappointment, whether done formally or informally, is inviting and involving people into the process to coincide with the category into which they fit.

Whilst this may seem a bit contrived, here's the thing: the gain far outweighs the pain. People need different things to turn and drive them on. This is the only way in which frictions and factions can realistically be prevented from blocking the way to progress, and the phased approach can create and manage the diffusion wave that will get the innovation accepted and institutionalized, at a chosen pace (see Exhibit 7.1).

Each category should be brought into the process at different times:

The small, **activated** category is where 'points of light' are to be found, and should exclusively feature during the awakening phase. It is they who will vocalize discomfort and excitement about the new direction, and cultivate the sense of urgency and appetite to break with the past. They understand why this is being done, and they *get it*, and that is what motivates them to activate the process.

Hopefully these are the obvious influencers in the organization, but that may not always be the case. Especially in traditional-type enterprises. The representatives these activated people choose, the allies they seek, the coalitions they build and the team they bring together initially, will start to include the next category, the enlightened and **motivated**.

This group aligns when they see *action*. They should join the activated, and be more prominent during the discovery process, when the 'market space' definition and work on the customer activity cycles are being done. As well, they are often chosen for their experience

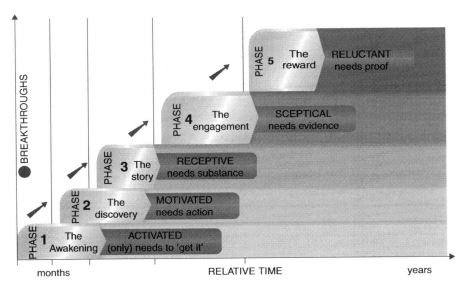

Exhibit 7.1 Internal categories' take-up and motivators

and knowledge of the markets and customers. Together with the activated, they take the process through to the next stage.

The **receptives** buy in next. Being part of the action isn't enough for them. They want to see something tangible and they seek clarity and *substance*. They will probably stay neutral, while the motivated align.

But once the story has been formulated and has begun to be told, they take a more active interest and will buy in, especially when presented with the numbers, even though they may only be on paper. They, together with the activated and motivated, keep the process going.

It is only during the engagement phase, when buy-in from colleagues and customers, partners, investors and the press begins to swell, and positive proof of concept comes back during the modelling phase that the **sceptical**, the next group, become converted. They will doubt at the beginning until *evidence* is provided.

Until then they may be reluctant to participate, more comfortable with business as usual, rather than any new initiatives. It usually won't be until success is declared that they will be completely won over.

The last group are laggards, the **reluctants**. They need *proof* that everything is working and that there is no turning back; sometimes they never buy in and continue to live with old mindsets in the past. They should be left in the background, and they will probably show a high attrition rate.

Here is more detail on the attributes of each category:

Activated: a small group, distinguished by the fact that they react and act first. Generally, this small group not only accepts change quickly and instinctively, but also is outward facing in seeing and sensing things, which is why they are good at customer perspective. They enjoy change, even upheaval, not for its own sake, but because they genuinely see remaking and reshaping as a natural part of an organization's growth and evolution. Determined, they look for ways to win, using foresight, are provocative, and courageous: 'willing to push through closed doors if necessary'.

They are creative but, unlike some of the classic innovator types, this is not to the exclusion of the structure and discipline that they deliberately use to get the concerted balance needed to follow through step for step. These people are single-minded about a goal, but also handle ambiguity well, and are gifted at operating in existing milieus, while at the same time trying to alter them.

They also have cross-sight, the ability to transcend boundaries, and they look for how everyone can gain, as well as the company. This is what makes them ideal candidates for both catalysing, and leading customer centricity transformations.

Motivated: this is a larger and critical group, because its members influence others, have a high interest level, see the point, and want to be integral to the transformation, but only once they have really understood it. Although typically they will be looking for a defined model and route, they collaborate and participate, as the big picture emerges. While they look at the details, they don't necessarily demand facts to support ideas. They admire the activated types, and use them as role models, tolerate change well, and are happy to work for the good of the whole.

These individuals can play an important role because they will go back into their silos and, through them and lead players, the next group will be influenced.

Receptive: a larger group, particularly in traditional environments, they are more conservative and make their move to avoid any loss rather than chase wins. Its members have difficulty deviating from what they know and understand, and have to be invited in. They can be engaged, but they will wait for the story to be clearly articulated, and they will monitor reaction to it. Once the prize becomes clear, they become more comfortable. Although they are not as receptive to change as the activated and motivated, they will cooperate and be prepared to make the leap to commitment, (only) once they see substance and the financial viability, moving nonetheless with a degree of caution.

They are often in the operations side of the business and therefore fundamental to success, and they will start to influence peers once they are convinced that the story makes sense, and they understand more about how it impacts them.

The most significant shift that must take place with operations is the realization that the real asset is the customer, not the hard assets such as factories, equipment or real estate, which is what they are used to managing.

Sceptical: holding back until they see customer acceptance, risk averse by nature, these people will want visible signs of success, and will look for evidence and examples of customer acceptance before they commit themselves or release their resources. They are preoccupied with processes, policies and procedures, and stick to rules and routines. And they may even have difficulty understanding the need for change. They will be concerned about consequences for their own patch, and will buy in only when it is clear that the transformation is irrefutably working and they have no option.

Reluctant: these people will only truly buy in once the transformation has gathered sufficient momentum for it to be an irrevocable triumph, though some may never be able to identify with the change. A number may elect to leave early on – and others will simply have to go.

Involving customers

The engagement stage is also the time when outsiders need to become actively involved. The innovative way of doing things for customers, consisting of the most important new value-add opportunities – however that is defined – needs to be modelled and made to work. The best way to do this is with customers, who themselves become part of the commitment to action, and therefore the implementation.

The notion of a trial with customers before going to market is not new. But note: this is no pilot test, where the object is to attempt something new but abandon it if the experiment doesn't work. By now a great deal of time, effort and resources will have gone into building a view of the future, knowing full well that traditional methods cannot be expected to reveal this or extract it from customers. Model concepts mean what they say: the enterprise believes in an innovative approach *to* customers, and then proceeds to get it right and make it work *with* a select group of customers, before rolling out and scaling up.

The principles hold for all situations – B2C and B2B. Choosing the correct customers is essential.

Initially UT Bank in Ghana focused on traders, who needed bridging finance, such as exporters who had orders and had to meet deadlines on delivery dates. Or people who needed a cash stopgap to finish a project they already had. Prince Amoabeng acknowledged that the new enterprise needed to prove that they could do it right from the outset and get quick wins. From that came the platform for more and more successes, including its expansion into other parts of the world.

End users can't be randomly chosen. They need to be interested enough in the issue to help make it work. In IBM's work with energy conservation in cities like Dubuque, Iowa, in the USA, the company used a select group of volunteer households interested in conservation in order to model a water and energy system, monitoring their sustainable behaviour changes, which included taking shorter showers, fixing leaks, buying water-efficient appliances and altering water systems in gardens.

In B2B it is important to choose the correct enterprises or individuals within those organizations. These are 'points of light', like-minded in the sense that they respond positively to change, but still want to see something tangible to be gained. If they do, they are usually prepared to collaborate, be transparent and open, help to get the correct people on board, share risk and, importantly, comply.

In over 100 cities, IBM has had to challenge local government leaders to think differently about how decisions are taken, and how they can get things done more proactively. Initially, they worked with high-profile cities, with innovative leadership and a strong commitment from the mayor or city manager. Decisions were taken so that the chances of making benefits real and measurable were high. People were willing to share information, open doors in communities, and help IBM engage with the correct citizens, officials, engineers, town planners, environmental experts, NGOs and whoever else was relevant.

Pilot tests versus model concepts

During this stage of engagement, when chosen customers agree to model the new customer concepts, another breakthrough will have been made.

The significant differences between the product-based pilot tests and customer-centricity approach of modelling the customer concepts are summarized in Table 7.1.

First of all, modelling is about getting the new way of doing things right, instead of testing and then throwing it out if it fails. And getting it right with a select group of carefully chosen customers, instead of behind closed doors in laboratories or factories.

Table 7.1 Pilot tests versus model concepts

	Pilot tests	**Model projects**
Object	Test it, and drop if it fails	Make it work
Commitment	Minimum resources required to start	Put best resources behind it
Choose customers	Representative	Innovative prepared to do different, untried things
Time frame	Defined beginning and end	Can be ongoing – used as laboratory and reference point
Relationship with customer	Keep intentions and experiment low-key for fear of failure and exposure	Transparent – jointly make it work
Assumption	Terminate if it fails	Keep going until you get it right
Intention	Sell to customer when perfect	Do with customer in the spirit of collaboration
Approach	Make it perfect	Experiment, learn

With old logic, companies test and retest in order to get perfection before they let it into the market, and often move too slowly or are too late as a consequence. This doesn't work with disruptive thinkers. Paul Polman of Unilever, speaking about his move into sustainable living, comments: 'If we had tested the thing to death, we would have sat here until the end of the next decade – and the ship will be sinking.'[61]

Concept modelling is more in keeping with a disruptive customer-centric mind and model. Experimental by nature, it allows for adaptations to be incorporated, as learnings take place. This learning may never stop and the model may be used as an ongoing laboratory in the quest for, say, sustainable living or the ideal banking experience.

To model concepts, the people chosen also need to be prepared to experiment. In IBM's Pennsylvania efforts, for instance, the company has set up a living laboratory for transportation. Everything in the network is addressed, from bus scheduling to parking, from pothole monitoring to automated traffic light switching, and nothing is set in stone – it is always changing, as the learnings kick in.

The nature of commitment is different from a pilot test. In a pilot test, generally as few resources as possible are used, in case it fails and wastes money. In contrast, model concepts use the finest people, talent and resources, because the main object is to do whatever it takes to make it work.

Pilot tests have a clearly defined beginning and end. Model concepts evolve, as people learn as they go along. So in B2B situations working arrangements can develop and grow, far beyond what was originally anticipated or agreed, exposing opportunities to work together, including joint ventures.

Intentions and experiments are contained and given a low profile in pilot tests, for fear that failure may damage the brand. If the pilot doesn't achieve the required response, it is quickly abandoned. Good customers are preferably excluded from the test in order to minimize risk, and only exposed to it once the product or service has been accepted and perfected. With customer-centric modelling, the enterprise and its customers work together transparently, in an atmosphere of sharing and learning, achieving results that are mutually rewarding.

In classic tradition, a good pilot test would choose a representative market or group of customers with which to work. Average responses from average customers would be the guiding force for a go/no go decision.

But average customers or responses cannot help make landmark change. So to disrupt, the enterprise must try to engage those people who are unafraid of bold moves, prepared to make the unknown happen, if they believe in it.

Rules for successful modelling

The length of time involved in model concepts can vary greatly, depending on, among other things, the number of markets chosen to work in initially; the number of customers within them; the spread of geographies; the time taken to get customers to agree; and the extent of the commitment. The great thing about doing model concepts with customers is that, at their conclusion, and even while they are under way, the new customer-centric approach is in fact being implemented, not merely tested.

So instead of having a thick piece of research to report on at the end, executives can now claim that the new customer concept is demonstrably working. Also people are given time to adjust to the changes while they are doing something tangible, rather than hearing an announcement about something new and then having to execute it.

For an enterprise like IHI, a group of independent customers or employees could work through how a new health plan can be built up and monitored on the website over a couple of months. In a B2B setting, BP could choose a sector like shipping, and work with one or several firms to reduce the amount of energy used by a fleet over a working period of a year, or work with many different sectors simultaneously in order to deliberately capture the overlaps and differences between them.

Getting customers to a workshop is the starting point, with the following as the main objectives:

- To test assumptions, interpretations and views on the future direction.
- To validate the new concept, captured in the 'market space' definition, and customer activity cycle analysis, and fine-tune these if needed.
- To find out what customers consider to be the most important value components or 'hot spots', emanating from the string of value-adds in the customer activity cycle mosaic.
- To involve sponsors internally in order to retain and increase share of mind.

While validation and feedback are essential, equally pressing is to get customers to buy into the idea of participating in actually modelling the concept, either in its entirety or in part. The overriding objective for the enterprise when entering this vital phase is to be able to demonstrate proof of the new customer concept, and so showcase some visible results internally and externally.

The burden of getting proof through modelling is greater for people who are disrupting, making groundbreaking changes, than for those who are simply making incremental additions. But when disruptors get proof of concept and proof of value, another huge breakthrough will have been achieved. Confidence will be bolstered, which will mobilize the positive energy that accelerates more buy-in inside the enterprise, freeing up more time and resources for projects, which in turn boosts confidence and so creates still more buy-in.

However, a warning: in the same way that success breeds success, so failure will engender expectation of more failure. That can become self-fulfilling and is known to do a great deal of damage to creative initiatives. That is why it is so essential that some important rules be followed:

Rule 1 – position the workshop as a research event

If workshops are used as a kick-off, to which selected customers are invited to participate, it should be conceived and positioned as a research event, rather than as a pitch or platform to broadcast and promote what the enterprise has already decided to do.

The event should expressly be designed to share opinions and information, allowing active dialogue and rich forums for exchange. The customer activity cycle exercise can be used to facilitate this and validate and prioritize the new opportunities identified.

Rule 2 – choose customers carefully

Choose customers that have the best chances of making it work, is the best advice anyone can give. This goes for consumers and organizations. Unfortunately, the biggest (in size or sales) enterprises aren't always the best for a model concept, because they won't necessarily be the most forward thinking or collaborative. In fact, they can sometimes be the most conservative.

The questions below should be asked when making the choice of customers with whom to work on modelling:

- Who are the innovators, free and novel thinkers, like-minded and collaborative?
- Who are the influencers in this market who have the potential to viralize positive behaviours?
- Who is likely to invest time and resources to make it work?
- With whom do we have high-level relationships that can be leveraged?
- Who is likely to provide immediate or follow-on business?
- Who is the most experienced at what they do and will be indicative of, and indeed influence, trends?
- Who will give us access to the correct people and resources?

Rule 3 – involve senior executives

These research forums should include high-level executives, including, where relevant, CEO presence. Discussion needs to transcend day-to-day talk or operational grievances, and instead get into high-ground strategic conversations about the new approach, and working together to achieve it.

When dealing with B2B customers, the same principle applies to the participating institution. If the correct level in the customer organization does not actively support and attend the event, its impact will be lost, and the follow-up needed to get the proof of concept may never materialize. As a result, the enterprise may soon be back to the product price shackle with customers.

Rule 4 – be flexible on incentives

Behind this exercise lies the implicit assumption that once the very carefully chosen customers see the gains to be had, they will actually want to play an active role in helping them manifest.

It is okay to incentivize people in lieu of time and resources spent, to help get the new proposition right, which is after all the aim of modelling. This is different from having to keep people objective enough to give feedback and advice, and not be incentivized, which traditional pilot testing has to do.

These incentives can take many different forms. Sometimes consumers are prepared to collaborate as volunteers, interested in the brand or the new proposition, as we saw with the IBM water conservation modelling in the USA. Or because they are getting something free, as with MTN Ghana's student modelling.

Enterprises that are expected to gain from the modelling may require a concession like a special price, or first-mover advantage. Or even the prospect of a joint venture, if the opportunity is enticing enough. This is what happened with BP during one of the sessions with a haulier customer, when the idling – or rather elimination of idling – while drivers slept, was exposed as a value-add, and turned into a new business.

Rule 5 – cover the basics in the agreement

Compliance is also an issue. People must agree to cooperate and go through the motions that make the process work. So before an agreement to proceed is reached, certain basics have to be acknowledged, especially who is responsible for doing what, and what resources will be allocated by the respective parties.

It is likely that some unforeseen irresolvable issues will have to be faced along the way, because new ground will be covered and explored, unknown and unfamiliar. This will mean that both parties have to tolerate experimentation, jointly finding solutions for longer-term gains.

Gains may even be uncertain: BP could not say exactly what shippers would save if they switched to new ways of managing their integrated energy needs, so it decided to guarantee a minimum, and then gain share in the results.

For all these reasons, if expectations and accountability are agreed at the outset, with transparency about intent, roles and how to apportion benefits, the chances are multiplied of solving problems as they arise, and of success overall.

Rule 6 – quantify results

Nothing motivates people like seeing tangible results. Therefore, the more the modelling can demonstrate measurable before and after gains the better. This can be in the form of data or case studies, provided they can be used as a reference point and benchmark.

This evidence from the modelling is important for two reasons: it increases appetite for the new ways of doing things within the participating customer constituent groups, and it adds more credence and confidence inside the transforming enterprise, during this important buy-in stage.

In IBM's sustainable water project with households in Dubuque, Iowa, for example, they measured everything associated with water usage changes, including increases in understanding, decreases in use, and savings in cost. Once the figures came back, for example a 716 per cent increase in leak detection, and conservation of nearly 7 per cent of the water used, it was enough to get proof of concept to drive the project still further and attract other cities.[62]

Rule 7 – create role models

Model concepts serve as reference points and role models for other customers. Reputation, trust and credibility expand, which leads to word-of-mouth diffusion and becomes the platform for attracting more customers. Hence the importance of choosing customers well.

An enterprise may even use itself to model the concept: 'You get so much more credibility if you can say we are doing it ourselves.' IHI did this when they introduced a 'get well feel well' customized canteen experience for staff, matching food to their personal energy profiles and intolerances in order to raise productivity levels.

Getting early wins

While it may sound paradoxical, model concepts are both a new form of customer R&D, and an opportunity to actually demonstrate early wins that have been unleashed from the customer activity cycle. What is more, these two possibilities are not mutually exclusive, because when the ingredients to produce value are more service-intensive, the distinction between development, design and delivery blurs.

People get engaged during the model concepts, so they learn, adapt, refine and improve as they go along. If they are working with customers to develop a new value-add – say to build a health plan online, or help to reconfigure a production line in a factory, or to enable the customer to reuse energy or use less water or heat – a large part of what they are doing is also the actual delivery.

This is foreign to traditional organizations, which research design and develop in laboratories, produce in product or service factories, pilot test in confined areas, and then finally sell the innovation out into the marketplace.

Whether the emphasis and agreement on how to conduct the model concept will be customer R&D, or straight delivery, is impossible to say, because so much depends on the organization and its circumstances, and no one-size-fits-all formula works. Depending on where the emphasis goes, so the financial ramifications will be different.

Some enterprises may be confident enough to produce benefits for the customer immediately, and charge them during this modelling period. Others will be content with viewing model concepts as customer R&D, gaining in other ways such as:

- Powerfully demonstrating the customer approach in action.
- Quantifying measurable returns early on.

- Building a body of reusable knowledge.
- Learning new skills and approaches.
- Building case studies and testimony.
- Gaining access to information that has never before been available.
- Showcasing early, visible, promotable wins.
- Making connections and enhancing relationships.
- Getting into the higher ground in organizations.
- Building advocates for the brand.

BREAKTHROUGH 8

Get People Working Together

Key idea

There are ways of getting internal engagement, but there are also tripping points such as distraction, which must be anticipated and managed. If a customer-centric, 'one company' outcome is to be delivered, these will need to be identified and eliminated. People will have to work together across company, and new account management elevated to drive coordination and collaboration throughout the customer activity cycle. Concurrently, external engagement – mobilized through creative ways of partnering, including with customers – creates virtuous circles and plus sum gains.

Tips and tripping points

Getting people to want to work together and turn motivation into action is the next breakthrough to be achieved, if customer centricity is to take hold sustainably in an organization. This will have been a continuous thread and theme managed by the leader, which includes matching people to the process, according to their ability to take on the change and pace.

If the implementation protocol is maintained along the breakthrough milestones, 'stickiness' will result. People will begin to talk with more authority and conviction about customer centricity, and the new story. Executives claim that this is one of the strong signs 'that the transformation has finally taken root'.

Concepts and language are bedded down, and start to become 'a code or shorthand during discussions that no one questions any more', and, at meetings, customer value and its delivery dominate discussions.

Some of the other signs that this is happening include:

- More people volunteering to take part in new initiatives.
- More questions about what is happening, from all parts of the organization.
- Active participation and experimentation.
- Talking with customers to get their formal and informal feedback.
- Customers, board and press begin asking about new initiatives.

Warnings of distraction

The implementation process can be badly tripped up, however. The opposite of the traction that keeps things moving forward – is distraction. That can pull the transformation process in other directions and slow down the pace. And, at worst, it can lead to disillusionment about whether the process is working. If distraction comes from senior influential people, who may previously have been supportive, this can potentially unhinge the process. As Steve Jobs warned about being out-front, you will go through a period 'when everybody tells you that you've completely failed'.[63]

It is difficult to predict when to expect this distraction, because it can happen anywhere in the process, but it's important to understand the signs, and manage and manoeuvre through it.

And to understand that although it is different from resistance, it is just as predictable and equally potent.

Part of the problem with distraction is that although people support the transformation, they don't always understand what it takes and how strategic the implications are, so they become side-tracked and may even become critical.

Jeff Bezos famously said:

> *You do something that you genuinely believe in, that you have conviction about, but for a long period of time well-meaning people may criticize that effort and when you receive criticism... first of all, search yourself, are they right? And if they are, you need to adapt what you're doing. If they are not right, if you really have conviction that they're not right then you need to have that long-term willingness to be misunderstood.*[64]

Understanding that the implementation process never works in linear fashion can help. As one executive put it: 'Be prepared for highs and lows, it looks more like spaghetti than a straight line.'

What everyone does agree, though, is that as long as the direction is upward, that's all that really matters. When leaders have faith in themselves and what they are doing, it's always easier to ride the tough times. FNB's Jordaan maintains that fundamental to success is that he stuck to his strategy he believed in, but learnt along the way and was prepared to tweak it until he and his team got it right.

Here are the main causes or signs of distraction to watch out for:

- An unexpected change in business conditions that frightens the powers that be, who postpone or interrupt the initiative.
- Impatience with pace, so meetings are cancelled by parts of the organization, and their participation dissipates.
- Initiatives in different silos proceed in parallel, each with its own plans, without commitment to the overarching customer vision.
- New consultants brought in, who start the process from scratch.
- A sudden decision to prioritize some other initiative, which takes up people's time and energy.
- A new model or approach brought in that is considered hot.
- Loss of focus due to a change in the position of key people.

Some quotes from executives who have made the customer-centric journey:

> *It takes a combination of courage, patience and time – more than you think.*

> *It requires tenacity and persistence that you cannot do without.*

> *Staying the course is the main thing – if you can do that you can get through the tough times.*

> *The landscape is constantly changing. You must have a game plan which helps you use your personal informal network, to get around the politics and bring who you want on board.*

> *The most important tip I have is: get and keep it on important meeting agendas.*

Fear of dampened demand due to poor economic conditions can of course be a huge distraction. However, if one examines the enterprises that have managed to thrive, even during tough years, they do so and outpace competitors by not deviating from their customer-centric goals.

To quote Angela Ahrendts, who said of Burberry when she was its customer-centric transformational CEO, 'We always said we're not immune to the ebb and flow of the macro economy, but that doesn't change our vision. We have absolute clarity and commitment to our proven strategies, which gives us confidence for the long term.'

Getting silos unified

Although from the outset cross-silo teams move in concert along a clearly defined process and set of breakthroughs, positive and motivated, they may never before have had to confront the multifunctional challenges that lie ahead. They may have to work with quite a different set of people in order to make this customer-centric journey. And whilst colleagues may be part of the same organization, they may hitherto have been cut off from each other, even though they may share customers, have spoken over the phone or e-mailed each other. It is not unusual to hear people say, 'this is the first time we have worked on a common project'.

The good news is that the process and the tools are designed to consciously pull together all of the relevant bits of the organization, in order to produce a unified customer outcome. When this breakthrough becomes timely, alignment should be in place, with sufficient numbers mobilized to get the needed engagement. The bad news, executives always say, is that it is *the* most challenging and perplexing part of the transformation process. It is infinitely more difficult, they insist, than finding outside partners.

The following quotes illustrate:

> *Beating up your colleagues was more important than winning in the marketplace.*

> *Our main divisions have been constantly at war, battling each other instead of working together for common customers.*

> *We couldn't get them [another division in the company], to even tell us what price they quoted our mutual customer.*

There is long-standing agreement in academic and practitioner circles that, in any innovative initiative, the sooner the process fragmented silos and diverse people unify and work together the better, if engagement and pace are to be accelerated.

Selected individuals from each silo should be invited to join in and work with the lead team early on, when the 'market space' is being defined and the customer activity cycles are being worked through. Not only to tap into expertise and knowledge, but also to make them feel involved. However, again and again executives warn that this only works if 'you choose the people very carefully – the most receptive and the best people, not just those that can be spared'.

Clarity on roles in the delivery process follows directly from the customer activity cycle analysis, which is the unifying template for who delivers what, in the customer experience 'pre', 'during' and 'post'. Any function or activity that doesn't have a part to play in delivering this value either directly, or indirectly to internal customers, has to be seriously questioned.

Unfreezing the silo mentality

Managing the experiences of a diverse customer base (new way) is very different from managing a diverse portfolio of fairly standard products or services (old way). The latter is based on separation for the sake of accounting and accountability. In contrast, whatever goes to make the customer experience has to be connected, based on interaction, irrespective of who does what, from which silo. Coexistence, cooperation and co-creation with internal colleagues becomes as important as the specialist job, therefore. This new way of delivering unified brand experiences requires either transcending silos, or finding creative formulae for mixing and merging them, to knit the customer concept together.

Many enterprises struggle with huge restructuring exercises. That customers don't care how companies are structured is ironic, given all the time, money and effort that is spent on this restructuring, of which, it is said, between 50 per cent and 70 per cent fail.[65] Largely because putting people into new boxes in a formal restructuring often doesn't change anything. And this is especially true when high-end knowledge-intensive skills are involved, which is what we are interested in. Customers also don't care about the capabilities an enterprise has, as long as value lands in *their* space, seamless and integrated.

It's not the silos that work against this. It's the silo *mentality* that gets in the way, the likes of which we have already discussed. Great customer-centric change makers concentrate their efforts on how the silos deliver together in this way, and how to unite multiple functions, instead of how to restructure entire organizations. With customers as the centre of gravity, and the strong shared story and mission providing direction, their object is to take from each component, remarkable in its own right, and produce a 'one company' proposition. IBM's Gerstner, for example, despite pressure from the press and other stakeholders to carve up the company because it made more financial sense, stuck to his guns and kept IBM whole, because it made customer sense.

Some enterprises find that if they change the way they mix and match people, they start to behave differently. Ogilvy & Mather South Africa grew organically around silos. This way they worked to become best in breed, and that's what customers wanted, especially those who work in a fragmented way themselves, using different agencies for different things, for example advertising, social media or PR. But as the trend moved towards integrated customer engagement, and one-partner relationships, Mokgwatsane and his team created 'brand liberation teams', which consisted of specialists who had great silo skills but shed these identities when delivering an integrated offering.

As part of Marks & Spencer's customer-centric remodelling it combined people and units horizontally. In the past, silos had been built around the vertical merchandise slices, from clothing to books, furnishings to financial services. However, how the products or services went onto the physical or virtual shelves was totally unrelated to the customer's lifestyle experiences, which cut across these categories.

Then the silos were merged into teams responsible for joined-up outcomes. For instance, stripped beds, bedding, headboards, electric lamps and TVs had all been sold separately before, and the customer bought them in separate transactions, and maybe on different floors, or even from different stores. Once the emphasis switched from the bed to the bedroom, everything that belonged together became the basis for the brand experience.

Ways to accelerate engagement

Getting engagement internally can include workshops, roadshows and/ or training sessions, which align new thinking in a concerted effort to change mindsets and behaviours throughout the organization.

The greater the level of involvement by the CEO, lead player or the senior coalition in this, the swifter and more enduring the engagement is likely to be.

Customer-centric disruptors find as well that these activities, itemized below, accelerate the kind of buy-in internally that turns to action.

Demonstrating the gains

This impetus to do things differently and together for customers can be strengthened by demonstrating that the silos will not lose and, on the contrary, they have something specific to gain.

The more this can be quantified, the better. The evaluation formula may have to change, however, to reflect contribution or a new kind of contribution, instead of just sales. Sometimes a parallel system is used initially to reflect this.

At BP, even if a customer's total energy bill shrank due to newly offered consulting advice on how to buy better, use less and reuse energy, the silos still got a deeper share of customer wallet: a greater number of ships, sites, fleet trucks and buildings to fuel.

There are also gains from closer and longer relationships. It is particularly motivating for executives when they begin to deal with customers in the higher ground, more senior and more strategic, escaping the old price syndrome. 'Our people were used to dealing with buyers along a traditional selling path. Now they are included in conversations with people at levels and in parts of the customer's organization that has totally changed the relationship, opening up fresh opportunities for new business never before possible.'

Proliferating the tools

When people actually use common tools they become commonplace, common talk, common practice, making the old preconceived notions, dictates and formulae obsolete. This helps the culture switch.

Not only do people start to use the language and the concepts, they also begin to tell the story as if it were their own.

> It's when people start echoing your message, and the story, that you know you have broken through.

> Sometimes they forget where it came from, and begin to think it's their own – that's really good.

Executives in my work have repeatedly confirmed that these are the behaviours and remarks to signal that engagement has taken place, and that people have accepted not only the direction, but also the means to get there. Ease and familiarity turn previous reserves and closely guarded agendas into the behaviour platforms needed for the implementation process to take on its own momentum.

Finding the forums to facilitate this is part of the secret. People remember when they get this take-up because they say, 'you can feel the energy shift'. From one executive came this remark, 'All the market owners came to the usual annual strategic investment meeting to put forward their two- to four-year resource requests. One by one, they began showing customer activity cycles to motivate their investment requests... That's when I knew we were there.'

Heralding and showcasing victories

Especially motivating for employees is when victories resulting from the model concepts are heralded and showcased. They are held up as examples, and the positive feedback and public recognition draws in more people and more innovation.

When customers buy into modelling and are willing to collaborate, a signal is sent across the organization. If successes are deliberately celebrated, new role models will be built, further enticing people to join in.

That's why it's so important to choose value-adds that are promotable to model initially. This should be synchronized with an internal marketing communication programme, a branded exercise, linked to the external marketing and communication.

Rewards and showcasing victories is an ongoing exercise, which must clearly include employees. Jordaan believes fervently that the power of incentives has driven much of the behaviour and innovation responsible for the FNB turnaround. Employees who excel are rewarded for new creative ideas and behaviours that can bring about tightly focused customer goals, and are celebrated as heroes, given financial rewards and points, in a deliberate attempt to get and sustain staff engagement and motivation.

Building a common technological infrastructure

Most product-based structures have data lying in different silos. At worst they may have different systems, which may not talk to each other. Customer-centric logic pulls this all together, and builds a single repository for information and decision making. With a common customer concept as a frame of reference, and common technological infrastructure built around a customer experience, people from different parts of the organization get to align more quickly.

Burberry, FNB and the Overseas Chinese Banking Corporation all did this very deliberately – they provided one view of the customer that each and every person in the organization saw in real time. This significantly accelerates how, and when, the silos collaborate.

And in the public sector the same trend has emerged. Rio's attempt to produce integrated decisions and responses for Brazilian citizens has relied on one integrated technology infrastructure. Previously each of the bodies was getting different kinds of unrelated data, at different times, and responding in different ways. Data was captured from various devices, such as sensors, video cameras and so on, and each was analysed in isolation. To knock down silo walls everyone's data was brought together, bringing massive advantages to citizens, as well as saving costs to cities, country and cosmos.

Building customer outcome into performance loops

Linking performance criteria and promotion to achieving a customer outcome is a powerful motivator in changing behaviour. Unfortunately, all too often inward mentality enterprises are afraid to relinquish performance metrics that showcase sales of their origin products, and so hold on to the old schemes, confusing and confounding people who want to move on, and seriously jeopardizing progress.

Instead of rewards being the first thing to change, it's often the last. Without a modification in the reward and promotion system, engagement will be slow and the behavioural transformations needed for a lasting cultural change can disintegrate.

Once organizations let go of what is often the last vestige of product-mindedness, they find the transition to customer centricity that much swifter. For instance, in the old days at Lexis Nexis, success meant selling subscriptions. Now performance metrics are linked to the return customers get from the use of data, and this has significantly altered the way people think and prioritize.

The crux of this important point is that the performance of the customer and the performance of the enterprise from the delivering teams is integrally linked in one reinforcing loop.

New key performance indicators (KPIs), which are usually quantifiable, will have to be aligned to the modelling initiatives from inception, in order to reflect new goals and drive new behaviour. These may be combined with strategic performance objectives (SPOs), which will be broader and indicate direction rather than specific results.

For example, a KPI may be:

- increased speed of delivery;
- decreased cost;
- reduced risk.

Whereas an SPO may be:

- Are we being included in important strategic meetings?
- Is advice given being taken?
- Are we getting to influencers in the high ground?
- Have we been asked advice about competitors' offerings?
- Are we getting advocacy voluntarily through social media and blogs?
- Are we getting new ideas for joint improvements?

The sooner KPIs are built into the implementation process, the better. Recently I was involved with a company which had four teams, each working on different market customer activity cycle exercises as part of a transformation. What became apparent was that one of the teams was working better and seemed to be more engaged, eager to move quickly. As it turned out, a good portion of the value-adds that this team was working towards had been deliberately put into their KPIs with deadlines by the head of that division, in order to get acceleration.

Making customer-centric goals and enablers integral to the CEO, or sponsoring coalition's performance criteria, significantly alters the clip, pace and level of engagement. Michael Jordaan of FNB who has been through this measures his Exco's performance, using the same criteria that appear on his scorecard. Scorecards are not purely profit-oriented but are based on criteria such as transformation, innovation, employee engagement and customer feedback.

What is measured is as important as *who* is measured. Eighty per cent of what Amazon measures relates to customer objectives.

Everything else is a function of that ultimate end. Unilever has 50 economic environmental and social targets that emanate from its multifaceted and multilayered customer-centric formula.

A passion for caring

With a higher purpose, walking the talk takes on new meaning. How the enterprise conducts its business, and how its staff, suppliers and partners behave, becomes as important as what the organization does or makes.

As we have seen, the groundbreakers today embed a sense of self-transcendence into their missions and stories, seeking something beyond personal or corporate gain. These seek to serve not just consumers, but also society, embracing the citizens, communities, cities and countries – and cosmos – in which they live.

Research reveals that leaders who embed contemporary values into their endeavours are more likely to attract young millennial workers, who want to work for enterprises that demonstrate good corporate citizenship.[66] They build this deep into the DNA of their employees, so that this ethos and behaviour manifests on the ground, not just in the board and strategic meeting rooms.

Somehow, BP failed to do this. Years after its innovative customer-centric UK head office transformation, its Gulf of Mexico oil spill disaster caused untold damage to itself and the environment.

Raising levels of consciousness and aspirations to higher levels can be an extremely powerful galvanizing force in bringing people from different parts of the organization together during the transformation, because they hold similar beliefs and are dedicated to the same ideal.

Engagement along the various stages of the process must therefore be a deliberate attempt to link and align people to the higher order beliefs, backed by projects that have consciously been integrated into the customer-centric narrative, and manifest in day-to-day operations.

For example, Unilever staff participate in the behaviour hand-washing-change training for kids in schools. To become better global citizens, IBM actively encourages its employees to take initiatives in their own time, to make a better smarter planet. Cleaning up the streets of Bangalore in 'spot fixing', volunteers from the company literally look for spots to clean such as a stretch of a street or an area in a community. Another project in India was a 'no to plastic' drive involving some 30,000 IBMers working with different communities and NGOs.[67]

New models for customer engagement

Getting people to work together requires a mechanism that pulls networks together and so binds the expertise that delivers value along the customer activity cycle – when and where and how it is needed.

This goes well beyond the old customer relations management (CRM) models of yesteryear, fundamentally a system of collecting historic customer data and buying patterns and record keeping, supposedly to give sales people the ability to generate more sales, and monitor performance.

I would argue that the notion of sales is old logic. With customer centricity, what is relevant is that the right employees are empowered to ensure that customer outcomes are accomplished, wherever, whenever and however needed, to fulfil the promise. From that, sales follow.

Account management undergoing a reformulation of its own is closer to what we need today. This can be crucial in building the customer-centric culture. Especially if the multiple customer touchpoints that go to make up a one-customer experience are managed by different functions in the organization. Significantly, it can act as a funnel through which silo expertise is filtered and combined to bring about customer outcomes in an integrated way.

Account management reformation B2C: collaborative consumption

Another paradox challenges the customer-centric disruptor. How to create an advantage from two polar opposite trends – more individualization and increasing collective consumption.

On the one hand, engagement today is more about having conversations with individuals than selling to target segments. In B2C situations this may be done for premier customers, as some banks do. Customers have a relationship manager, for instance, for whom they may have to pay, who has a single and coordinated view across the organization, ostensibly to solve individual problems.

On a daily basis, cutting-edge technology is changing B2C account management capabilities. It is able to hardwire enterprises to enable them to drive enhanced individual customer engagement across omni-channels and multiple touchpoints, en masse. Linked digital, social and mobile channels, as well as media, can connect them to the enterprise 365/24/7, in as many languages as necessary, anywhere and everywhere.

Take Burberry: its interactive website connects customers to several fashion sites, including features videos and new cool music discoveries. Through personal portals customers can have discussions with store employees and provide feedback on anything related to the enterprise. All conversations are tracked and analysed, allowing Burberry to monitor everything that customers say about the brand.

At the other end of the spectrum is another equally prevalent trend pushing for B2C account management reformation – collaborative consumption. Customers are sharing, acknowledging that it is no longer necessary to own or consume everything themselves. This means that customer-centric enterprises no longer sell to customers – they facilitate shared purchase and use in creative new types of offerings.

Millennials seem to be more inclined than their predecessors to collaboratively consume.

Car sharing, for example – although it is not new, what makes it a disruptor and potentially explosive today in places like Singapore Germany and the USA is that these millennials are making an effort not to have to drive, or drive alone. Possibly to avoid the hassles of it, but also because of the obvious social ramifications. Added to that is that technology – GPS and smartphone applications – allow customers to access and drop off a car wherever it suits them, instead of having to pick it up and bring it all the way back to a lot, saving them time, energy and money.

In Silicon Valley, where driving is no pleasure, Google has used its capability in commuter transport to provide mass transportation for its staff – around 132 trips every day – mastering traffic patterns and routes to bring them to work stress-free, with their bikes on exterior racks, and their dogs on their laps. This shared system not only attracts and keeps the best talent, they believe, it also reduces congestion and does a whole lot of other good, such as minimizing the amount of land set aside for parking spaces and reducing fuel usage, carbon emissions and congestion.

Sharing is the norm in many emerging markets. In Africa, for example, phone sharing is practised widely. In Kenya around 30 per cent of the population share a phone, in Tanzania nearly half.[68]

Given Russia's collective heritage, it is not surprising that part of its new building innovations include new ways of allowing customers to share. Not just services but products – for example, food; clothes; sport equipment such as skis, ice skates and golf clubs; children's toys and equipment such as strollers, or baby seats for cars; kitchen utensils; and particularly things seldom used such as tools – drills and hammers, food processors or blenders, and cleaning equipment.

The nature of how enterprises engage with customers changes with collaborative consumption, requiring learning how to deal with group or team buying, not just individuals.

Groups can be self-organizing. Customers wanting the same product are increasingly using the Internet and social media to form groups online, meeting virtually or face to face, with a view to negotiating better bulk prices, in a trend that originated in China called Tuanguo. Various sites have sprung up, which act as an aggregating force to leverage the collective power of these groups, dramatically changing the balance of power.

Groups also get together to borrow and save money in emerging markets, jointly taking responsibility for repaying loans, and applying peer pressure to make repayment rates high enough to give them more buying potential. Cemex deliberately put customers into mini 'socio' savings groups. They discuss plans and do the design with architects and technicians, get and distribute the materials, and make the payments. The group also evaluates the distributors, and decides as a group which one will get future business.

In Brazil, *consorcio* (consortium) sharing, run by financial institutions, has been popular for buying high-ticket items such as motorcycles, automobiles, commercial heavy equipment and residential properties. Each person continues to pay an affordable monthly sum, and ownership is acquired through auction or lottery over time, as each sum adds up to cover an item.[69]

Leaders are used in various ways to keep the groups together and facilitate interaction with the vendor organization. In China, the Tuanguo use a team leader for the negotiation. India Tobacco Company has lead farmers as the interface between them and individual farmers. These leaders set up community portals in their homes, which the farmers access, backed up by support provided per village, and 24/7 helpdesk services. They also aggregate the individual farmer produce to sell back to the company.

Account management reformation B2B: collaborating for mutual rewards

Old B2B account management models focused primarily on contracts, negotiation and managing the terms and service level agreements. Very often this led to win–lose situations, and zero sum gains.

Customer-centric models concentrate on new forms of engagement, based on collaboration and win–win. The degree to which this applies varies according to the size of the customer and contract, and other factors that have to do with appetite for engaging differently.

Here is a format (see Exhibit 8.1) that is useful for deciding where a customer enterprise fits, and how to approach a portfolio of customers, to drive longer, stronger relationships.

Central to this model is that advantages are mutually rewarding. Parties are interdependent – neither wants to default, or the other to fail – both have a vested interest in everyone succeeding.

Collaborative account governance

Working from the top of the diagram shown in Exhibit 8.1, tier 1 customers, by virtue of their size and importance to the enterprise, require an approach that I will refer to as collaborative account governance. There is an equally valid case to be made for tier 1

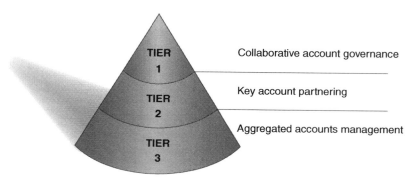

Exhibit 8.1 Account management engagement model

customers being those who have great potential, are willing to be open and receptive to new ideas, and are actively seeking true collaboration. And these may not be the largest customers.

Ogilvy & Mather chose to work with top clients in their new engagement model, but specifically selecting those at the outset who themselves were moving to a customer-centricity model, and using contemporary ideas to get there.

T-Systems (a subsidiary of Deutsche Telekom), providing outsourcing IT services to Old Mutual, the financial services corporation headquartered in the UK, tried to obviate the old methods of contracting in South Africa. With tendering and renewals costing both sides dearly, the object was to find a new way to work together, where both parties irrevocably gained.

Contracts between the two enterprises sometimes went into thousands of pages, and meetings were complex with highly defined service quality levels (SQL); they had 400. These were the focal points of the relationship before the new approach was taken, with penalties and termination being the punishment for default. This changed into a collaborative model where both parties decided on objectives and KPIs, and took joint responsibility for getting and reporting outcomes. Leaders were jointly elected to head up the team, with common motives and incentives driving the relationship.

The executive who led the innovative approach from T-Systems South Africa pointed out that the problem with contracts is that often they are rigid and static, whereas customer needs are constantly changing. T-Systems had therefore been more concerned with complying than delivering what was actually required. Now, instead of the two parties looking through a magnifying glass at contracts to see who was doing what wrong, they spend their time and efforts jointly finding ways to get it right.

The difference between traditional contracting-type account management and collaborative governance for B2B is shown in Table 8.1.

In this new way of engaging, joint teams co-create the boundaries, rules and terms of agreement. Rather than these terms cast in concrete, parties negotiate new conditions, as and when they arise, which may alter the signed deal.

Relationships are cultivated based on constructive dialogue, which achieves common goals. Conversations are strategic. On a daily or regular basis, physical space is shared, and systems and processes are

Table 8.1 Comparing old and new B2B engagement models

Old contracting	New collaborative governance
Separate decisions	Joint decision making
Conversations operational	Conversations strategic
Negotiation	Open discussion
Dictates briefs from customer	Workshops to examine what is needed, and potential barriers
Sell to customers	Joint briefs and contract building
Termination contract, renewal	Formal mechanism for ongoing, joint problem solving
Penalties	Common incentives
Service level agreements	Gain sharing as well
Closed book	Transparency on cost
Measurements done separately by buyer and seller	Measurements done reciprocally
Separate accountability	Joint accountability
No contact competitors	Collaborate with competitors, if necessary

integrated. As problems come up they are jointly solved. And results are driven by the team that is accountable.

Ogilvy & Mather calls this 'CoLabs', to connate a joint venture between it and its clients. It has made a deliberate attempt to get rid of the 'fake silo walls' and amalgamate people and purpose to create trust and commitment instead of division.

CoLabs contain the best dedicated talent from both sides, and other skills that may be necessary, such as neuroscientists or sociologists, as added when needed. Some enterprises use project managers in these teams as well, who play a central role in facilitating relationships and outputs.

For tier 1 customers, vendors should allow products and services to be brought in from outside, if internal partners cannot perform. And span collaboration to include competitors, if they are part of or related to getting the customer outcome, even including them in the team.

Relationship scorecard

Measurements on engagement and performance are done reciprocally. T-Systems and Old Mutual use a 'Relationship Scorecard'.

How each behaved to facilitate success is examined in the interest of retaining a sustainable relationship.

Interdependently, vendor and customer rate each other on set criteria that impacted on each other's ability to perform, with questions like:

- Did they involve us early enough in planning?
- Did they give us accurate information?
- Did they engage with us at the appropriate level?
- Did they create barriers to achieving the value and impact?
- Did they enable us to make a profit?

Collaborative account governance, or a version of it, requires a transformation of its own to get it to work. The right partner, who genuinely gets it, needs to be found and will help drive the joint venture. It also requires high-level sponsorship from both the supplier and customer enterprise, and a phased-in approach, with experimentation allowed at the beginning, and some early wins (rather than tackling the most difficult issues), so that credibility can be gained before it is taken on as the new standard.

The best projects to choose initially are those with business impact that can display measurable results. Not only will that make an impact, it will also be a testing ground, to agree on how to share the benefits that have been unlocked due to the collaboration.

Key account partnering

Tier 2 customers, who are fairly sizeable and form the bulk of the client portfolio, fit the principles of account management, and of becoming a trusted partner. A significant part of key account partnering is that it cannot be done by one person. A proper relationship may require multiple coordinated contacts and coverage of the customer organization.

Old industrial interpretation of account management is often having the product knowledge to sell more. With customer centricity, presence begins early on in the customer activity cycle, when strategic decisions are taken in the high ground. Research confirms that companies that specifically engage with decision makers in their B2B interactions will get over 90 per cent in referral rates, versus 28 per cent for those who don't.[70]

Delivery or advice-giving teams may be virtual and can be created when and where needed, coordinated by the key account partner, as the sole entry point. Even if they belong, and are used by several teams, people in them have a single company face when it comes to customers, using team communication and signatures on correspondence.

Account partners need to be able to have strategic conversations with customers about their business issues, and be part of the growth and change agenda. This requires knowledge of trends and futures in end user markets, and being or having access to experts in the field.

Dealing with competitors can be an issue, which may require separate teams or some format, whereby 'chinese walls' protect confidentiality. There can still be opportunities to share industry knowledge on a broader basis.

Getting into the higher ground requires not just understanding the intimacies of the customer's business, but also making a strategic contribution to thinking, and how the vendor has impacted success. KPIs are done and evaluated jointly. Account partners need to feature in the customer's 'post' evaluation of plans, and quantify their role in it.

Fundamental to successful key account partnering is being able to pull on the various silos for inputs. So yet another success factor is that the KPIs of the silos are linked to overall customer outcomes. When silo mentality rules, people who manage the most assets usually have the most power. Here the power goes to the people managing the most customers, as assets. If account partners are expected to exert influence to get the job done well, but are not given the commensurate authority, the model cannot work.

A good deal of energy shifts when account managers are given seniority and clout, at least equal to the heads of the delivering silos. This is a signal that priorities have moved to the customer.

In this paradigm account partners:

- Act as a single point of entry for and to customers, for advice, enquiries, problem solving and trouble shooting.
- Act as the customer's representative in the organization, even its advocate.
- Are able to move the emphasis from selling and order taking, into higher ground advice giving and consulting.

- Provide the much-needed communication between the customer or customer organization and the enterprise.
- Are responsible for collaboration between the customer and the various internal and external silos and partners, to source, brief and provide a unified offering.
- Coordinate the efforts of the various players, to ensure a seamless outcome.
- Monitor compliance on the part of the enterprise and customers, so that performance targets can be met.

The same principles apply to global accounts. Customer operations across the globe are treated as one account. BP illustrates this: it has switched from single-product or single-region performance contracts, to ones where rewards and recognition are global, spanning silos. Highly skilled individuals sit outside of any single business unit structure, accountable to someone who works cross-stream, reporting to the highest level in the organization.

Aggregation account management

The customer-centric question for tier 3 smaller corporations, who each on their own have little or no buying power, is how to make them more competitive, through aggregation accounts management. The object is to take advantage of the size and strength of the vendor enterprise, to the benefit of smaller corporate players.

This aggregation is easily done with technology. Lexis Nexis, for instance, built online communities for individual lawyers, so they can find other professionals who may have expertise or information they need, and so benefit from collective expertise in the field. MTN Ghana does this for doctors, to help them spread their expertise, share cases, and build knowledge in particular medical fields that are significant to the development of the country.

Kenya's HealthStore uses its collective buying power and centralized procurement operation to drive down drug costs, and ensure drug quality for its franchisees.

And instead of letting the many Indian micro farmers struggle with inadequate government help or subsidies, India Tobacco Company provides information and knowledge to each farmer, and buys farming supplies and equipment in bulk, which it then distributes for them in small lots. It also buys commodities from them in small parcels, which are aggregated up in order to get higher market prices. In this way, micro farmers get the benefits of ITC's scale, which they could never have enjoyed as individuals. It also provides its R&D clout, to bring more eco-friendly inputs to these farmers, such as seed, fertilizer, chemicals and machinery.

SMEs in Ghana cannot afford the high costs and capital outlay associated with IT software and hardware, but they have to improve productivity and business systems in the same way that larger companies do, to stay competitive. Aggregating facilities is part of the MTN new value proposition. It brings SMEs together, and offers cloud computing services (based on the aggregation principle), which enables them to share files and minimize the cost of doing business, paying with airtime or MTN mobile money.

Finding external partners

Creating and coordinating a constellation of partners is what customer-centric enterprises know how to do. The more ambitious they are in defining their 'market space', the more likely it is that partners will be needed.

This partnering will be expressly to plug and play where there are value gaps to fill that the enterprise doesn't possess, or they don't want to get involved in. This is what Amazon does with couriers, or IHI does with international experts in personal security.

As the offering becomes progressively layered, more extensive collaboration usually becomes necessary. To truly mitigate customer risk, for instance, Lexis Nexis needed to partner. Customers, they discovered, had binding contracts, which had emanated from different parts of the organization, but needed to be managed by others, who were not aware of the details. It had to get fuller visibility of these contracts, which had to be integrated into one system, so that legal teams could manage their contract universe more effectively.

Enterprises may even partner with competitors if the outcome needs something they don't have. Or, if they run out of capacity or stock, partner with a competitor to tap their excess, rather than risk a failed delivery.

Emerging markets pose their own kinds of partnering challenge for multinationals, including a lack of suitable resources whom they have to train and fund in order to get them up to scratch. Together with universities and NGOs, GE is training up 'green managers' in China to build a fresh supply of ecologically minded individuals, which will back its clean tech initiatives. McDonald's in Moscow famously had to actively seek out, train and finance Russian farmers and bakers, import their own cattle from Holland and potatoes from the USA, and bring in specialists from Canada and Europe to help upgrade farming management practices.[71]

Starbucks provides agricultural and technical expertise to the small farmers of Rwanda and Chile, including helping them with crop stability, soil management, increased yields, reducing cost of production, and infections, all to improve coffee quality and get the special varieties produced that it needs. As well, it makes loans to coffee growers, who cannot get funds in the traditional way for either capital improvements or for cash flows at harvest times.

For a variety of reasons, mostly to do with local cultures and contacts, a good deal of partnering in emerging countries is done in conjunction with governments, civil society organizations, international aid agencies, businesses and NGOs, who have links with communities and leaders within them. These people and institutions play an active role in the affairs of citizens and, through established, trusted relationships and reputations with locals, have an understanding of the complex rules and rituals that can make or break take-up.

HealthStore partners with this range of parties, in a public–private partnering business model typified in Africa. It buys hundreds of government-approved, tested drugs centrally for clinics, at highly competitive prices per treatment. This it can only achieve because it partners with the Mission for Essential Drugs & Supplies (MEDS), who work with churches, health facilities and other non-profit health care providers in Kenya.

Franchisees partner with local authorities to engage in community outreach efforts, educating on basic health care in schools in order to meet the Kenyan government objectives to reduce childhood mortality and the spread of infectious diseases. HealthStore also works closely with the Kenyan government at many levels to lobby for a health care policy that is of the widest possible benefit to its underserved communities. Educational activities help to establish trust within the local community, and build the franchisees a reputation for health care rather than just medicine.

Forming the extended enterprise

With customer centricity, the enterprise is no longer a whole mass of different, unrelated product and service factories, or distribution or processing channels that are legally owned by the same organization. The new, networked enterprise is a conglomerate of diverse players, held together by a common purpose and set of customers.[72] It's what they do and accomplish in the marketplace *together* that binds them, not to which legal entity they happen to belong.

There are a whole variety of possible formats and formal working arrangements for partnering. Alliances and joint ventures, franchising, minority stakeholdings, licensing, as well as working with developers on applications, or straight outsourcing and co-branding – and there is plenty of literature on this.

Some enterprises prefer more informal collaborative schemas where people work together when the occasion arises. Or they may simply link into a network of specialists to supplement their skills or knowledge base when needed. Others prefer something tight and binding. The legality, however, is clearly less important than how they operate in concert together.

And, fundamentally, that means collaborating to build a better customer experience. Research on practice confirms that, irrespective of the arrangement, the stronger this collaboration, the more each party will gain.[73]

A matching of equals

External partners can be fundamental to getting a new concept accepted and into the hearts and hands of customers. Finding the right partners will therefore go beyond merely filling in for shortfalls: they can be fundamental to success, and their involvement can speed up transformation and take-up.

They can also create more awareness quicker and enhance credibility and image.

A dramatic example comes from M-PESA. It is a well-known fact that had the Kenyan regulatory authorities not behaved like 'points of light', the innovation may never have happened as well, or as swiftly. True, M-PESA had the advantage that the system was not designed to fit a regulated financial institution. But then, other financial companies had had this advantage as well, and still not been as successful. Once M-PESA reached its inflection point, and the banks finally did try to stop them from operating, the regulatory system backed it. What this means to the transforming enterprise is that decisions on which outsiders to work with are far from trivial and go way beyond the financials. Here are some of the criteria that executives say are vital in making the choice:

- Are they excited and motivated, like-minded in terms of the customer concept and direction?
- Can they work at our pace?
- Do they understand and believe in the concept of lifetime customer value?
- Are they prepared to collaborate for the good of the whole?
- Are they willing to share information and contribute other resources such as time, energy and expertise (and even funds when relevant) to make the new way of doing things work?
- Are they seen as leaders who will influence and attract others?
- Do they have our higher order beliefs, time frames and standards?

Foremost in what works and what doesn't in the long term is that external partners have to be regarded as equals rather than merely suppliers. The enterprise is not just engaging partners in simple transactional behaviours, out only for its own competitive advantage. It is looking to create mutual advantage for and with them. (see Table 8.2).

Table 8.2 Collaborating for mutual advantage – what doesn't work and what does

What doesn't work	What does work
Control and dominate	Trust and transparency
Owning everything	Having access
Providing specifications	Working to common service standards
Contracting	Jointly developing, co-innovating and co-creating
Separate technologies	Common technology platform and sharing

Control and dominate versus trust and transparency

Previously, enterprises controlled and dominated vendors, from which they bought goods and services as inputs to their businesses, or through which they distributed their stuff. Behaviour was largely a function of buying clout, size, and the strength of the brand. The net result of this was invariably contention and controversy, with players often pulling in opposite directions, in complete disregard of the impact down the line on the end user.

Now, enterprises work together with a common purpose and vision, and with end customers placed squarely at the forefront of decision making. This is more akin to the Latin word *competere*, meaning to coincide or to strive together, than compete, where someone wins to the detriment of someone else.

Sometimes today they must do so with others, whose brands may be as powerful as their own. With this comes the need for trust and transparency, which can take many forms but, most importantly, requires a clear understanding of who does and has responsibility for what, and a respect for who owns what, particularly customers avoiding trespassing.

When Amazon uses a courier or postal service to deliver its books around the world, it outsources the service. However, the delivery service can be as important to the outcome as the choice of the book itself. And since this is the only physical contact the customer has in the entire experience, any default could seriously reflect on the Amazon brand.

Owning everything versus having access

By owning everything the enterprise protected itself, or so executives used to think. It also kept information, knowledge and technology proprietary, for fear of losing control. That is no longer the case. As enterprises move from competitive to mutual advantage, who possesses what is less the issue than having access to get the end result to customers, with innovation open and shared.

A system that is proprietary, isolated from a collaborative network and unlinked – no matter how proficient – can be distinctly disadvantageous to achieving customer centricity.

Scientists, lawyers or teachers don't want to have to click into different libraries and files from different US states in order to find the answer to a question. Lexis Nexis, now a pioneer in using technology for the legal and professional markets, partners to provide these customers with access to the best and most relevant information no matter what it may be, no matter who owns it. Only then can they hope to reduce their risk when making a presentation, winning a case or developing a breakthrough product, irrespective of where that information originates. 'Which is quite amazing if you think that in the past everything had to be proprietary and owned,' as one executive put it.

Provide specifications versus working to common service standards

Being a touchpoint, filling a critical value gap, means the partner becomes an integral part of brand quality. Although customers don't care if partners land some of the value, the enterprise should retain ownership of the experience. Amazon does this very well. They use couriers for delivery, but if they default and goods don't arrive, the contact made by the customer is with Amazon, who takes responsibility for rectifying the problem.

Providing specifications works fine when dealing in discrete products and predictable and standard customer needs. However, when real-time actions and interactions are required, many of which may be personalized and complex, this simply doesn't work.

There needs to be symmetry of purpose, principles and priorities for dealing with customers, including a unified customer perspective, so that customers experience one view of the brand.

Common standards include social and environmental ethos. Unilever is constantly looking to bring its products to customers more quickly. In its move to double its size and halve its environmental footprint, in a strategic agreement with DHL, it is finding ways to enhance worldwide logistic capability, whilst reducing waste and carbon emission.

Contracting versus jointly developing, co-innovating and co-creating

Whereas previously a purchase order and supplier compliance was what kept a deal going – 'contracts were placed and they were simply told what to do' – now partners are integral to innovative attempts to get and stay ahead. Here, enterprises work together to co-create value, solving problems and exploring opportunities together to magnify markets and customer experience.

Rather than lose kids to video games Lego is partnering with Sony Japan to co-create new-age toys, bringing physical bricks and inter-active electronic games together. This involves miniaturizing video technology so that the tiny bricks can include motors, cameras and actuators. In another example, because research shows that the chief snack in the USA now is fresh fruit and yogurt, surpassing chocolate and potato chips, Starbucks is shifting into a better-for-you brand gear. This has led to co-creating its new portfolio of nutritious Greek yogurts with Danone, the French fresh diary conglomerate.[74] First in the USA and then around the world, these offerings will be sold multichannel, in both Starbucks and other retail stores, co-branded Evolution (the juice company Starbucks acquired) – inspired by Danone.

Separate technologies versus common technology, platform and sharing

One overarching technological platform that spans the entire cus-tomer experience is needed for internal silos, as well as across the entire partner network.

Health care costs in the USA have been a disruptive impetus for changing the approach to patients, and dialogue and debate continue not just on how to handle customers better episodically for a specific malady, but also how to best manage them across the whole con-tinuum of care, over a lifetime. Before, each player in the system worked independently and in isolation. Today, hospitals are proac-tively innovating to find ways to manage population health by pull-ing partners together in one community of care.

Behind this movement is GE Healthcare, which provides the tech-nology and services that enable hospitals and care-providing institu-tions to link together, so that all doctors and nurses – the customer touchpoints – have real time and transparent access to records on immunization vaccines, referrals and so on, and so have an integrated view of each patient and his or her specific needs.

In reality, the collaboration could range from a minimal exchange of essential information when necessary, through the limited ability to access each other's customer data, information and databases, to the much more ambitious open sharing, via integrated and digitalized technology and cloud computing, platforms and processes.

Either way, the closer the collaboration and exposure that partners have to one another, the more likely that joint developments and co-innovation will be successful. And this largely depends on people sharing the same tools, procedures, work flow, software and methods of operating.

Amazon, for instance, has communities of developers using common tools, and its gigantic unlimited cloud computing power, in order to keep its mighty machine innovating – at next to no cost.

Getting the plus sum gains

The first step is to get the correct partners to buy in. Then this take-up becomes exponential, thanks to networking effects. Once partners, including developers, join the network, it attracts others, and so the potential for creating value grows, swelling the enticing still further – success breeding more success.

Of course, this will mean having an ethos that fosters sharing wealth and financial gains. That is not something we can automatically assume happens with traditional minds and cultures.

Often in the battle for margins on discrete products or services in these settings, executives assume that if someone else wins, they will lose. This ultimately contaminates thinking and leads to a zero sum gain. Customer centricity makes a concerted leap to allow all constituents to thrive, and partake in the added wealth.

Safaricom (Vodafone's Kenyan subsidiary), which had the dominant market share in telecommunications in Kenya when it launched M-PESA, saw the synergistic potential and leveraged their brand power to make the new venture a success, in which everyone would eventually gain. The collective effort to produce customer value dictates who they work with, and what they do with whom, in order to bring a fuller set of options to their customers, and today this includes banks, instead of just existing channels.

The principle behind this customer-centric behaviour is that networks that join forces to deliver value prosper more together than apart, through co-involvement, interdependence and mutual effectiveness. And it results in a plus sum game, which becomes the binding glue.

Cemex developed such a network in Mexico, working in concert with several players consisting of, amongst others:

Professions: an associated network of qualified masons, which provided high-quality building services, thereby enhancing both the quantity and quality of local professionals.

Suppliers and distributors: partners, suppliers and distributors, which implemented just-in-time delivery and storage, as well as being a conduit for a credit scheme for overseas Mexican customers, who could send money home so that family members could buy materials from distributors of their choice.

Public sector actors: government, public sector and NGOs who had connections with the market.

Interfunctional teams: teams consisting of a general manager, engineer, technical advisor, and/or architect, supplies manager, and customer services representative, jointly responsible for getting customer outcomes.

Local individuals: a group of promoters who were recruited and trained by Cemex working on a commission basis (when they sign up they get points, which can be converted into cash or materials) to enrol customers.

'Socios': approximately 5,000 residents were organized into self-financing cells or 'socios', responsible for buying, and making sure loans were repaid. Groups are made up of women (following the Bangladesh Grameen experience that revealed that women are more reliable borrowers) and are kept small in order to make sure there is the bonding needed for on-time loan payments.

Enterprises which understand the long-term implications of customer centricity are happy to allow others to benefit. They may have to be patient and wait, but this is in the knowledge that ultimately they will reach a point where their success will be irrefutable and irrevocable.

Take Amazon: since its inception it has consciously sought to allow partners to gain, even before it did. How else would it have attracted such a network to drive its relentless growth? And gain they have, including those merchants who, stuck for finance, have been invited to join Amazon's lending programme in order to buy inventory and increase online sales. The interest rates that Amazon offers are competitive and the process of signing up and paying much easier than with traditional banks. Merchants only have to wait days to receive monies, and payments are automatically deducted from their Amazon merchant account, without undue administration.

Enterprises that disrupt also have to be willing to invent new ways for people in the organization to think about how to work with others, so that sharing can extend beyond traditional mental barriers. For instance, Amazon helps associates learn from their interactions with customers. A 'Performance Tips' section shares ideas on how they can sell more items and make even more money from the Internet. A 'Build A Link' tool enables associates to easily create a variety of links, tailored to each individual site's content, so they can learn from each other. Amazon also hosts the 'Associates Discussion Board', where questions or messages can be posted and advice given. In addition, it makes available to partners the 'Marketing Resource Centre', with expert resources to help them understand better how to market themselves, online and off.

Creating virtuous circles

With higher purpose built into mission, customer-centric enterprises build virtuous circles.

This is more than redistributing wealth, where money is made in one way and distributed in another. It involves disruptors creating a plus sum gain for all, by expanding the pie, with the express intention of everyone, including them, gaining in the process.

Let's go back to the city of Moscow. Beyond just improving the buildings, developers and builders in Russia are now actively embedding lifestyle infrastructures into apartment blocks: 'Low costing housing is not just about them being affordable to buy, rent and maintain, but also low-cost to live in.' Also, a broader view has been taken of what 'living' really means for Russian residents, with developments outside of city centres and services hitherto difficult, costly and time consuming to access. Now shared services such as childcare, laundry, affordable health clubs, cafés, restaurants, shops, and so on, are part of apartment complexes. An online community has been created, where neighbours can swap products and services in order to save time and expenses.

But the intention is to go further: to boost not just the players in the existing building industry, but to also provide small business opportunities for the community members, furthering neighbour-hoods, inhabitants and regions.

And in what can best be described as an emerging 'micro economy' people can also pay neighbours for services such as cleaning cars, fixing bikes, laundry, gardening and so on in order to elevate standards of living.

Virtuous circles take the changing enterprise (or country) from thinking about linear growth for some, to a systems approach, where a beneficial cycle of growth is activated for all. This is done by purposefully creating a gain in one area that kicks-in a process that has positive effects on another, in what turns out to be a reccurring and positive ever-enlarging loop.

Google can only take search to the mass remotely located markets of the world, and create capacity to demand, if it first creates capacity to supply, hence its 'Project Loon'.

FNB Connect is supplying free data packages to build customer demand to up the use of social media, converting once digital-passive customers to become more digitally capable and, in the process, increasing Internet demand and penetration in South Africa. This has enabled it to cement its social digital lead, as well as attract new customers, which in turn allows it to harness more resources to innovate further in an ongoing positive loop.

In emerging markets, virtuous circle thinking and practice is particularly prevalent, where customer centricity may encounter paucity of supply and demand, and have to create both.

So instead of separating the supply and demand chains, the customer-centric organization makes them interdependent. Put another way, they create demand in communities and societies where there is no capacity for demand, by creating supply often by involving locals in employment opportunities mostly through funding and training, which triggers demand and, in turn, more supply and then more demand. Which of course is what is giving rise to the aspirant middle class – everyone is better off in this self-perpetuating system (see Exhibit 8.2).

Looking at examples from emerging countries to illustrate:

In the personal hygiene space Unilever India has built up a direct network using its own customers as salespeople, which started off as a handful of women in hinterland India to nearly 50,000 who reach 3 million households. These consumer-producers are equipped with

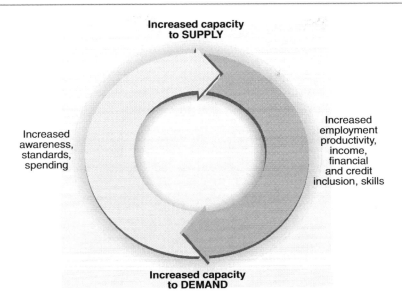

Increased capacity
to SUPPLY

Increased
awareness,
standards,
spending

Increased
employment
productivity,
income,
financial
and credit
inclusion, skills

Increased capacity
to DEMAND

Exhibit 8.2 Virtuous circle of supply and demand (simplified and generic)

business skills and micro financing, and as they earn income they would never otherwise have been able to do it feeds the capacity to *supply*, which fosters *demand* for personal hygiene amongst families, friends and communities, as well as the wherewithal to buy products in that space, further driving *supply* and so on.

The Cemex model is similar. Whilst it creates *demand* for better housing, transforming its customers' lives through home ownership, it also creates *supply* by upgrading communities, providing microloans to community residents in order to help pay for paving, schools and sidewalks built with cement, and training locals as masons and salespeople. Paying and upgrading lifestyles thereby creates a virtuous circle of more *demand*, which triggers more *supply* of everything related to home ownership and associated activities.

The franchise model that Kenya's HealthStore set up is a symbiotic relationship between the establishment and micro entrepreneurs. Local talent is given the opportunity to own and operate stores or clinics to provide *supply* of medical services and drugs in rural areas. This means a rise in income for these community members, and for the qualified nurses and health care providers, which creates more *demand*, thereby further attracting *supply* of a variety of services, bringing and keeping more health providers in these rural areas, earning more, creating more *demand*, as well as countering the brain drain.

The brilliance of the India Tobacco Company system is that through the e-Choupal small farmers can deal with large or small food processors, so intermediaries are no longer needed as brokers, dramatically reducing costs, which combined with better information, know-how, methods and materials has increased the capacity to *supply*. The result? Farmers obtain higher prices. This has positively impacted 10 million farmers and entire communities, pushing up capacity to *demand* better farming materials, equipment, systems and technology, which has reinforced the positive effects, drawing in even more farmers into the system, leading to better *supply* of quality farming and high-grade ecological crops, increasing *demand* for the increased stature of the entire Indian agricultural system.

Additionally, in India, local leaders have been developed, and farmers as first-time Internet users have been elevated, unleashing small-scale entrepreneurship by the e-Choupal. Intermediaries are still used where they add value, for instance for storage, transport quality control and risk management, which has improved the entire logistics function.

Not only has M-PESA in Kenya transformed customers' lives for the better, research has shown that in Kenyan rural households who have adopted M-PESA, incomes have risen by 5–30 per cent.[75] It also has provided education and development to retail operators, taking them into state-of-the-art thinking and technology, enabling them to earn, influence and develop themselves and their communities. Additionally the brand has opened opportunities for developers, building new applications, and spawned a whole lot of start-ups with all the benefits that ensue. And, as more people use it, more vendors come on board who accept payments by mobile phone, which means more sales to more people who use M-PESA for a wider range of products and services, in another virtuous loop of its own.

Evidently it has been inspirational for young entrepreneurs in Kenya and all over Africa, to do things they would never have considered possible. Additionally it has forced down the price of transferring money in the country on the part of competitors, the money transfer companies, and compelled them to improve their services. In some cases, traditional money transfer players are working with M-PESA to offer an integrated service to expats living outside Kenya, sending money home to people who can now receive and access this money from a ubiquitous network of ATMs.

And the winner is... everyone

In sum, with customer centricity, the underlying driver is not only to win, but to have the formula and power to make everyone else win as well.

To ensure easy engagement, the sentiment and structures that foster a plus sum gain must be built into the customer concept early on. Often, what might previously have been conflicting goals between different parties, have to deliberately be made harmonious and synergetic.

Cemex purposefully designed a system that created this. Despite enabling customers to buy fewer raw materials for any given construction project, the expansion of the total market for these projects has been exponential.

Everyone continues to gain:

- **Customers win** because they get better quality homes, at a cheaper cost, lasting longer, even over generations. Market values of houses go up. They get access to credit to buy other goods. And aspirations grow as individuals plan for a better life.
- **The suppliers and distributors win** because they sell more product, at no extra investment.
- **The community at large wins** because it is uplifted, upgraded and made more ecologically sustainable, which benefits in more ways than one, including attracting better calibre residents and suppliers.
- **The locals** win because they are trained and enjoy fuller employment and rising incomes, with all that that can bring.
- **The governmental system wins** because the people and economy prosper.
- **The enterprise wins** because they sell more to more people for longer periods.

The Cemex narrative is also about the linkages between these wins that create and foster virtuous cycles. It becomes both possible and feasible that, as communities are empowered to buy better materials and build better homes – and as people like masons and promoters, architects and technicians, are involved and earn more income, and build awareness for what is possible and available – so communities grow and thrive, inviting in better stores, artisans, schools, banks, developers and so on, which leads to more work, more taxes, better infrastructures and demand for better quality housing, and so the positive cycle continues.

Customers as partners

Customer-centric disruptors amass and mobilize customers as an external resource, no longer just relying on inside people or part-ners. These communities of like-interest come together of their own accord, or are brought together by the company, on demand, to jointly solve problems.

They may be fans and advocates, users or super users. But they are not just allies. They are deeply involved and bonded to the brand. And they are not just used for inspiration and ideas. They actually work.

The enterprise benefits from this work and the combining and aggregating of collective intelligence, for real-time exchange of ideas, fresh insights or concrete usable innovation. It invests in digital platforms and physical forums, in which these customers can go or crowd in order to converse, collaborate and co-create, with input being anything from designing new advertisements to helping to build or improve a product.[76]

If managed well and creatively, they benefit exponentially from the networking effects of these wide and self-sustaining circles of influence. Because as they grow more people gravitate to them, so they grow still more.

The advantages of using customers as partners is listed in Box 8.1 But the real value comes from the cumulative benefits of the activities.

Lego is a dramatic example of this. When Jorgen Vig Knudstorp became CEO in 2004, he announced that innovation in the future would be open, and come from partners including Lego users. Since then, Lego has facilitated user connection through online business,

---

Box 8.1 Benefits of customer communities

Getting new ideas for R&D and design.

Building global advisory and discussion boards.

Developing new products, services and applications.

Finding new ways of using products and services.

Creating content.

Ranking and rating.

Instant feedback and refinement on products, services, distribution and promotion.

Ironing out prelaunch problems.

Reducing time to market.

Scale and diversity of feedback.

Availability on demand.

Tapping specialized knowledge.

Cost saving.

---

social platforms and special events, almost blasphemous in the past when top management was obsessed with keeping R&D and its intellectual property sacred and secret.

It makes use of the brainpower of its customer base through online crowdsourcing, whilst it simultaneously increases customer engagement. Sometimes they are more formally assigned tasks. But mostly, its strong community of hundreds of thousands of users and groups, now intrinsic to Lego's innovation and development process, design prototypes. And if there are 10,000 participants who like an idea it will be considered by Lego for product development. Both adults and kids are involved with this experimentation, and share their creations virally on YouTube and other sites.[77]

IBM's connection to its huge customer base means that over a million people are in contact virtually, collaborating on developments using IBM technology, expanding markets and applications. This has also switched its relationship with customers from enquiries to active participators. Responses to phone calls and providing website manuals on site have been replaced by support staff and customers as content builders, as what is learnt is institutionalized.

From conversations, discussions and exchanges, knowledge is turned into specific content value that is searchable, and constantly updated as customers add to and modify it. Additionally, in this way it can pre-test marketing and communications content, and new designs, in real time.

Social and financial motivators

With crowdsourcing the norm for the twentyteens plus, catching on daily in the wider marketplace, come new challenges to get the unprecedented gains. Perhaps one of the most important is to get the right people attracted, retained and incentivized – like any other workforce – to enrich content creation.

The main questions to ask in building customer communities are:

- What kinds of people do we need for what purpose?
- What will attract and entice them?
- What do we need to provide in order to bring them together, and forge the interactions that will bring the values we want?
- How do we capture and use these values?
- What impact will this have on us?

As to what motivates customer communities: they engage and are energized by the desire to be involved, participate and learn, interacting as they do with people with whom they share values and interests. Mostly their object is to build social, not financial capital. They value the experience and connection with like-minded affiliators, who are either part of their community or who they can locate or discover. They build networks, and are motivated by the opportunities to contribute and develop mastery. When recognized by the group, it endows stature and a sense of accomplishment.[78]

Some companies do pay for these services. Lego pay in products or even hire on a fee-based basis. IBM provides money, or points that go to make up funds for favourite charities. Prizes are sometimes offered to attract high-calibre professional participation.

In emerging markets the patterns are the same. In Ghana each campus has Y-Cliq ambassadors, who MTN use to organize meetings and act as liaisons between it and the club. These ambassadors receive a monthly remittance, a month of free airtime.

And, once again, the model is self-perpetuating. YouTube, in trying to move to paid subscriptions for some of its channels, is constantly upgrading its offering. In so doing it is attracting real professional talent. To drive this still further, it is allowing some of its select providers to monetize the content they provide. By sharing revenue with customers they make them fully-fledged partners, attracting the best content, building a stronger and more diverse customer base, drawing in still more and more diverse better content providers, increasing its social value even further.

The Reward

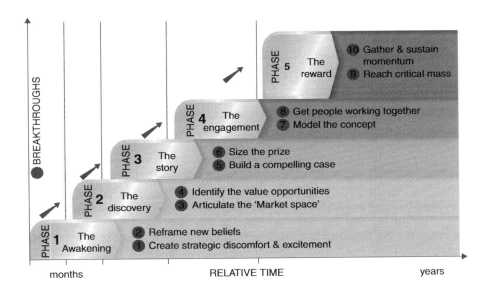

Reach Critical Mass

Key idea

Customer-centric transformation relies on getting insider and outsider conversion rates and the adoption process right, for which there are critical success factors. At this point, internally people are influencing each other and are influenced by market reaction. Externally, through a powerful combination of marketing and engagement, based on trust and authentic ongoing value, social proof, public approval and positive sentiment, the brand becomes contagious. The trick is to get the two internal and external energy forces to coincide, which leads to rapid multiplication and exponential rewards.

Compounding customer take-up

When an enterprise has reached the stage where there is a critical mass of take-up from customers for the new way of doing things, a breakthrough will have been achieved that finally unlocks the promised exponential rewards. This starts to culminate in the fifth and final phase. Then comes a groundswell, as the market buys, and keeps buying, into the new concept innovation.

Thanks to word of mouth, intensive marketing and carefully crafted methods to entice people into physical and virtual places at the correct time, the take-up builds scale, in terms of numbers, and spend, in a snowball effect. This comes about when the enterprise has successfully appealed to customers on the three levels we discussed in an earlier chapter, on employee take-up, which applies equally here, namely:

Cognitive – get customers to *think* a certain way about a brand or enterprise: then there should be good reason to deal with it.

Emotional – get customers to *feel* a certain way about a brand or enterprise: then there should be an association and affinity with it.

Social – getting people to *care* about how the company does, and who deals with it: then there should be positive public sentiment and approval of it.

The model is this: by appealing to customers on all three levels, the enterprise gets customer 'lock-on', which results in more and longer spend from the existing base, and through new marketing methods it attracts new customers, and so it keeps growing, building on its success.

Internally, it means that the customer-centric logic and behaviour has reached a threshold, which then spreads and becomes *the* way of doing business. Externally, it means sufficient numbers of customers and partners have taken it on, which draws in still more customers and partners.

The effect of this is compounding. Again, Amazon is a classic case. Why did it take 27 months to acquire the first million customers and less than 6 months to acquire the next million? Not because Bezos was the first to think of selling books on the Internet. Because, from the very inception, he drove a cumulative and compounding customer-centric business model.

Making the brand contagious

Some of the take-up will already have been accomplished through the model concepts. If they are clever, enterprises will have intentionally selected a group of customers – the 'points of light' within their market domain – and used them to energize and drive the conversion process. Newcomers, bringing customer centricity focus into a stale industry, will need to do the same. The challenges may be different as they build a brand from scratch, yet starting with a clean slate.

Either way, the principle remains the same: use various marketing and social media activities to attract individuals for the correct reasons, and through their changed behaviour patterns and affiliation they will spread the word and influence others.

Marketing, if it is based solely on traditional hard-sell promotion and broadcasting techniques, cannot get the compounding effects of take-up that customer centricity needs.

Once the initial investment has been made in take-up, the object is to become ever more involved with individual users, proactively interacting with them, to bring about stronger and self-reinforcing engagement throughout the customer activity cycle.

After adoption by sufficient early entrants comes the mass take-up, and then, as the new way of doing things becomes increasingly contagious, more and more customers respond. This is the turning point for the enterprise. Because if it is done properly, conversion should spread at the desired pace, to get the brand to go from:

being ***indispensable*** to each customer
to
penetrating the wider market and becoming ***infectious***
to
finally reaching a critical mass, becoming the new standard and ***indigenous***.

Getting rapid multiplication

Getting adoption rates right, and reducing lead time to convert to new ways of doing things, is a big part of making the transformation work. Although so-called big bang disruptions may not follow the normal distribution pattern, because they trigger lightning-quick conversion, the reality is that most times the adoption process has to be carefully orchestrated.[79]

There is no one recipe. But there are some critical success factors.

Marketing's makeover

Whilst conventional marketing aims at mass markets or target segments to ultimately reach individuals who aggregate up to market share, customer-centric marketing aims at individuals and getting the exponential potential of their lifetime spend advocacy and viral influence.

There are good reasons for the new marketing approach. Exhibits 9.1 and 9.2 try to capture this visually. In Exhibit 9.1 the industrial-minded enterprise pushing products or services communicates and promotes one way and, by and large the same way, en masse to

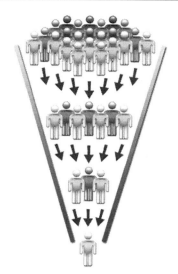

Exhibit 9.1 Old marketing: mass, targeted reach

Exhibit 9.2 New marketing: individualized and viral

them. They handle individuals, on an on-demand basis, to comple-ment this, for instance in call centres. With new marketing, shown in Exhibit 9.2, the customer-centric enterprise engages and interacts with individuals through multiple channels and social media, who then directly and indirectly, through behaviour and advocacy, influ-ence others in their tribe or affinity group, driving the multiplier effect. Mass-targeted cross-channel integrated communication com-plements this.

First, contemporary approaches are geared to individuals whose 'lock-on' is anchored in the quality of the individual customer experience creatively communicated, not just mass or targeted asso-ciations, cleverly conceived to coerce groups. Second, the integrity of the brand promise, and the trusted voluntary bond with the enter-prise, is a personal affair. It is individual people who advocate and share with others, to whom they relate.

The challenge of cross-channel marketing is to bring about real change. Like changing the way people bank, or buy food, or drive, or approach disease prevention. Take for instance Unilever's hand-washing Lifebuoy initiative in the 'personal hygiene management' 'market space'. In a combination of one-to-one and various media interventions, it aims to have 1 billion people involved in washing hands by 2015. It delivers its message in a series of interconnected social media, seminars, face-to-face events and communications combined for multiple private and public stakeholders, including delivery partners, governments, universities and NGOs. Not to forget school contact programmes designed especially to creatively (and scientifically) engage and educate children to wash their hands.

In 2013, at the Maha Kumbh Mela in India, the largest religious festival on the planet, Unilever creatively managed to promote its mission and message to people by heat stamping the question 'Have you washed your hands with Lifebuoy Soap?' onto roti (Indian bread). Over a period of 30 days over 100 Unilever people stood in 100 kitchens stamping the over 2.5 million rotis to present to people to eat with their meals. This event and others are captured in advertising and video messaging, viewed by consumers and other stakeholders through social media.[80]

The principle of engaging individuals first-hand (no Unilever pun intended), complemented by wider promotional and communication spread, to get high conversion, applies across the B2C and B2B spectra. Influencers can be multi-fold, ranging from industry specialists through vocal customers – early adopters or users in the know – to bloggers, analysts or partners. The object is to find these target influencers and work with them in order to leverage advocacy.

We know that customers who have tried products become better advocates, especially if the benefits are tangible, visible and easy to quantify. Experience has shown that every time a farmer in India sees another farmer getting a better deal or better equipment, they join e-Choupal. Or, when a person tells a friend what they have saved on their petrol bill, the chances are that they will actively set about finding out about the Discovery Insure driver programme.

Research tells us that huge numbers of consumers are turning to friends, family and colleagues for advice on what and where to buy. The figure for banking is around 70 per cent.[81] Ever-larger portions of the market use the Internet today to look for information to make important buying decisions, or get through life-changing episodes. Evidently 83 per cent of all global customers go online before they begin the car-purchasing process, nearly 80 per cent say they trust online reviews as much as personal recommendations, over 80 per cent of US consumers go online before buying books, music or movies, and 60 per cent of all global customers (including Chinese) do the same before buying clothes, shoes, toys, health and beauty products.[82]

Influence, however it is gleaned, can of course be negative as well as positive, which makes the need for authentic engagement so much more compelling. As Bezos says: 'If you make customers unhappy in the physical world, they might each tell six friends. If you make customers unhappy on the Internet, they can each tell 6,000 friends with one message about you.' And he said this in 1998 before the social media came into its own!

Creating consistent experiences

Consistency of the customer experience is high on the to-do list for accelerating take-up.

One of Ahrendts's first moves when she got to Burberry was to get all design and marketing decisions into an integrated brand protocol to be applied globally. Some of the decisions taken were tough, including unpopular ones such as closing down a factory in Wales, for which she had to testify before Parliament. She explained: 'We stood behind our decision. As a company we always do what's best for the brand because our job is to protect it and keep it powerful and relevant.'

This consistency principle applies equally to emerging countries. M-PESA stores – tens of thousands – all had the same look and were instantly recognizable. From the moment a customer entered a store the experience was consistent wherever they went. This was achieved through intensive selection of people to participate in the store network, based on their knowledge of languages in the area, rigorous ongoing training, plus supervision of the store network (for which M-PESA demanded operator exclusivity).

This consistency can bridge seemingly disparate companies, as Virgin demonstrates. Says Richard Branson: 'It should not matter whether you are on one of our planes or trains. A member of one of our health clubs or talking to a friend using one of our mobile phone services: the experience should stand out as distinctly Virgin.'

Franchising is being used extensively in emerging markets to achieve this consistency because it:

- Provides a uniform standard of quality throughout channels.
- Speeds up learning for franchisees.

- Accelerates take-up of both supply and demand.
- Gets scaled-up distribution more quickly for the enterprise.
- Requires relatively low capital investment.

Start-up costs for each HealthStore franchisee, for instance, was under US $2,000, with HealthStore Foundation providing up to 88 per cent of this capital, via a low-interest micro-financing scheme. So low is this, that it has attracted licensed nurses and qualified community health care workers as micro-franchisees, and stores have scaled up to serve more than 1.5 million patients a year, from 200 locations across Kenya. The franchise controls levels of quality and consistency in areas such as systems and training; selection of key locations; product and service standards; and inspections.

Building trust to make brands contagious

Whether the brand exists or is new, if it is geared to a new way of doing things it has to earn the market's trust in order to build demand. A lot of this has to do with getting credibility by delivering the promise, because the concept works and delivers outcomes with integrity. Only after this is accomplished with the first customer entrants can the brand become contagious to a wider audience. In other words, the brand's trust and consequent popularity arises from what customers get, not merely from creative campaigns.

This is especially true for emerging markets. Great pains were taken by M-PESA to build trust at the outset for the new payment system. Users, many of whom had hitherto no experience of dealing with financial institutions, let alone mobile wallets, were particularly sensitive to risk, and had to be made to believe that systems from a non-banking supplier would work.

Part of how this was done was to use the existing well-known Safaricom (the company that commercialized M-PESA) reputation and airtime stores when it introduced M-PESA and asked customers for deposits to build up their e-floats. This way, customers already knew operators, with whom they had built relationships and integrity, thus reducing fear and hesitancy.

Once the brand became accepted, Safaricom began to build M-PESA branded agencies. The brand was visible all over communities and meeting places, where people gathered and worked. Trust also came from leveraging public goodwill, because Safaricom already had a reputation for its fair practice and public work in communities.

To maximize the chances of getting trust, the brand enjoyed a full-blown national launch, making sure that the store network covered all geographic areas advertised on TV and radio. This was not just done to expose the brand, but also to explain how to apply for and use the service. The message was deliberately simple initially, 'send money home'. To avoid the impression that M-PESA was a low-value brand for the poor, the messaging was aspirational, backed by face-to-face outreach programmes, through road shows and tents, travelling around the country giving first-hand advice and demonstrations.[83]

Making it easy for customers to say yes

Getting compounding take-up at this stage, taking brands from indispensable for each customer to infectious to many, to ultimately indigenous for all, means having made it easy for customers to trial and engage. The aim here is to make people less reluctant to try something new, even if the outcome is not entirely clear at the outset.

Making it easy for customers to engage is more about mastering the art of thinking differently than just about being operationally adept. For instance, it's not merely that Amazon has a technological capability that is driving it forward, making the brand synonymous with popular culture. It's that it consistently makes it easy for people to become involved in its multifaceted machinery: from entering the site, navigating, ordering, obtaining the goods, complaining, getting rectification, sending a gift to a friend, chatting, giving an opinion, buying a second-hand book, buying almost anything that is difficult to get elsewhere, and getting as much shipped as wanted, at one flat rate.

Easy-to-use systems are essential in getting compounding growth in emerging markets. GE Imaging has gained both hospitals and doctors as proponents in China for its low-cost portable ultrasound devices. Making this happen meant not only getting clinics to buy the machines, but encouraging doctors to try them. These doctors were not specialists, as in richer countries, so ease of use was *the* most important criteria for trial and then take-up.

By making M-PESA's system akin to airtime, based on simple text that all mobiles could use, it was made as familiar as possible to customers, which gave the brand the initial impetus it needed, and made it an indispensable part of people's lives. When money is deposited, it takes a minute or less. Registering is made simple, done at an agent, gas station, food market or local store for free, and requires only an ID or passport. Sending money or paying a bill is equally simple, and the sender and recipient each receive an immediate text message. Customers can transfer money with ease to any person with a mobile phone, even if the recipient is not a Safaricom subscriber.

M-PESA's new M-Shwari (Swahili for 'cool') loans can be opened instantly by existing customers, and accessed from any mobile handset. It needs no minimum balance, and offers a small overdraft facility with a negligible set-up fee. If customers default they lose their phone number, which hurts more than being recorded in some database for poor credit compliance.

Amazon employs the same easy-to-use principle for retailer partners, whose sites it helps to develop in order to drive compounding growth – both theirs and its own – which are closely related. Amazon makes it simple for retailer partners to get more business online, by providing them with a technological platform that is easy for their customers to operate. Though the retailers maintain their own branding 100 per cent, the layout of the site is deliberately very similar to Amazon's, so that customers, most of whom are familiar with the Amazon site, can easily navigate.

Similarly, Amazon's patented one-click technology is available to the merchant's customers, so that once their details – credit card preferences, mailing, invoicing, friends' addresses, and so on, are in the system, they don't have to fill them in again every time they place a new order. The system also recognizes customers and, based on previous purchases, will offer suggestions that might be of particular interest to them, all to improve the merchant's ability to easily get their end users' purchase rates up. If a problem does arise, Amazon offers recovery services to the merchant suppliers.

Ease of use is closely linked to reducing complexity.

There are a lot of variables that go into making a safe driver. The key is that drivers know their own and their car's capabilities and limitations according to the CEO of Discovery Insure. What top management learnt was that to make great driving a reality, the system had to be made simple enough for people to understand. They need to know exactly what they have to do to get what outcome. For example, 'don't speed', 'don't slam on brakes', 'don't drive late at night', and so on. And what they also discovered was that the easiest behaviours to understand were the easiest to change.

Another learning was not to make the rewards too complex. When people were getting some of the benefits linked to travel, some to credit cards, and some to petrol, the response wasn't great. As soon as the bulk of the benefits were made for petrol, engagement rates and levels soared.

Making it easy on the finances

Making it easy on the finances is not to be confused with discounting in order to get customers to buy more of the same. The aim here is to make an investment in getting customers to 'lock-on' initially, so as to leverage future compounding returns, and not making the price so prohibitive as to build up resistance.

When Amazon went into Prime it exceeded all forecasts with membership, mostly because they made it easy for customers to make a decision, and it is aiming for 25 million members by 2017. Once a US subscriber bought in, for under $100, shipping became free, and paperwork automatic. This investment on the customer's part encouraged more to buy more. Amazon's investment, which included heavy promotion, such as free access to the Amazon library, was cardinal to reaching the tipping point as quickly as possible, so it could then reap future returns from compounding numbers, from whom it now gets much more customer spend, compared to non Prime members.

The arithmetic is simple, and there is probably margin for bringing down the price of Prime. But the point is that with customer-centric logic, if value is embedded early on, benefits manifest later and, in theory, can continue into perpetuity.

Sometimes it's necessary to offer free trials. MTN Ghana achieved take-up of its new doctor information-sharing site by giving opinion leader medical specialists from various hospitals free devices. Also an 'e-contact' service was created for them to share information, experiences and knowledge. They also enjoyed discounted prices on calls among themselves in order to encourage interaction.

To drive acceptance and penetration in India, rural clinics and doctors were offered no-interest loans as part of the GE deal, thanks to a partnership with the State Bank of India (some companies fund these loans themselves). Some clinics were given free equipment, and investments by doctors were made easy, through a credit facility by the bank.

M-PESA actively used the same principle to encourage Kenyans to experiment with its new offerings. For instance, it allowed users initially to register for free, and customers requiring a SIM card upgrade received one without having to pay. Despite this, however, the store operator got a registration commission upfront. Once the brand started taking off, this was split and operators got half upfront and the other half after the first customer deposit was made. Balances were given free to customers after a transaction.

Enterprises may also need to incentivize partners early on, and make it easy on their finances. MTN Uganda's MobileMoney had one of the most successful take-up and conversions to mobile wallets in the world, namely 1 million subscribers within the first year, largely because it took the historic step to give 70 per cent of the new value to its distributors.

Educating customers

The process of shaping expectations and changing attitudes and habits can be quite complex. Customer-centric disruptors don't simply meet or exceed customer expectations: they mould them. Customers are asked to adopt concepts and change habits in ways not yet encountered or even consciously needed.

Getting take-up therefore entails being able to ride the paradoxical waves of educating the market, while at the same time creating and compounding it. Unless you factor this into the go-to-market strategy, take-up may not be as fast as you had hoped, or high enough to get to a tipping point.

GE Healthcare always initially concentrated their efforts on education and training, which is part of its success formula. To this end, training on-site and virtually was emphasized in India and China, supplemented with online guidelines, simpler keyboards, and presets for certain tasks.

M-PESA missed this when they went into Tanzania – and paid the price because it affected take-up initially. It consequently rectified, making its marketing campaigns more educational.

Changing habits requires finding ways to work closely with customers, in training and coaching sessions. Unilever does this wherever it goes in Africa, South America and Asia in the 'personal hygiene management' 'market space'. Part of getting critical mass has been giving training in schools in multiple classroom contact sessions across countries and continents, reaching millions of youngsters. This training, which mirrors what has been done across the world, involves quite sophisticated techniques to show children that 'visibly clean' is not the same as 'hygienically clean', or why a liquid hand wash is more effective than a bar of soap.

And having also realized that children are more likely to commit if a promise is made in public, it gets them to sign up to hand washing in front of peers in a campaign it has called a 'Classroom Soap Pledge', complemented by local soap jingles, celebrity events and comic-book characters.

Education is best done by the enterprise itself. M-PESA did countrywide road shows to teach customers how its system worked. When Ghana MTN took SMEs into cloud computing, employees spent time with customers in their own premises, in order to demonstrate that it worked and, even more importantly, that their data was safe and easily retrievable.

Discovery Insure uses brokers as its customer risk coaches. They are trained regularly, with interesting speakers brought in from all over the world, constantly bolstered with up-to-date data and interesting facts about driving safety. And especially the driving and engagement status of their own customer base, which they are expected to follow-up on.

Broker emphasis is to get customers to engage. They go into the Internet with them, and take them through questionnaires and the reward scheme. They work through their scorecards, and show them what they can gain under various scenarios. Experience has taught Discovery that the more that brokers do this with customers, the greater the engagement and take-up.

Call centres do the same job. Customers can see at a glance where they stand, and what the value is of their benefit at any moment in time. If they have queries, the call centre will have conversations about what they may be doing, or not doing, to earn the rewards.

Even in sophisticated economies like Sweden, education is needed to change habits. Stockholm authorities wanted to get people out of cars and onto public transport. Public opposition was very high. IBM worked with the authorities to design and run a system that involved educating customers to see the value of this switch.

Customer education requires upfront investments in time, money and energy. We have already discussed Apple's efforts in retail and the huge Apple-like store follow-ship on the part of other vendors. These retailing concepts are also being used for education.

South Africa's FNB, with its emphasis on digital platform banking, has opened dotFNB cashless concept stores, so that tech-savvy customers can discuss and get trained by trained staff on how to install and use applications and devices. This is combined with high-tech virtual-type environments using tablets and augmented reality with conference cubicles for video consultations.

Lego's venture into retail stores is not an attempt to vertically integrate and control the distribution channel to sell more boxes, another old product idea. Rather, it has set up stores around the world, including in the USA, the UK, Europe, Australia, Singapore and Japan, expressly to make these stores part of the brand 'showrooming' experience, where the customers can come to terms with how to interact with the play materials, software and interactive technology. In these educational settings Lego has found a way to communicate and educate its customer population, making sure they understand how to follow instructions and, more importantly, use their own creative abilities to build models beyond their wildest expectations.

Quantifying the benefits for customers

Closely allied to education is demonstrating value to customers. Here the enterprise must actually be able to show that customers are better off with the new way of doing things, rather than without it. Needless to say, it's only when this happens that the innovation really takes hold, to become part of customers' daily lives and routines. This is when the implementation moves into a new gear and starts to show returns.

Results have been spectacular for Cemex customers, partly accounting for the incredible take-up. Not only have millions of Mexican families and communities benefited; time, money and energy have also been saved. The system enabled a family to build a typical home in just 1.4 years, compared to the average four years for families not participating in the initiative. Cost reductions for a construction project are as high as 30 per cent, with savings of 60–70 per cent in time. Families are also taught how to minimize water and energy usage and to practise better waste disposal. Efficient appliances further reduce resource utilization.

IHI used its Wellbeing University as a vehicle to educate the corporate market, and also to quantify the huge benefits to be gained from investing in wellness programmes. While corporations mostly still look at pulling down direct health costs, they could instead be getting huge returns on their investment from interventions that not only save them costs (both direct and hidden), but also bring in extra monies from increased productivity and performance. Together with leading global corporate lights and experts, IHI's various education initiatives included joint research, forums and publications.

Through the new IBM system, traffic in Stockholm has been reduced by 25 per cent, traffic delays by 50 per cent and air quality has also been improved, all of which has been quantified for the public. Now the majority of the public is in favour of the change. And the IBM Rio de Janeiro project, which aimed ultimately to create a single real-time integrated view of the city, to provide citizens with enhanced safety in a coordinated and efficient way, measured response times which have improved by 30 per cent so far. This has helped IBM to compound take-up from other cities and countries.[84]

Google's push for driverless cars has been motivated on the basis of measurable data and this has made the case more compelling inside the company and out. The goal has always been powered by the quest to make driving safer and to save lives and customer time, which has been constantly backed by data: for example, accident rates, which are high in most countries – the fact that these are mainly due to human error, and they are one of the chief reasons for premature death, traffic congestion and all the costs associated with accidents. As much as one-third of the land in some cities goes to parking spots and 30 per cent of driving in business districts is to find parking, all of which can be saved. Coupled, of course, with the fact that it can reduce the hours wasted in commuting by 90 per cent, as well as increase productive use of people's time.[85]

Discovery Insure, in a very short space of time found that it had substantially fewer bad drivers, more good drivers and more excellent drivers in its policyholder base. Customers have less reckless accidents or incidents – with all the concomitant extra expenses and hassles removed. This resulted in a drop in claims of 46 per cent, and less costs for repair.

Collating before and after data

To be able to make the investment in quantification, the enterprise needs to collate both before and after baseline statistics. This means having to build new capabilities that can produce tangible and intangible evidence of customer value.

The entire Discovery Insure driver safety programme is based on an algorithm that measures before and after results. They have perfected a way to link driver behaviour and accidents. Everyone knows that speeding causes accidents, but no one has really quantified the connection in ways that are meaningful. Discovery Insure takes the macro data and brings it down to the level of the individual customer, linking cause and effect, and demonstrating before and after changes to each person.

It also knows that stolen vehicles and hijackings are huge problems for customers in South Africa, costing the insurance industry billions of rand per year, with very low recovery rates. Through Discovery Insure's expertise, it can identify changed driving behaviour and alert drivers to a possible hijack or theft 85 per cent of the time, within minutes by text message, and send help to the scene.

Unilever has developed a model of hand hygiene behaviour change, on how to increase soap usage during the five most critical health impact moments in a person's day, such as before eating lunch, or after a visit to the toilet, or playing. It collates before and after data and finds correlations with hand hygiene, diarrhoea and other diseases, such as eye infections.

Using smart sensor technology inside soap it measures hand washing behaviours in three dimensions over time to gauge the impact before and after interventions and monitors how different types worked. The diaries of mothers and children are also checked to record changed behaviour and patterns. Importantly, the research it uses is not just evidence-based, but ascertains whether behaviour change is sustained over time and why.

In some countries, soap usage is up by as much as 50–75 per cent, so contributing to its social value as well as sales. And it has also got the multiplier effect of changed behaviour, because kids who use soap tend to influence the soap habits of their family, which accelerates total reach and take-up.[86]

As well as tangible data, statements can verbalize the intangible benefits of new ways of doing things, 'often many times as important as the monetary'. This may entail jointly building a list with customers, putting words around some qualitative statements.

If a company like Lexis Nexis is able to state that independent research showed that its customers outperformed their competitors by 26 per cent, that is a very powerful motivator for take-up. And it can do this because it collects, collates and measures the appropriate data.[87]

But it goes further. It got employees to sit down with insurance claims assessors, and ask them for their definition of success. As it turned out, this was the number of times that fraud had been identified, and money recovered. Then executives obtained 'before' success rates, looked at the information Lexis Nexis had injected into the customer activity cycle to reduce risk during critical decision points in the workflow, compared them to 'after' success rates, and built a formula to quantify its contribution.

Celebrating and rewarding results

Rewarding customers is mainstream practice, particularly in B2C business. But customers are simply rewarded for coming back and doing what they have always done, backed by the kind of loyalty programmes in a product-based approach that we have already discussed.

Cut to the notable exceptions, coming from customer centricity, which link rewards to the omni-channel customer experience, meaningful linkages and the thrust of what the company is trying to achieve in the marketplace. Starbucks, for example, has a cross-channel multi-brand loyalty programme. Customers can also get the integrated benefit of buying Starbucks-packaged coffee, tea or ice cream in grocery stores. And from new brands such as purchases in the Teavana retail stores, with 'stars' redeemed for food or drink.

Also customer centricity links rewards to desired customer behaviour. Discovery Insure rewards customers for improving driving behaviour as well as choices made, such as no late-night driving, no drinking while driving or no driving at high speed. Improvements and good driving go into a safe driving bonus, and drivers are rewarded by getting rebates of up to 50 per cent on petrol bills using the Discovery card.

It has been found that customers change behaviour if rewards are substantial enough. This behavioural change is also sustainable because the rewards are designed to get customers to continue to drive well, in order to be able to earn points against petrol cost. Not only are good driver claims almost half that of poor drivers, they have quicker response times and better safety habits, which lead to fewer accidents and less chance of fatalities.

If you want to enhance take-up, you need to think about making results visible, and celebrating the new behaviours and successes of all the stakeholders, which include customers, employees and partners. Examples are:

- **Customers:** Cemex, for instance, organizes a party and presents a food-and-drink kit when a house is completed. Friends and family in the community are invited to celebrate with the home owner.
- **Employees:** In Marks & Spencer's landmark turnaround to customer centricity it was fastidious about training for and celebrating great service, and embedding that into performance systems. This was done through regular recognition programmes, and annual customer service awards.[88]
- **Partners:** Unilever gives 'Hand Washing Champion' rewards to public and private partners. For example, the government of Mali for their national hand-washing campaign that reached 70 per cent of the population, and the governments of Kenya for getting the most number of people ever to wash their hands at a single location, on Global Hand Washing Day, now a regular event worldwide.

Expanding the positive energy

Critical mass is needed both internally and externally to get the compounding effects of customer centricity. Insiders influence one another, and together their successes, which should be highly profiled, set an example for others who then become more comfortable, confident and courageous. Getting the 'points of light' and some of the activated group to see the logic and feel strongly, and then behave differently, drives first principles of conversion. This has been used in some of the most celebrated cases of best practice, tipping point change management in the public and private sectors.[89]

This see-feel-change sequence takes the enterprise through the milestones in an ongoing process of getting the correct people involved, at the correct time.[90] Tuned in and turned on, the activated group buy in, attracting the motivated group and then, suddenly, enough people start to think and behave differently, drawing still more people in, which causes a 'push' for the new way of doing things for and with customers. As a consequence, the speed of take-up gathers, culminating in accelerated internal buy-in, which drives up the internal take-up curve.

External take-up follows the same principle. Once the model concepts and marketing efforts begin to show results, customers start to affect the opinion and behaviour of other customers, creating social proof, and making the brand infectious and then indigenous, effectively setting a new standard through increased market 'pull'.

The two expanding movements of internal and external energies move in tandem as people inside influence each other, and as customers and other interested parties outside do the same (see Exhibit 9.3).

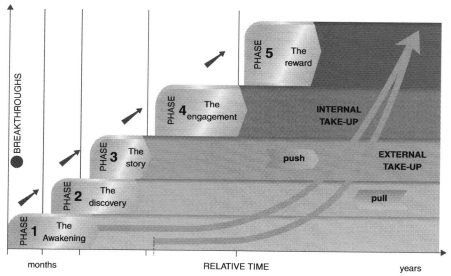

Exhibit 9.3 The internal 'push' and external 'pull' take-up

Managing the 'push/pull' rhythm

These two streams affect one another, making them inexorably linked and reinforcing. This implies that the systematic timing and management of their interconnecting rhythms is critical to successful implementation.

This fact is often missed by those executives who manage internal and external buy-in separately, as two distinct activities. For example, at this stage, often marketing departments will have taken over the external promotion and communication. And the human resource department will most likely be doing the internal communications campaign, along with the people, cultural and transformational work.

This can slip out of sync unless managed jointly in one interlinked process, especially with disruptions, either because the enterprise can't get the market to take what it is ready to give, or because the market can't get from an enterprise what it is ready to accept. This separation in effort cuts off the positive feedback dynamic between internal and external forces, which could otherwise be used to power the process.

This power comes about because of the synergistic interplay between the internal and external energy streams. They nourish each other in a rhythm of 'push/pull' that, when carefully managed, can help drive the implementation to reach its critical mass.

Effectively there are, therefore, three dynamics at work. Let's take a look at them in more detail:

- **Dynamic 1: inside 'push' rhythm**
  When the model concepts with customers begin to show proof that the new approach is working, more traction is created among insiders and more people start to use the concepts and language, institutionalizing the customer approach. This then becomes manifest in new thinking, behaviour patterns and rewards. As evidence of success from early wins is heralded, and enthusiasm and confidence levels increase throughout the organization, it produces a *'push'* to do more, more quickly.
- **Dynamic 2: outside 'pull' rhythm**
  Externally, as the model concepts start to take shape and/or early adopters begin to buy, demand compounds to create a *'pull'* from the outside. Add to this the increased press coverage, heightened interest and involvement from partners and developers, curiosity and receptiveness from investors, and positive influence by advocates,

and the demand starts to accelerate, so that it finally produces sufficient critical mass of take-up through the marketplace.
- **Dynamic 3: 'push/pull' rhythm**
  The more the support and engagement grow inside, the greater
  the chances of early victories, because more people and resources
  are committed and people discover extra innovations to add. This
  internal *'push'* in turn boosts involvement and interaction with
  customers, which increases their commitment and the *'pull'* from
  the external world, which reinforces the appetite and case internally for more attention time and investment.

In essence, these linked positive feedback loops result in a rhythmic
flow of energy and support:

> *through the enterprise*
> *and*
> *through the markets*
> *and as well*
> *from the enterprise to the market*
> *and then*
> *from the marketplace back into the organization.*

So in fact the reinforcing internal and external take-up looks more
like an interconnected positive reinforcing spiral (see Exhibit 9.4).

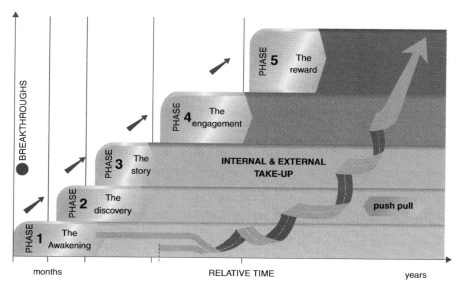

Exhibit 9.4 The interrelated dynamic of 'push/pull'

BREAKTHROUGH 10

Gather & Sustain Momentum

Key idea

Customer centricity builds a customer base from which it leverages increasing value over time. This requires making the investments that look further down the line, and developing the intangible capabilities – the high-value ingredients – that lock customers on and competitors out. These intangibles have unique capabilities that build new types of capital, which need to be measured and reported differently. Customer-centric enterprises acknowledge that great transformations are never-ending, and great disruptors never stop disrupting to make their impact felt and their lead enduring.

Leveraging the investment

Rewards come to customer-centric disruptors who make investments in an ever-growing customer base, from which they then leverage increasing possibilities for growth.

The ultimate breakthrough occurs when, having built these platforms, the internal and external 'push/pull' rhythm produces enough unstoppable momentum to generate rewards, usually starting around the 18-month mark or later, depending on circumstances.

Some key points on these investments are given below.

Investments should bring rewards that are lasting

The real question is not just how good an organization is at building the investment, but also how good it is at using it to power growth enduringly.

With Tim Cook at the helm Apple is poised to grow by investing anew in concepts that outwit competitors. And use Angela Ahrendts's combination of retail and digital expertise to make luxury affordable, online as well as off. For us interrogating customer-centric success the real questions are these: what could Apple do with its strong customer-base investment? How can it ensure the 'lock-on' continuity of its 400 retail store customer base, and expand that through elevated seamless online and offline shopping experiences? How can it leverage its 600 million customers with iTunes accounts?[91]

With such a customer base, a company is well positioned to build growth through revenues projected into meaningful customer life expectancy, through longevity, breadth, depth and diversity of their spend at low costs. And if this is done well, it can leave traditional players behind, battling over price and annual, monthly and quarterly sales quotas.

FNB's boundary pushing and investments in its social media persona and capability has proved to be fruitful in getting new customer spend. And, apart from banking, disrupting several other industries, such as electronic retailers, it is now the largest reseller of Apple iPads and iPhones in the country (the bulk of its digital app user customers use iPhones and iPads). Within the first year, it was receiving applications for two iPads/smartphones every minute. The telecommunications industry will also inevitably feel the disruption, given the up to 100 per cent discount off customers' monthly ADSL accounts, free unmetered Internet data access to any of its websites and social network channels, and cheaper voice calls and free calls to FNB and FNB customers.

To the uninitiated it could look like a gimmick. To the serious customer-centric mind, making an investment so that customers can easily get high-tech products is a good way to fuel use of FNB's apps, which brings about the 'lock-on', driving increasing returns – more spend at almost no cost – which in this case has come from both existing customers and new customers. Customers can buy the smart products online, in an experience that includes delivery and post-sales services, and funds are provided by attaching the purchase onto an existing account, at a discount, interest- and hassle-free.

In emerging markets, investments are not only to capture today's wealth. It's also to look to a future, when opportunities arise to upsell to these customers. GE investments have been high in China and

India, with margins slimmer than usual, but markets are expected to move to more advanced machines in the not-too-distant years ahead.

Investments should cover the total customer constituency

Many of the examples we have talked about illustrate this. Look at India Tobacco Company, which had to deal with a poor infrastructure, poor power supply bandwidth and connectivity shortages, and so on. Investments were not just made in its relationships with customers. It went beyond this to develop infrastructures in communities, to facilitate its e-Choupal innovation. And, in line with environmental commitments, batteries were charged by solar panels.

GE has successfully demonstrated that development costs in frugal innovation can benefit the entire customer spectrum. Its affordable cardiac and portable ultrasound equipment not only benefits patients and saves lives, it also lowers costs for government, doctors and hospitals and makes a contribution to the overall economic health of countries. Included is alternative energy and eco-friendly infrastructures, all part of Jeff Immelt's 'green is green' metaphor, which captures his customer-centric vision for GE to do good, and do it well.[92]

Investments may be sizeable

The nature and size of the investments needed to change habits and social and business practice may be considerable. But they come with huge payback. Every example we have looked at is testament to this.

Amazon deliberately overinvested in technology, customer acquisition, branding and fulfilment (warehousing and logistics), initially forfeiting profit, after which the accumulated power created for Amazon could be – and still is being – leveraged to amass positive returns.[93]

Investments may have to happen before a concept is totally proven

By definition, the great disruptors and disruptions need to make investments before that something being actualized is proven.

Ocado spent nearly a decade investing in a customer-centric offering, backed by state-of-the-art technology, which then disrupted retail incumbents. It continues to penetrate the spending of nearly half of all British consumers who are now radically changing their habits by buying groceries and non-food remotely.

M-PESA made heavy investments in the design and delivery of its agency network and marketing in Kenya, without really knowing if and how much take-up they would get. But that's what grew its brand exponentially, as demand and supply increased, thanks to networking externalities and customer viralization, feeding each other.

Investments in customers should be continuous

To keep and grow a customer base from which to leverage, means to keep investing in innovation all the time in multiple ways to add customer value. Tesco's success in virtual shopping will be layered with augmented reality so that shoppers can see the images three dimensionally. And no doubt this will be followed by being able to touch and feel them as well.

UT Bank in Ghana started a service called 'phone for loan'. Typically entrepreneurs and SMEs can't come to the bank because they would have to close their shops, or trading stations. Now they don't have to: they can call in for a loan. The bank does the initial process over the phone, and in the first five minutes if managers think it's a yes, they go to them for the next part of the procedure. This saves everyone time, effort and money.

This led to UT 'Banks on Wheels', the first of its kind in Ghana. At certain set times, the bank literally goes to the doorstep of the customer, such as schools or communities that have no access to banking, or entrepreneurs who have no time to travel long distances into town. Equipped with state-of-the-art technology, these roving units do everything, including foreign exchange, savings and loans, and they have safety features to protect customers withdrawing cash from the ATM.

This continuous investment in customer value is not to be confused with short-term promotions. Here is an example to demonstrate the difference. When one of the long-awaited Harry Potter books came out, Amazon discounted it by 40 per cent. Pre-sales hit 1 million copies, of which 250,000 gushed from buyers who had never before made a purchase from Amazon.

Most traditional booksellers also discounted the book to attract customers into their stores. There was one important difference: they saw the book as a classic loss leader to get people to buy more books. Amazon's aim was to use these books (which, if stacked one on top of the other, would be more than twice the height of Mount Everest, the world's highest peak!) to get customers on-site so that it could get to know them.[94] Here was a very cost-effective way of making an investment (not a sales promotion to get rid of a pile of stuff) to get customers on board, an opportunity that would pay off in the long term (not just for the moment).

Investments should be proactive and focus on customers not competitors

Customer-centric disruptors don't look to obvious competitors to decide what investments to make. They build customer value, which is the stock in which they trade.

Says an executive from IBM: 'We can see a clear correlation between investments that are lined up behind specific business values for a customer and revenues. If investments are made in order to give customers a specific outcome, then the returns we get are not only larger, but more predictable.'

Bezos maintains that his overriding driver in making investments comes from a focus on giving customers added value, not looking at what competitors do. Investments are proactive and push boundaries, rather than reacting to external pressure. Amazon now contracts directly with authors for releasing their print and online fiction and non-fiction books, in a new disruptive approach aimed to connect writer and reader and bypass traditional publishers who use old models and mindsets.

For example, Amazon Publishing moves quickly and has massive distribution and, consequently, is wooing some well-known authors into its camp. Ignoring industry norms, Amazon is providing services previously offered by agents, publishers and critics. It makes the entire process easier for writers, including instantly getting access to data on book sales, promoting books vigorously to the correctly matched individuals, connecting authors directly with fans, and paying authors monthly, instead of the standard once or twice a year, which is a major issue for professionals who write for a living.

Good reasons to take intangibles seriously

For some time we have known that executives who are product-focused don't spend enough time thinking about how to use the intangibles to create customer value and wealth for enterprise. And that having the tangible rather than the intangible assets and investments on a balance sheet is no sure indicator of their long-term growth, or of sustainable performance.[95] We also know that not having intangibles as an integral investment can seriously hamper the ability of the enterprises to drive change.[96]

The intangibles are the very assets that are often referred to as the non-sales or non-financial drivers. Investing in these intangibles doesn't come easily to conventional players. They still prefer to put their money behind the tangibles, the assumed sales or financial drivers in which they have more faith.[97]

Decisions about new buildings, new acquisitions, more factories and equipment, more branches, feel safe. They are more measurable and less subjective than the intangibles, and they seemingly show returns more quickly. But in ignoring and underestimating the intangible assets and their significance to performance, and how they correlate with growth, executives and their enterprises miss out on two important performance drivers. The first is the ability to compete for the longer term, by building a customer base and a true barrier to entry; the second is the ability to drive real scale and speed, at low cost. On the other hand, if investments have been made in intangibles, they have the potential to deliver exponential rewards. To see why, let's summarize their ten unique attributes:

1. Intangibles are abundant, so instead of diminishing as they are used, they do the opposite, which means that they don't lose value, as happens to hard assets and resources that suffer depletion, wear and tear and depreciation: intangibles appreciate in value, enjoying positive depreciation the more they are reused.
2. Once the investment is made in these intangibles, not only do they last longer, but the cost of using them decreases as they are recycled, so marginal expense to serve customers go down and can even approximate zero.
3. Since they are expandable, the initial outlay in investments such as technology infrastructures, user communities, platforms to

capture data information and know-how become a baseline cost, requiring occasional refreshment and update. It involves none of the expensive replacements that traditional investments need, which bring diminishing returns.

4. While traditional hard asset investments do appear to bolster balance sheets, they don't actually drive the much-needed increased customer spend, whereas the intangibles such as applications, software, social media networks, collaborative partnerships and service cultures produce ongoing value that is also personalized.

5. Intangible investments give the enterprise organic growth potential that comes from internal strength and capability extension, which it can continue to use rather than expanding just through acquisition.

6. Tangibles have to be maintained from time to time. This is costly. In contrast, intangibles are always being maintained and upgraded on a monthly, daily, hourly or even minute-for-minute basis, at no or minimal cost.

7. Enterprises get intangibles free from customers, such as know-how, expertise, personal data, information and content. So they can entice customers in through creative pricing mechanisms, including new concepts of 'free'.[98] Or they can pass these benefits on to customers in other competitive ways.

8. With user communities facilitated by the Internet, intangibles can be grown exponentially at low cost, and can become speedy, scalable and saleable content.

9. Brainpower, wisdom, experience and know-how can be made collective, at very low cost.

10. This collective know-how is searchable, discoverable and accessible instantly, globally, any time, from any device, at low or no cost, in ever magnifying quantities.

Reaping the exponential reward

Exhibit 10.1 shows the exponential reward curve that comes from increased revenue and the lower-cost formula, thanks to new customer economies. This is what customer-centric executives aim for ultimately, in managing the breakthroughs. Let's go through it in more detail.

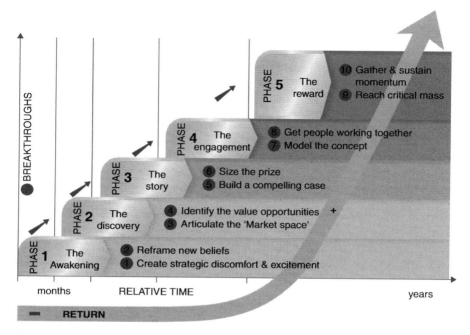

Exhibit 10.1 Conceptual exponential reward curve

Initially, there is a negative cash flow as the enterprise releases funds, and invests for perhaps months or years, depending on the circumstances, without revenues necessarily coming in. That's the bad news.

The good news is that, once the initial investments are made up front, because of its high intangible component the bulk of that investment can be refreshed at very low cost. As well, the initial investment will be spread over large numbers of customers and, in time, other ventures and countries speedily (economies of spread).

In addition, the initial costs are offset by data content and feedback gained on an ongoing basis, to build the algorithms and case studies that provide testimony, expertise and better personalized customer outcomes. These can be reused at low cost, relatively speaking (economies of skill).

Further along in the curve, the enterprise benefits from longer, stronger and new revenues, and gains from economies of sweep (people e-linked, getting personalized services en masse). As the brand gains power, and relationships deepen and thicken through customer 'lock-on', advocacy increases and sales are pushed up at low cost (economies of stretch). Later the enterprise begins to diversify its customer spend into totally new 'market spaces' economically.

Quite apart from this, costs may also be pulled down further, because from the spill off of customer 'lock-on' comes the more efficient utilization of hard assets and resources, and employees and partners. Additionally, networking effects lead to more resources, systems and information shared between company customers and partners, so expenses can decline still further, with disproportionate returns.

The result of all this, for the customer-centric transformer? Remarkably simple and powerful: as momentum builds, there is real potential for exponential rewards.

Outpacing through know-how

Another contributor to getting the promised reward, once momentum has gathered pace, is the fact that, thanks to know-how, the major ingredient in creating and differentiating customer value, not only can exponential returns be produced, but the enterprise can be kept irretrievably ahead.

First, the enterprise uses the know-how to get customers engaged and entrenched, something that other assets cannot sustainably do. Then, it uses it to grow and move up the curve at a steady clip, to keep it ahead of the game, widening the gap between the enterprise and rivals, as it learns and applies that learning faster than anyone else. This is especially effective when the knowledge is complex, or if it is not easy to codify because it emanates from several disciplines and sources internally and externally, which makes it difficult for others to copy.[99]

Leading by knowing

Knowledge turned into tangible customer value is what makes the enterprise potentially the undisputed expert in a 'market space'. This can't really happen with discrete products and services – even the most elaborate. Think about it: GE have sophisticated scanning and diagnostic hardware that enable more detailed and personalized predictive capability than probably any other company. But so far doctors still have to detect and analyse the problem, diagnose and prescribe treatment and perform surgery.[100]

How does the enterprise stay ahead? There is only one way. By making sure that doctors get the outcome. GE constantly builds and passes on its know-how to doctors, on how to analyse data from the scanning, so that they can detect diseases even earlier, diagnose even more accurately to prevent or prolong the onset of the disease, and so enhance the speed and success of recovery rates, to help institutions better manage the health of its population.

When knowledge is explicitly linked to individual customers and constantly updated, relationships can't be easily snatched away by competitors. It then becomes an asset, potent enough to enable the organization to gather momentum and hold its ground.

Prince Kofi Amoabeng of UT Bank Ghana knows there are always banks trying to emulate UT. But they are constantly ahead because by the time the others do copy, they know their customers so well that they have something else to offer.

This know-how that keeps the enterprise ahead relates as well to internal practices that deliver customer centricity. 'Minivations', at FNB, are all the small innovations that lead to small behavioural changes internally, tied to its imperative to be thoroughly customer centric. These (nearly 6,000 since the transformation) add up to make a formidable powerbase that is increasingly giving them the edge. Other banks, Jordaan reiterates, can copy products but the ways in which FNB does things he believes cannot be copied.

To get the resulting happy returns, top of mind for the transforming enterprise therefore must always be:

- Do we have the necessary know-how that makes us the expert, indispensable in our 'market space'?
- Are we developing it, collecting, using, combining, updating, disseminating and reusing it to gain and maintain the lead?
- Are we creating content from this that promotes our leader status.

Discovery Insure, for example, have positioned themselves as *the* experts in great driving practice. And it is leveraging this know-how quickly across its worldwide operation.

But to retain its lead has required ongoing commitment, including making the data ever more granular, useful and relevant to customers. So, for example, they already give weather reports, but this will soon lead to alerts, depending where exactly the person is at that moment in time. Because analysis tells them that young new drivers are at risk at night, they now provide night driving courses. And because 80–90 per cent of decisions made while driving are based on visual information, they have invested in EyeGym, a visual training program to help customers train their eye muscles, and so improve visual skills and awareness, for which they get rewarded.

It also means being prepared to develop new skills, and discard or complement the old, as Amazon did with Kindle. Tesco's Homeplus in South Korea was not just about knowing how to open more physical retail stores. The real question was how to get ahead of the curve in South Korea, by learning to build virtual concepts that were just as good as, or better than, the real thing.

From an emphasis on know-how, will come a competitive lead in the following ways:

Keeping competitors out

What better way to stop others from jumping onto the bandwagon than blocking them before they even have a chance to get close?

Undoubtedly Amazon's MayDay concept of remote humanized support will be copied, and probably become a new standard for communicating remotely with customers. But Amazon characteristically will retain its lead in two ways: (1) technologically by making the investments that keep them ahead, and (2) using the information and know-how it gleans from customers, which it will kick back into the system to keep providing better personalized value.

Knowledge, once accumulated, makes this possible, because it can be easily, quickly and cheaply adapted in order to progress the enterprise. As happened with India Tobacco Company which scaled up from one commodity, soya beans, to several others such as coffee and wheat, and from one province to many others, at low cost and high speed. Or Discovery Insure, which continues to compound its lead by building know-how onto its already considerable knowledge base on great driving.

Given Amazon's well-earned skill base in technology, most other companies would keep it a secret and simply send merchants more and more visitors from its site, or provide links in exchange for a commission. Why would it decide instead to share the technology with retail merchants, and make them more competitive?

The answer is this: staying ahead means being so darn good at it that it makes it too difficult for others to enter or offer an alternative, without being seen as the follower. Perhaps that is why no other airline has managed to offer a limousine service to business-class customers that supersedes Virgin's service?

Having a knowledge base is a major factor in being and being seen as the expert. Amazon Web Services Inc. uses its considerable skill to bolster its multi-billion-dollar revenues at next to no cost, by building branded sites for merchants so that they can capture sales using the Internet.

Expanding smartly

Starbucks have unique skill at in-store experiences in urban neigh-bourhoods for people throughout the planet who want to sit around and do things while they also drink hot or cold customized beverages. Teavana carry a large high-class range of bulk and loose tea, but have no seating areas to serve customers tea. Starbucks can change this at very low cost and speed up the conversion from selling tea to tea bars, because that's what they did for coffee, and that's what they know how to do.

Leveraging from its know-how may get the enterprise into new revenue-generating opportunities. So successful was HealthStore's evolving knowledge of the health of its Kenyan customers that it could quickly ramp up operations to work with governments, expanding into other relief areas such as lab testing for malaria, tuberculosis and AIDS; AIDS counselling; and maternal health ser-vices; as well as go into a micro-insurance health plan.

This know-how may also start with products or services that the enterprise needs for itself and then replicates for others. UT Bank built capabilities in service areas such as collection, warehousing and logistics, goods clearing and handling, property validation and life and goods insurance, and security, which were all needed in order to build their own customer experience. But they became so good at it that they made each one into a fully-fledged business.

Expansions are not only quicker; they also cost less. A classic example comes from Virgin Blue's low-fares airline debut into Australia. Using knowledge as its capital, Virgin's investment there cost a mere £5 million! Since then Virgin has led the incipient space tourism business. Leveraging off technical know-how in air travel and the knowledge and expertise gained from balloon trips across the Pacific, together with partners, it has managed to make this new way of touring technologically, economically and ecologically feasible, using low-energy access launching ships from the air, instead of the ground.

Enterprises from emerging countries internationalize in this way. Cemex accumulated knowledge and then used it to spread its wings globally. 'The Cemex Way' catalogues and stores superior practice into a centralized database and then makes it an enterprise standard rolled out into other countries or acquisitions. It has been estimated that 70 per cent of Cemex's practices have been acquired in this way, with the cumulative and substantial effects on its ability to expand effectively very quickly globally.[101]

Massifying the knowledge

Part of the trick is to capture knowledge obtained from the behaviour unique to an individual customer, consolidate the findings, and transfer the relevant bits for use on other customers – when, where and how they need them. Or to make these gems mainstream in offerings.

For instance, Lexis Nexis conscientiously and continuously observes the behaviour of customers such as sales departments, financial managers or scientists, tracking how users link information in their decision-making processes. It then takes these connections and brings back the components into new value-adds for other customers.

Through a never-ending flow of improvements, real-time opportunities bloom. The net effect of this is that it can continuously produce superior value at low delivered cost, thus setting up protective barriers against any and all predators waiting in the wings.

This may require creating a venue for people to learn from each other. In IBM's quest to take SmartCities worldwide, the experience and know-how of mayors and municipalities, with their collective learning, are pulled together and pooled into platforms, white papers and special events. The inputs are from diverse people and departments, such as builders, artists, social activists, engineers, planners and local government officials, the object being to learn from each others' successes and failures.

And internally IBM have created special platforms where its so-called Blue IQ team can leverage social media, where knowledgeable people can mini-blog and share insights and practice with colleagues within and across the organization.[102]

Spreading leading practice

By virtue of constantly updating its know-how and best practice, the customer-centric enterprise can maximize its chances of getting and staying ahead. Despite Virgin's eccentricity it is not just hot air that gives it the brand power that has enabled it to attract customers. Virgin Atlantic became the new standard-bearer for passenger experience in its lounges, which includes libraries, Internet cafés, stylish cocktail bars, full restaurants, sleep alcoves, billiard areas, computer work spaces, and organic food and drinks served at delis.

Ever updated, its hospitality know-how has been taken to Virgin Money UK customers. Standalone lounges are now placed in banks, where customers can sit down, have a coffee, charge a phone, make a call or just relax, with no tellers or sales people around. And the response has been rewarded with more customers gravitating to the branches and brand.[103]

Unilever stays ahead not just because it got in first to transform hand-washing habits, but because it knows how it is done, and it is constantly updating and codifying its know-how to stay ahead. For instance, it knows the relative effectiveness of different media and interventions in changing hand-washing behaviour. Studies are run all over the world to build best practice to get superior results and then transfer these, with Unilever so far ahead that catching up would be almost impossible.

Answers to these questions are needed to make this work:

- What country is getting the best results?
- What region in this country is getting the best results?
- What person/institution within the region is getting the best results?

Then a template is created of exactly what is done, how, when in the intervention process, how often, and for what kinds of customers. From this the best demonstrated practice is collected, and disseminated across the enterprise, constantly updated to become leading practice.

When such knowledge comes from unique experiences with customers and resides in people's heads, appropriate systems need to be in place to motivate these people to share and update their experiences, so that the entire knowledge base can be continually elevated, and each person's capability when dealing with a customer can ascend into content representing that collective whole.

Ideally, this means that the people interacting with customers need to be encouraged and rewarded for bringing knowledge back to the enterprise. At IBM, for instance, consultants are expected to consciously look for what is replicable, and then record it in a global database so that others can use and refine it. Their contribution is weighted in their appraisals, to ensure an ongoing flow of knowledge that executives believe keeps the enterprise ahead in environments that are changing at enormous speed.

Alternatively, cross-functional and global teams can be formed specifically for this purpose, namely to collate collective knowledge, and allow partners internally or externally to leverage from it, as we saw with the Cemex case, where teams are especially formed for this purpose.

Taking this one step further is Apple University, which aims to impart the Apple DNA into future generations and so sustain a culture in which people understand why and how Apple is unique. And then replicate this knowhow to try and perpetuate its legendary innovative capability.

Pushing performance boundaries

Product-dominant logic uses financial capital to compete. With its *input output* mentality it manages, measures and reports on hard tangible resources assets, used and gained. This is ironic because, as many writers now point out, financial capital is more abundant than ever before.[104]

Customer-centric logic competes with intangibles, which produces the customer *outcomes* – managed, measured and reported in performance metrics. Add higher purpose to the equation and it goes a step further, to include social **impact** – positive or negative – in goals and measures. Here the object is for the enterprise to be a positive net contribution by trading in social as well as individual outcomes.

For instance, Unilever created a special low-oil soap, so as not to contaminate the water as many poor Indians wash in rivers. And in its preventative child death initiative, getting people to use soap to wash hands can decrease diarrhoea by 25 per cent in India, and hence 13 per cent of the deaths of under-fives and all the suffering that brings to their families, as well as improve school attendance and entry levels for education.[105]

Counting and accounting for intangible capital

But a mismatch exists between what creates (or damages) value in a customer-centric contemporary world, and what is traditionally measured and reported as value. Current accounting and financial practice and instruments simply cannot count or account for resources, investments or assets when:

- The real value is infinite, not finite.
- Labour is brains, not bodies or time.
- Some raw materials, like know-how, are abundant not scarce.
- Marginal costs can approximate zero.
- Some resources, such as water or fresh air, are scarce and no longer free.
- Value is increasingly tapped externally, often at zero cost.
- Social returns are as important as financial returns.
- Relationships are precious, but often not quantified and measured.
- Upstart competitors can disrupt, with minimal amounts of capital.

As enterprises increasingly enter a world where the engine for growth is the customer, and the major ingredients for achieving this are intangible, more effort has to go into genuinely valuing these intangibles in a standard way so that comparisons are equitable. The rules of accounting are trying to catch up, and develop more relevant and expanded definitions and performance measurement systems, and there are several initiatives afoot.

Widespread concern from US legislators and policymakers, the European Union and members of the OECD resulted in increasing efforts to take up this not insignificant challenge of how to incorporate non-financial (intangible) data into financial statements. This was all in the spirit of being able to present a more realistic picture of good or poor decision making, and makers.

The US Securities and Exchange Commission and the Financial Accounting Standards Board now recommend that, in addition to the usual financial statements, enterprises should publish supplementary information on their new business models, giving more emphasis to the intangibles.[106] Recently, the US Bureau of Economic Analysis categorized R&D and software as fixed investments, rather than expenses. This decision was made on the basis that these investments are long lived and therefore need to be capitalized and amortized.[107]

Notwithstanding, it is becoming increasingly important to give a fuller picture of company performance, especially if new approaches need to be motivated, sold and institutionalized in organizations.

Pushing performance boundaries to show true value earned, and how that is reflected in company worth, can never happen, however, until the intangible resources and other non-financials are incorporated into performance and accounting measures and reporting, as difficult as that may be. Which is why market capitalization due to earnings of frontrunners often continues to far outweigh their book value.[108]

Some of the issues are as follows:

- The real value of the enterprise cannot be quantified unless all its assets are shown. Company value used to be 80 per cent tangible assets and 20 per cent intangible assets. Now it is the other way around.[109]
- The real cost to an enterprise cannot be quantified unless all inputs used are shown, including those that are free (for example, customer R&D or design), received from user communities.
- The real value achieved by the enterprise cannot be quantified just by financial capital, used and gained. It needs to account for all forms of resources used, quantifying the resulting positive and negative impacts (we cannot think we are adding value for one set of customers while at the same time we are destroying value for others).[110]
- Similarly we need to measure natural resources renewed or restored, for example, trees or natural watersheds.
- Digital assets contain tangible hardware and systems and models, but also intangibles such as software and software development skills, which enable competitiveness and growth. While not on

the balance sheet, these are nonetheless investments that need to be capitalized.

- Investment decisions and investment cases cannot be realistically made, compared or assessed, or ratios such as return on assets (ROA), return on investment (ROI), return on capital (ROC), return on equity (ROE), or economic value added (EVA) used, unless there is an acceptable transparent standard way of quantifying an asset, capital, equity or investment (versus expenses).

The new capital

Some of the new capital measures that are being quantified on balance sheets or profit and loss accounts in customer-centric organizations include:

- **IQ capital:** store of expertise, knowledge, abilities and skills that are used directly or indirectly to produce customer value.
- **Relational capital:** value of brand and/or customer relationships, which give positive sway to the enterprise.
- **Social capital:** value of networks, including partners and customers, used in order to produce customer value, for ideas, R&D, design and other innovations, as well as referral value.
- **Digital capital:** value of the digital assets, which include unique models, designs, systems (including software), big data and analytic capability that enable the enterprise to create value for and with customers.
- **Natural capital:** value or accumulation of natural resources, which may be free or scarce, used in production of the offering, such as minerals, forests and water, depleted or replaced.[111]

We still have a long way to go to disrupt accounting methods and give the world a new way of measuring that makes sense where stakeholders, including press and investors, will be able to make the all-important connections between:

- What has been done to advance customer centricity and why?
- What has actually been spent, used/used up in the process?

- What has been achieved/lost for market constituents – consumers, citizens, cities, communities, countries, the cosmos?
- How has the enterprise therefore performed? What returns has it achieved?
- How does this impact its prospects for enduring growth?

Lead and lag measures

Another important question is what numbers to look at and measure, and what tools to use to more accurately assess direction and progress. In a process that is phased and managed over time, it is important to distinguish between the lead and lag indictors.

Lag indicators are goals, but photographs of a measure at a moment in time. By the time they are known, they have already happened and, therefore, they are always lagging. Lead indicators are measures that indicate a direction and foretell how the desired result will be achieved. The probability is that if they are met, the enterprise will achieve its mission and the ultimate performance it wants. Cause and effect.

The difference between lead and lag indicators is that lead indicators are **predictive** and therefore can warn the enterprise if the implementation is off course, so that pre-emptive actions can take place. Lead measures are also **influenceable**. They can be directly influenced by the enterprise, which can take proactive action when they fall off track.[112]

Let me give you an example. After Burberry's move into customer centricity came the global recession, which also hit the luxury market that was experiencing a slowdown in global traffic. But Ahrendts started looking at different data. She said: 'With better insight into the numbers, we were able to report that although traffic was down, the quality of our sales was actually improving.' The enterprise was getting more spend per customer, more conversing from their digital efforts, and greater demand for its more elevated lines, which was part of the objective. Also, the brand was resonating more strongly with core customers. A fact that she believed would make the brand power enduring.

It is yet another irony that executives often focus exclusively on the lag, and not the lead factors. Clearly the transforming enterprise needs to establish its lead indictors, and then find a way to track them during the transformation process.

Shifting emphasis from profit to cash flow

If we look more closely and compare traditional balance sheets, and profit and loss (P&L) accounts to cash flows, we quickly see the relevance of cash flow analysis to customer centricity (see Table 10.1).

Let's begin with the fact that traditional financial accounts are a snapshot of how the enterprise stands today. In contrast, the whole point of customer centricity is to perpetuate the flow of giving and getting customer value over time, by capturing the major proportion of spend in the chosen 'market space', expressed in a statement of the prize over the contemplated years.

Cash flow encapsulates net present value (NPV), which provides an assessment of what the future value of the customer base is today, given certain actions. It also indicates what cash will be freed over and above what is required to make the customer-centric initiative work.

Cash flow analysis has the added advantage that it invites the much-needed high-ground discussions by boards, executives, investors and journalists who influence the public at large on what exactly it is that is driving the performance today and for the future. This makes the connection between customer-centric logic and lasting growth.

Then comes the fact that what matters is the *meaning* behind the metrics. The balance sheet and P&L can't provide this, certainly not if considered exclusively on their own. How much the organization sold this year, for instance, says absolutely nothing about its prospects for the next.

Table 10.1 Traditional accounting versus cash flow

Balance sheets and P&L accounts	Cash flows
Show financial standing of enterprise today	Show potential for customer value in the future
Show profits, assets and liabilities at current scale	Say how cash could be used to grow the business
Look at tangibles almost exclusively	Look at intangibles as well
Used to assess past performance	Used to track ongoing performance
Identify financial health of silos within the organization	Tell overall story of how well the total enterprise is doing
Encourage short-term behaviour	Drive the long-term

Profit does say how well an enterprise did and is doing today at covering its expenses to benefit from its revenues. However, the cost of goods sold, which is the most important component of the equation is, firstly, a function of what is expensed whereas, secondly, it may not even be a meaningful figure for enterprises that live in the intangible and Internet-enabled world of value and, thirdly, may be looking for social as well as financial returns.

This leads to questions such as:

- How do we cost the time spent on relationship building?
- How do we cost the know-how transferred to and from customers?
- How do we charge for time when less time may be preferable?
- How do we pay/cost the information and expertise that we use as an ingredient for value creation?
- How do we pay/cost the value we get from customers and the public, including advocacy viralization, and aggregated sentiment?
- How do we measure the wider social losses and profits?

Making measures meaningful

Profit is a static snapshot at a moment in time. Cash flows are measured over time. Profits gear attention to what can be done with the current capacity and scale. In contrast, looking at cash flow tells executives how the enterprise has been doing, or could be doing, in using its cash to invest to grow its customer and advocacy base and potential.

Added to this is that balance sheets may look rich and fabulous, but may in no way contain the assets that will bring the enterprise from a product to customer centricity, or that will sustain its growth into the future through investment. What does appear on the balance sheet could be good, bad or neutral, today or tomorrow, depending on all sorts of developments or disruptions that the enterprise could either wait for, or itself decide to make happen. In contrast, what does *not* appear on that balance sheet is probably what has produced the value, and it is this that needs to be accounted for.

So the next point is that the intangibles that should be put to work and linked to the performance drivers and financial results are not on most balance sheets. Nevertheless, although they are ignored in conventional accounts and valuations, they are embedded in or can be extracted from cash flows, where their effects can be seen, felt and discussed.

The bottom line, so to speak, on cash flow is that it fills out the picture and is transparent about what matters. It provides executives with insight and opens up avenues for discussing where the money was spent, and whether the decisions taken were good or bad, in as much as they have yielded and are likely to continue to yield the economic, environmental and social returns over an extended time span, even multiple generations. When they understand this difference, executives are better placed to evaluate the decisions made to date, and line up resources for investments that will continue to bring the long-run returns they want.

Instead of terminating initiatives that may require more time or making pronouncements about cutting costs across the board to bolster profits quickly – which may sound naïve but happens all the time, often to the detriment of customer value – boards and executives are more likely to be able to see what actually created the value, and what didn't. They will therefore know what to keep, and what to cut.

Cash flows are meant to illuminate how the enterprise has used its resources to shift its market position, and what returns are likely to be coming in over time, and at what cost. The good thing about them is that they track financial health, which makes it difficult for the powers that be to ignore three important factors:

- where the enterprise began;
- how far it has come;
- where it is headed.

Another deficiency in conventional accounting tools is the same old problem of silo transactional mentality being perpetuated through reporting. Silo reporting does nothing to motivate customer-centric behaviour, and it says nothing about where the organization is headed. When each bit is examined separately, it gives no clue as to how individual silos may have contributed to overall customer value, or how well the total enterprise is doing to deliver integrated experiences. This further tempts and encourages behaviour that leads to poor decisions, not the good and strength of the whole.

Put all of this together and it is easy to see that the practices and instruments used to measure and communicate success can either herald in the new customer era for all time and be the engine for continued momentum and growth for all – enterprises and economies – or they can hold it back.

Leading questions

Traditional accounting is notoriously retroactive. That is not exactly conducive to making the breakthroughs that the forward-thrusting enterprise has to accomplish in order to disrupt and reinvent itself and the future. Not only is the fixation on the past out of sync with the thinking and actions that take an enterprise along a growth trajectory, it can also be dangerously misleading and, in the worst case, can result in outright failure.

So, in the end, the true mark of enduring customer-centric success depends on a more forward-looking approach that answers the questions set out in Box 10.1.

Box 10.1 Leading questions

1. Has the enterprise unveiled an exciting view about the future and told a compelling story?
2. Does this story disrupt current thinking and practice, and potentially create new opportunities for wealth, changing the way the industry operates?
3. Are investments being made to get customer 'lock-on', with future leverage potential?
4. Does the story and investments include wider customer constituents, and opportunities to get plus sum gains for all?
5. Have well-known partners and developers joined in?
6. Is a technology platform being built cross-company that has potential for enabling long-term success?
7. Is the brand becoming increasingly contagious amongst customers?
8. Is there customer advocacy and active involvement with the brand – is it being talked about positively?
9. Do cash flows reveal future potential for maximizing share of customer spend?
10. Has what has been done and used been fully reflected in relevant performance measures and reporting?

In for the long term

In many quarters, a different outlook on time is becoming apparent, with executives adamant that they are rebuilding their enterprises for the long term. Some organizations are simply refusing to hand over short-term financial projections, explaining that they detract from a more meaningful focus on the long term, and attract the wrong kinds of investors.

It helps that increasingly we are seeing living proof that customer centricity pays, and that doing well and doing good pays even better, and are not separable. It also helps that successful customer-centric disruptors have taken the radical view and refuse to allow short-term pressure to contaminate their behaviour, testimony to the fact that short termism is bad for business. Upon Paul Polman's arrival at Unilever, in his attempt to create long-term magic instead of short-term metrics, he immediately eliminated quarterly reporting. And although Amazon's revenues are exponential while profits are not, due to continuous investments in customer innovation, share price has managed to hold its own. Bezos reminds us: 'In the short run, the market is a voting machine, but in the long run, it is a weighing machine. We don't celebrate a 10% increase in the stock price like we celebrate excellent customer service. We aren't 10% smarter when that happens and conversely aren't 10% dumber when the stock goes the other way. We want to be weighed, and we're always working to build a heavier company.'[113]

Investors, boards, banks, directors, journalists, theorists, big-name organizations and others, all have a role to play in influencing this shift. But, at the end of the day, it is the enterprise making the ground-breaking differences in the marketplace that must take the lead in adjusting their mental and financial time frames, so they can better reflect an ability to generate real and ongoing growth, by making and then leveraging investments in customers.

Take Lexis Nexis. Previously, the huge investments in infrastructure, databases and partnering needed to get from subscriptions to customers would have been near impossible to get through the system, since such investments were expected to show returns in the normal, short time frame. However, when the customer-centricity implementation was started, a three- to five-year view was taken and, importantly, the decision was communicated to investor communities, including the fact that margins on origin business would have to take a knock initially, even though it would be more than compensated for.

This was accompanied by an explanation of how this all fit together with the story, what new direction the division was taking, why, how and:

- How long it would take to get the rewards.
- How the enterprise would perform better than in previous years.
- How it would do better than its competitors, because of the investments.
- How the advantage reaped would be enduring.

Sustaining success

Once there is a commitment to customer centricity, the enterprise enters a challenging period of eighteen months to three years, which can even carry over into five years if the enterprise starts from scratch or is in deep crisis. This is not without good reason: true customer centricity requires profound change to the way the organization or industry operates, if it is not only to deliver the substantial rewards, but make them long-lasting.

Leaders need to be prepared to take people through a systematic process with the five phases and ten breakthrough points we have discussed, none of which can operate in isolation and all of which are interwoven and reiterative, despite the seemingly orderly approach. It is ultimately their faith and passion, consistency and persistence that drive the implementation process forward so that, in the end, customer centricity takes on a life of its own. To make it work, leaders need to use an intricate combination of discipline and discovery; creativity and structure; emotional, social and rational appeal and anchor all actions in customers with a concept and story 'which people can't ignore, because it's just so obviously the right way to go'.

The moment the need for change is stated in a way that inspires people to feel and think differently and to willingly break with history – even if it means deviating from what happens to be working then – the enterprise enters a new era in its existence, and the implementation has begun.

As the milestones go by, the language and concepts become commonplace and, more importantly, the customer ethos that dictates what gets done, where and why, finally gets deep into the essence of the enterprise and its DNA – into what it is, what it does and what it prides itself on. It is then, that customer centricity becomes rooted in behaviour, shaping all subsequent priorities and actions both internally and in the marketplace.

It's just what people do.

Amazon is not a mystery and its success isn't about technology. Somehow Bezos has got customer centricity so deeply and unmistakenly embedded that it filters into everything everyone does, how they think, talk and behave.

Here is an extract of an e-mail sent to Amazon customers by employees, in lieu of the Olympics, which makes the point:

> *As London 2012 approaches, customers in parts of London may be preparing to make changes to their daily routine. We wanted to let you know about the steps we've taken at Amazon to ensure that your deliveries continue uninterrupted.*
>
> *We have worked closely with our carrier network to ensure that you receive your packages on time, from the moment the torch arrives in London on 16 July until the closure of the Olympic Park on 14 September. This includes residential and commercial addresses in or around the Olympic venues. The carriers delivering your Amazon orders have all planned for any disruption that the Olympic Road Network could cause. They're using a variety of different methods to ensure your usual delivery service continues including employing more staff, bicycle routes and foot deliveries, to name but a few.*
>
> *We're also pleased to let you know about a new way to receive your Amazon orders. There will be 25 automated Amazon Lockers situated at convenient locations like shopping centres, high street locations and some transport links. The Amazon Locker network is growing and will continue to be available even after the Games have finished, allowing you to choose where to*

have your Amazon order delivered – then you can collect at a time that's best for you.

Demystifying disruption

Disruption is a way of thinking, and a process of reshaping and reforming an organization that wants to change the rules by which success or failure are decided. As we have already discussed, it is not a product or a technology. These enable disruption. Customer-centric disruption only happens when a product or technology is used to change social and business practices, and create a new standard.

What is often forgotten is that when customer-centric leaders disrupt industries, in the process they invariably have to disrupt their own organizations in order to get from where they are to where they want to go.

Disruption stems from a crisis that some see and others don't. Something must be worth disrupting, because customers, and even the world, will be better off with the new way of doing things.

Disruption is not the exclusive domain of enterprises with deep pockets. Many of the greatest disruptions of our time have come about in garages by upstarts, who not only had an inspired idea, but also had the courage and format to oust the establishment.

Neither is it only for edgy entrepreneurs who enter a market, free of bureaucracy and baggage. Some of the finest customer-centric disruptions happen in mature companies, who successfully carry their legacy forward as they reinvent and remake themselves.

Disruption is not confined to technology and information-based organizations, though these components are integral to the success formula. And it is not only happening in rich countries – it is happening everywhere. And it is being used by locals to grow markets and mechanisms in their own countries, and by them and global enterprises to spread across the world.

And disruption doesn't just lower prices. Disruptors can operate at the high or low end of the market.

Finally, and perhaps most significantly, disruption is no longer a disruptor. It has become mainstream thinking in corporations, who want to be and stay future-fit.

What goes round can last

Customer centricity is a journey that has a beginning but no end. It starts when sufficient energy has been generated that impels the engine forward. Success will be felt throughout the process, as will failure, from which most executives will learn and encourage their staff to do the same. The first remodelling may have ended when the rewards are distributed, with enough investment to keep the momentum going inside and out. But then comes the next round.

The first time IBM went into a crisis, Lou Gerstner and his team breathed life back into it by going from just selling products to making services the heart of the business. Hurt but not hindered by the fact that increasing the quantity and enhancing the quality of PCs had not worked, but instead left companies frustrated and hopelessly out of pocket, IBM applied its remade power to disrupt itself. Reborn, next time round IBM didn't wait for a crisis before it took the courageous actions needed to push the enterprise yet further forward, which it continues to do, so customers can proactively use technology to meet and make smart futures.

Enterprises become programmed to creatively and constantly disrupt their own innovations or those of others in the quest to get ahead and stay ahead in a way that makes it difficult for others to catch up. And consistently, they create a desired future for themselves, for and with others, in a permanent state of innovation and reinvention.

The principles and template we have discussed hold for all enterprises, private and public, small or large, for profit or not for profit. Some, operating in relatively staid situations, may move more slowly; those in lightning-speed environments will have to work at a much more rapid pace. Some will struggle to open minds and doors; others will have an easier time of it. Some may find that the model fits as it is; others will have to adapt it.

Regardless of its unique situation, each enterprise will discover that, once it has successfully transformed itself, it needs to become resilient enough to adapt, easily renewing itself constantly, rather than undergoing radical reconstructions, in reaction to competitive threat or under severe pressure. Then the successes that ensue from getting customer centricity permanently imprinted into a culture are not just for the now. They are repeated over and over again, as the enterprise consciously and continuously refreshes itself, using a customer-centric compass in unknowable futures that it may even invent, with customers yet to come on-stream.

These successes play out on multiple fronts as no one wins alone, or at the expense of consumers, citizens, communities, cities, countries or the cosmos of which they are a part.

That's the ultimate object of customer centricity that lasts. The ability to unswervingly keep moving forward, with mindsets and mindsights that disrupt in big ways and small, to unveil futures, ahead of the game, to lock customers on, and the competition out.

Simply pumping more money into an old model that no longer works won't provide any organization with growth or help it regain lost ground.

Whatever the future holds for any of the examples discussed in this book, what every enterprise needs, is a model that is robust enough to enable it to continue to build on it, over and over again, in order to be enduringly successful. The customer-centric approach is such a model, because it has the power to transform and keep transforming.

What other option is there? The old models and mindsets are no longer working.

For those of you on the verge of taking up the challenge and beginning the breakthrough steps to customer centricity, Table 10.2 (overleaf) provides summary guidelines to help you on your way.

Table 10.2 Summary guideline sheet

Phase	Breakthrough	You know you have made it when…	Actions needed to get there include:	Implementation is driven forward because this:
1 (THE AWAKENING)	Create strategic discomfort and excitement	Enough of the correct people see and feel the urgent need to change	• Articulate the crises • Set new direction • Demystify numbers • Work through 'points of light' • Make disruption into an opportunity to add significant value	• Triggers discomfort and excitement • Raises levels of consciousness • Gets rational, emotional and social appeal • Instils passion and positive energy
	Reframe new beliefs	There is understanding on why and how customer centricity is different and more relevant to contemporary beliefs and models … and enduring	• Provides forum at high level • Embed beliefs as stimulators and guidelines for decision making • Show connection new beliefs to growth and performance	• Makes the case for customer centricity • Encourages new ground to be explored jointly • Aligns perspectives and spirit • Builds common language, principles and tools • Embeds higher purpose
2 (THE DISCOVERY)	Articulate the 'market space'	Agreement is reached on new competitive arena and how far to extend aspirations and boundaries	• Frame new 'market space' around customer outcome • Defines playing field • Express unified value cross-product - company and -industry • Cross-silo team makes educated hypothesis	• Makes the direction concrete and easy to communicate • Influences through involvement • Turns positive feelings to action • Is forward-thrusting • Links customer and mission
	Identify the value opportunities	People uncover specific value gaps and opportunities that become the potential for new wealth creation	• Choose lead markets • Use the customer activity cycle as organizing tool • Uncover gaps through unified customer experience • Define new value-add opportunities • Show role of silos	• Structured methodology boosts confidence and credibility • Takes ideas from the abstract to concrete • Packages unified customer concept • Builds traction for buy-in • Fosters creativity and imagination
3 (THE STORY)	Build a compelling case	A story unfolds and is told and sold around customers, and what needs to change and be done	• Build enterprise-wide picture around desired customer outcome • Mirror this in a new core purpose • Specify and scope the action plan	• Makes visual and cognitive impact • Embeds language and concepts in culture • Allows people to see where they fit • Gives the customer approach more meaning, relevance and take-up
	Size the prize	The numbers reveal growth and returns big enough to warrant the investment	• Motivate investment made on customer time value • Calculate total customer value (revenues up, costs down) • Anticipate social and environmental impact	• Stimulates confidence and trust • Attracts resources and budget • Lines up thinking and investments behind customer value • Give substance to story

Table 10.2 Continued

Phase	Breakthrough	You know you have made it when...	Actions needed to get there include:	Implementation is driven forward because this:
4 / THE ENGAGEMENT	Model the concept	Customers validate the concept and values and buy into getting it right	• Select relevant customers • Test and refine new value opportunities • Choose hot spots as entry points • Get proof of concept and early wins	• Provides the testimony that leads to heightened credibility and energy • Gets customers to influence others • Profiles successes and social proof that bolsters buy-in
	Get people working together	Silos and partners start to work jointly, becoming actively involved	• Involve customers, silos and partners in development and delivery • Demonstrate gains • Showcase and celebrate victories	• Makes silos work to same goals • Turns motivation to commitment • Grows familiarity and use of concepts • Develops new expertise and skills • Enhances customer experience and value
5 / THE REWARD	Reach critical mass	There is compounding take-up as the brand becomes contagious	• Invest in customer communities and engagement • Make brand contagious • Manage 'push/pull' energy rhythm • Internal marketing and communication	• Converts insiders and outsiders • Gets more partners and developers to join • Compounds demand through advocacy, public approval and sentiment
	Gather and sustain momentum	Rewards begin to be reaped with visible success and a lead that is sustainable	• Articulate rewards • Use cash flow to show progress and successes • Factor in intangible gains and new capital • Leverage know-how to stay ahead and expand • Leverage customer base	• Makes new concept the new standard • Shows connection customer centricity and performance • Hails and reinforces customer centricity and disruption • Attracts more investment • Provides platform for lasting success

REFERENCES

1　For more on the concept of shared wealth be it in mature or emerging markets, see S. Vandermerwe, 'The Transformation of Customer Focus: Lessons from Emerging Markets', *Innovative Marketing*, vol. 8 (2) 2012; M. Porter and M. R. Kramer, 'Creating Shared Value', *Harvard Business Review*, January–February 2011.

2　Statistics on failed implementation efforts from J. Kotter, 'Failed Strategy Execution Due to Oversight by Cooperate Boards?', 24 October 2012, http://www.forbes.com/sites/johnkotter/2012/10/24/failed-strategy-execution-oversight-by-corporate-boards; also for more reading, J. Kotter, 'Why Transformation Efforts Fail', *Harvard Business Review*, January 2007.

3　Further insights on reverse innovation from V. Govindsamy and C. Trimble, *Reverse Innovation: Create Far From Home, Win Everywhere*, Harvard Business School Publishing, Cambridge, MA, 2012.

4　This and all subsequent quotes by Angela Ahrendts from 'Burberry's CEO on Turning an Aging British Icon into a Global Luxury Brand', *Harvard Business Review*, January–February 2013. Another interesting read on Burberry's transformation in L. Burton and N. Pratley, 'Two Faces of Burberry', *The Guardian*, 15 April 2004.

5　Lego's view on different kinds of competitors in J. Riley, 'An Organic Growth Strategy Based on Innovation – Lego Powers Ahead', 22 February 2013, http://www.tutor2u.net/blog/index.php/business-studies/comments/an-organic-growth-strategy-based-on-innovation-lego-powers-ahead.

6　For case studies describing the early years of Amazon see for instance S. Vandermerwe and M. Taishoff, 'Amazon.com: Marketing the Go-Between-Service-Provider', European Case Clearing House, 1998; H. Mendelson and P. Meza: 'Amazon.com: Marching Toward Profitability', Graduate School of Business, Stanford University, 2001.

7　More on GE's initiative in China and India, see V. Govindarajan 'Reverse Innovation and the Myth of Cannibalization', April 2012 *Forbes Leadership Forum*, http://www.forbes.com/sites/forbesleadershipforum/2012/04/19/reverse-innovation-and-the-myth-of-cannibalization/. Also N. Musselwhite, 'Getting it Right at the Bottom of the Pyramid', http://www.geostrategypartners.com/GE%20Heathcare%20BOP%20Article.pdf.

8　C. Mui, 'How Kodak Failed: Unleashing the Killer Application and Billion Dollar Lessons', 1 August 2012, http://www.forbes.com/sites/

chunkamui/2012/01/18/how-kodak-failed/3/ provides insights into Kodak's oversight of the impact of digital technologies on its business model.

9 This and subsequent citations from Richard Branson in R. Branson, *Like a Virgin: Secrets They Won't Teach You at Business School*, Penguin, London, 2012.

10 For an interesting analysis of the history of IBM, and how the company has used that history to transform itself and move forward, see J. T. Seaman and G. D. Smith, 'Your Company's History as a Leadership Tool', *Harvard Business Review*, December 2012.

11 The *Harvard Business Review* information comes from M. T. Hansen, H. Ibarra and U. Peyer, 'The Best-Performing CEOs in the World', *Harvard Business Review*, January–February 2013. All other quotes for Amazon that are not separately referenced come from the following: K. Baldacci, '7 Customer Service Lessons from Amazon CEO Jeff Bezos', 10 June 2013; Jeff Bezos Q&A from *Business Week Online*'s Daily Briefing, The Free Library, 30 June 2013, http://www.thefreelibrary.com/Jeff+Bezos+Q%26A+From+Business+Week+Online's+Daily+Briefing.-a063064798; 'Inside Amazon's Idea Machine: How Bezos Decodes Customers', 4 April 2012, http://www.forbes.com/sites/georgeanders/2012/04/04/inside-amazon/; C. Salter, #9 Amazon, 10 February 2009, http://www.fastcompany.com/most-innovative-companies/2009/amazon; 'A Front Row Seat as Amazon Gets Serious', *New York Times*, 20 May 2001, http://blogs.salesforce.com/company/2013/06/jeff-bezos-lessons.html; R. Hof, 'Amazon.com: The Wild World of E-Commerce', *Business Week*, 14 December 1998.

12 The cost-cutting moves by the NHS, see S. Borland, 'GPs Told: Ration Cancer Scans', *Daily Mail*, 8 September 2011.

13 One of the numerous research pieces demonstrating the futility of price cutting for sustainable competitive success is M. E. Raynor and M. Ahmed, 'Three Rules for Making a Company Truly Great', *Harvard Business Review*, April 2013.

14 Gerstner quote in L. V. Gerstner, *Who Says Elephants Can't Dance? Inside IBM's Historic Turnaround*, HarperCollins, New York, 2009.

15 Interesting exposé on how disruptors operate and use data in S. Kaplan, *Leapfrogging: Harness the Power of Surprise for Business Breakthroughs*, Berrett-Koehler, San Francisco, 2012.

16 For more on Cemex see for instance J. Anderson, M. Kupp, S. Vandermerwe, 'Good Business Makes Poor Customers Good', *Business Strategy Review*, Winter November–December 2010; also the case study by T. London, 'Cemex's Patrimonio Hoy: At The Tipping Point?', Michigan Ross School of Business, 2006.

17 Steve Jobs quote in J. Markoff, 'Apple's Visionary Redefined Digital Age', *New York Times*, 5 October 2011, http://www.nytimes.com/2011/10/06/business/steve-jobs-of-apple-dies-at-56.html?pagewanted=all&_r=0.

18 On how some companies try to counter the 'nay sayers' and other points of resistance, see for example E. R. Kanter, 'Strategy as Improvisation Theory', *Sloan Management Review,* Winter 2002.

19 The impact of technology and big data on individuals and businesses is thoroughly discussed in E. Schmidt and J. Cohen, *The New Digital Age, Reshaping The Future of People, Nations and Business,* John Murray Publishers, London, 2013.

20 A great way to see the Tesco virtual store in action, and appreciate its unique customer benefits, is on video: 'Tesco Homeplus Virtual Subway store in South Korea', YouTube, http://www.youtube.com/watch?v=fGaVFRzTTP4. Also see J. Rayport, 'The Rise of Virtual Bricks and Mortars', *HBR Blog Network*, 22 May 2013.

21 The impact of digital technologies on consumer behaviour is discussed at length in D. Searls, *The Intention Economy*, Harvard Business School Publishing, Boston, MA, 2012.

22 Statistics on mistrust of and disenchantment with banks, especially amongst the young, in L. Bachelor, 'Millions Set to Switch Accounts as Study Finds Banks At Fault', http://www.theguardian.com/money/2013/apr/14/switch-banks-current-accounts. Also in 'A New Era of Customer Expectation: Global Consumer Banking Survey', Ernst and Young, 2011, 'Young More Likely to Switch Banks', *Financial Times*, 27 March 2013, http://www.ft.com/cms/s/0/af63d69e-954e-11e2-a4fa-00144feabdc0.html.

23 J. Kalan, 'Cashless in Kenya: A Mobile Money Experiment Using M-Pesa', http://www.wamda.com/2012/11/cashless-in-kenya-a-mobile-money-experiment-using-m-pesa; and 'What Makes a Successful Mobile Money Implementation? Learning's from M-PESA in Kenya and Tanzania', http://www.gsma.com/mobilefordevelopment/wp-content/uploads/2012/03/What-makes-a-successful-mobile-money-implementation.pdf.

24 OCBC's 'Frank' bank branding initiative discussed in D. Boumann and R. Tung, 'Challenges of Chinese Banking: The Complexity of Chinese Loyalty' *Marketing Magazine,* June 2012, http://www.marketing-mag.com.au/blogs/challenges-of-chinese-banking-the-complexity-of-chinese-loyalty-15261/#.UiQ_POEaJD8.

25 C. Gallo, 'Seven Customer Service Lessons I Learned In One Day With Richard Branson', http://www.forbes.com/sites/carminegallo/2013/05/09/seven-customer-service-lessons-i-learned-in-one-day-with-richard-branson-video/.

26 An interesting read comes from M. Schrage, *Who Do You Want Your Customers To Become?* Harvard Business School Publishing Corporation, Boston, MA, 2012.

27 B. Horowitz, 'Starbucks CEO Schultz on Digital Innovation', http://www.usatoday.com/story/money/business/2013/04/24/starbucks-howard-schultz-innovators/2047655/.

28 More on Casas Bahia's approach to lower income Brazilian customers in L. Costa and F. Fernandes, 'Successful Retail Innovation in Emerging Markets', Booz and Co. and Coca-Cola Retailing Research Council, 2006, http://www.booz.com/media/file/SuccessfulRetail InnovationinEmergingMarkets.pdf.

29 For Apple's innovations in retail store environments and experiences, see for instance L. Kahney, *Inside Steve's Brain: Business Lessons From Steve Jobs, The Man Who Saved Apple,* Atlantic Books, e-book edn, January 2010.

30 For further discussion of Burberry's innovative approach, see R. Arthur, 'Burberry's Personalizing New Collection With Embedded Digital Content', 17 February 2013, http://mashable.com/2013/02/17/burberry-rfid-chip/. For more on the 'art of the trench' see C. Parr, 'Social Media Leader: Burberry Top Luxury Brand on Facebook', http://pursuitist.com/social-media-leader-burberry-top-luxury-brand-on-facebook-socialmedia/.

31 Case study: 'Ocado Whets Customer Appetites through Tasty Content and Innovative Features on Google+', http://www.goevolve.co.uk/cms/wp-content/uploads/2012/09/ocado_casestudy.pdf.

32 The emergence of so-called humanistic values in the corporate and financial environment is a growing trend, sometimes called 'inclusive capitalism', 'sustainable capitalism' or 'conscious capitalism'. For an analysis of this trend and its implications on business in general, see for example J. Mackey and R. Sisodia, *Conscious Capitalism: Liberating the Heroic Spirit of Business*, Harvard Business School Publishing, Boston, MA, 2013.

33 M. E. Koltko-Rivera, 'Rediscovering the Latest Version of Maslow's Hierarchy of Needs', *Review Of General Psychology*, vol. 10 (4), December 2006.

34 For more on HealthStore's micro-pharmacy clinics and approach, see the case study by M. Fertig and H. Tzaras, 'What Works: HealthStore's Franchise Approach to Healthcare', *The World Resources Institute,* December 2005; also J. Anderson, M. Kupp and S. Vandermerwe, 'Good Business Makes Poor Customers Good', *Business Strategy Review*, Winter November–December 2010.

35 More on what is known as 'cause marketing' in P. Kotler, H. Karajaya and I. Setiawan, *Marketing 3.0: From Products to Customers to Human Spirit*, Wiley, New York, 2010.

36 The concept of 'market spaces' was coined by S. Vandermerwe in several publications, amongst them 'New Competitive Spaces: Jointly Investing in New Customer Logic', *Columbia Journal of World Business*, December 1996; *The 11th Commandment: Transforming to Own Customers,* John Wiley, London, 1996; *Customer Capitalism: The New Business Model of Increasing Returns in New 'Market Spaces'*, Nicholas Brealey Publishing, London, 1999.

37 Enthusiasm for driverless cars, including in the BRIC countries, discussed in P. Granger, 'Consumers Desire More Automated Automobiles, According to Cisco Study', 14 May 2013, http://newsroom.cisco.com/press-release-content?articleId=1184392&type=webcontent.

38 For data on M-PESA: 'Is it a Phone, Is it a Bank? Safaricom widens its Banking Services from Payments to Savings and Loans', 30 March 2013, http://www.economist.com/news/finance-and-economics/21574520-safaricom-widens-its-banking-services-payments-savings-and-loans-it.

39 For IBM SmartCities initiatives see 'IBM Helps City of Stockholm Reduce Road Traffic by 25% in One Month', http://www-03.ibm.com/press/us/en/pressrelease/19300.wss; N. Singer, 'Mission Control, Built for Cities', 3 March 2012, http://www.nytimes.com/2012/03/04/business/ibm-takes-smarter-cities-concept-to-rio-de-janeiro.html?pagewanted=all&_r=0; 'Mayors of The World May We Kindly Have 540 Words with You?', http://www.ibm.com/smarterplanet/global/files/us-en-us-cities-city leaders-wsj.pdf; 'How to Reinvent a City: Mayors Lessons from the Smarter Cities Challenge', IBM White Paper, 2013, http://smartercitieschallenge.org/executive_reports/IBM-SCC-How-to-Reinvent-a-City-Jan-2013-v2.pdf; and for 'Pennsylvania living laboratory' see, J. Bort, 'Pennsylvania Kills An IBM Contract That's 3 Years Late And $60 Million Over Budget', 3 August 2013, http://www.businessinsider.com/pennsylvania-kills-ibm-project-2013-8.

40 Growing acceptance by and usage of complementary medicine and naturopathy discussed in, amongst others, 'Alternative Medicine Industry: Market Research Reports, Statistics and Analysis', *The Report Linker*, http://www.reportlinker.com/ci02242/Alternative-Medicine.html; G. Bodeker and F. Kronenberg, 'A Public Health Agenda For Traditional Complementary and Alternative Medicine', *American Journal of Public Health*, October 2002.

41 The customer activity cycle as the tool and the foundation for implementing a customer-centric strategy was first postulated by S. Vandermerwe in 'Jumping into the Customer Activity Cycle', *Columbia Journal of World Business*, vol. 28 (2) 1993.

42 For an analysis of the frequently unexpected costs associated with expatriation of executives, see A. Vermeulen, 'Hidden Costs of Globalization', http://www.expatprep.com/library/the-hidden-costs-of-globalisation/.

43 The top- and bottom-line benefits of being in the customer's after sale, or 'post' phase, demonstrated in P. Baumgartner and R. Wise, 'Go Downstream: The New Profit Imperative In Manufacturing', *Harvard Business Review*, September–October 1999; M. Dennis and A. Kambil, 'Services Management: Building Profits after the Sale', *Accenture White Paper*, 2003; and J. Wright and T. Pugh, 'The Changing Landscape for After-Sale Service', *Frontline and Accenture Joint Publication*, 3 July 2003.

44 More on Amazon's recent growth strategies in A. Lashinsky, 'Amazon's Jeff Bezos: The Ultimate Disruptor', *Fortune*, 16 November 2012.

45 Amazon's move into the B2B knowledge-based services business model elaborated in the case study by S. Vandermerwe, M. Taishoff, 'Amazon Services Inc.: Using Knowledge to Drive Customer Growth Strategy', European Case Clearing House, 2004.

46 Some of the details on Capitec in this text come from H. Manson, 'Capitec's 6 P's of Marketing', April 2012, http://www.marklives.com/2012/04/capitecs-6-ps-of-marketing/#.UiRCP-EaJD8; and 'Annual Report 2013 – Capitec Bank', http://www.capitecbank.co.za/downloads/Intergrated_Annual_Report_2013.pdf. To view 'AskWhy' and car campaign video see 'Get Paid to Drive with Capitec Bank', Maties Marketing244, 15 September 2013.

47 M. Hattersley, 'The Managerial Art of Telling a Story', *Harvard Management Update*, January 1997.

48 The integral role of selling ideas to get buy-in during a transformation is based on research reported by S. Vandermerwe and S. Birley in 'The Corporate Entrepreneur: Leading Customer Transformation', *Long Range Planning*, vol. 30 (3), June 1997.

49 D. Kirkpatrick, 'The Future of IBM: Lou Gerstner Seems to have Pulled off a Miracle', *Fortune*, 18 February 2002.

50 For more on the role and impact of good storytelling in successful corporate transformations see R. McKee and B. Fryer, 'Storytelling That Moves People', *Harvard Business Review*, June 2003; P. Guber, *Tell to Win: Connect, Persuade, and Triumph With the Hidden Power of the Story*, Crown Business, New York, 2011.

51 Data on extent of preventable diseases and health disorders from 'Haelen Group Interview with CEO Julie Meek', *USA Today*, 21 January 2001.

52 On Starbucks' move into wellness drinks and into tea, as well as its overall new strategic directions reflecting evolving customer behaviour as well as quote see K. Nunes, 'Starbucks Is Redefining Brand Loyalty', 12 February 2013, *Food Business News*, http://www.foodbusiness news.net/Opinion/Keith%20Nunes/Starbucks%20is%20redefining%20brand%20loyalty.aspx?cck=1. Also see 'Starbucks Food, Tea Strategy Taking Shape', 18 June 2013, *Food Business News*, http://www.foodbusinessnews.net/Opinion/Keith%20Nunes/ Starbucks%20is%20redefining%20brand%20loyalty.aspx? cck=1; 'Global Coffee Giant Has New Growth Plans', January 2013, http://www.forbes.com/sites/walterloeb/2013/01/31/starbucks-global-coffee-giant-has-new-growth-plans/; 'Starbucks CEO Presents at 2013 Stanford C. Bernstein Strategic Decisions Conference' (Transcript), 29 May 2013, http://finance.yahoo.com/news/starbucks-ceo-presents-2013-sanford-183801144.html.

53 For some thoughts and perspectives on new accounting measures to better reflect the long-term value of intangible assets see J. Bughin and J. Manyika, 'Measuring the Full Impact Of Digital Capital', *McKinsey Quarterly*, July 2013; A. Kay, 'Baruch Lev on Intangible Assets – An Interview', *Knowledge Management*, 19 June 2001.

54 Jeff Bezos quote on investing in the Kindle see G. Anders, 'Inside Amazon's Idea Machine: How Bezos Decodes Customers', *Forbes Magazine,* 23 April 2012.

55 Economies of skill, sweep, stretch and spread consequent to customer lock-on elaborated upon in S.Vandermerwe, 'How Increasing Value to Customers Improves Business Results', *MIT Sloan Management Review,* vol. 42, Fall 2000.

56 Consumer faith in Virgin detailed in *Henley Centre's Report on Trust and the Media*, done for the UK Radio Authority Board, 2001.

57 Examples of digital innovations in the Turkish banking sector in B. Ensor, 'Banking Innovation in Turkey', 18 September 2012, http://blogs. forrester.com/benjamin_ensor/12-09-18-digital_banking_innovation_ in_turkey.

58 Data on relative ease of selling, once customers have locked-on, in A. Lawrence, 'Five Customer Retention Tips for Entrepreneurs', 11 January 2012, http://www.forbes.com/sites/alexlawrence/2012/11/01/ five-customer-retention-tips-for-entrepreneurs/.

59 For some of the different approaches to and accounting of customer lifetime net present value, see for instance J. Villanueva and D. M. Hanssens, 'Customer Equity: Measurement, Management and Research Opportunities', *Foundations and Trends in Marketing*, vol. 1 (1), 2007; S. Gupta, D. Lehman and J. Stuart, 'Valuing Customers', *Journal of Marketing Research*, vol. 41 February 2004; 'Research

Priorities, 2006–2008' Research Report, Cambridge, US, 2006; R. T. Rust, K. N. Lemon, V. A. Zeithami, 'Return on Marketing: Using Customer Equity to Focus Marketing Strategy' *Journal of Marketing*, vol. 68 (1) 2004; E. Ofek, 'Customer Profitability and Lifetime Value', *Harvard Business School Note*, 7 August 2002.

60 The first edition of Everett Rogers's *The Diffusion of Innovation* was published in 1962. The most recent edition was published in 2003 by Simon & Schuster, New York.

61 Quote from Paul Polman is from R. Barnes, 'Unilever's Paul Polman on Why "Advertising" Means Nothing to Him, Plus his Vision for Magic, not Metrics', 10 May 2012, http://www.marketingmagazine.co.uk/article/1130728/unilevers-paul-polman-why-advertising-means-nothing-him-plus-vision-magic-not-metrics.

62 Statistics for leakage: 'Mayors of The World May We Kindly Have 540 Words with You'?, http://www.ibm.com/smarterplanet/global/files/us-en-us-cities-city leaders-wsj.pdf.

63 Steve Jobs quote about being out-front, in L. Kahney, *Inside Steve's Brain: Business Lessons From Steve Jobs, The Man Who Saved Apple*, Atlantic Books, e-book edn, January 2010.

64 J. Yarow, 'This Is an Awesome and Inspiring Quote from Jeff Bezos on What it Takes to Make Invention Happen', *Business Insider*, 14 August 2013, http://www.businessinsider.com/jeff-bezos-on-how-innovation-happens-2013-8.

65 The various costs associated with restructuring, as well as low success rates of restructuring, from, amongst others, J. Clemmer, 'Overcoming the Abysmal Reorganizing and Restructuring Failure Rates', 31 May 2012, http://www.clemmergroup.com/blog/2012/05/31/overcoming-the-abysmal-reorganizing-and-restructuring-failure-rates/; G. Neilson, K. Martin and E. Powers, 'The Secrets to Successful Strategy Execution', *Harvard Business Review*, June 2008, http://hbr.org/2008/06/the-secrets-to-successful-strategy-execution/ar/1.

66 A. Herrin, 'The Employer of Choice: How Will Corporate Citizenship and Sustainable Shared Values Create a New Competitive Edge?', *Harvard Business Review*, August 2013.

67 See the article and video by A. Sharma, 'IBMers in India Go "Spot Fixing" to Help Clean up Bangalore', YouTube, 13 September 2012, http://citizenibm.com/2012/09/ibmers-in-india-go-%E2%80%9Cspot-fixing%E2%80%9D-to-help-clean-up-bangalore.html.

68 Figures and information on customers sharing phones, in G. Camner, C. Pulver and E. Sjoblom, 'What makes a Successful Mobile Money Implementation?: Learnings from M-PESA in Kenya and Tanzania', http://www.gsma.com/mobilefordevelopment/wp-content/uploads/

2012/03/What-makes-a-successful-mobile-money-implementation. pdf.

69 Sharing in Brazil, from thesis by A. M. Edward, 'Consorcios and Brazil's Consumer Credit Innovation', The Lauder Institute, University of Pennsylvania, April 2006, http://lauder.wharton.upenn.edu/pages/pdf/ student_thesis/Consorcios_and_Brazils_Consumer_Credit_Innovation.pdf.

70 Research on importance of getting to decision makers in B2B inter-actions, in L. Ramos, 'Live from Summit on Customer Engagement 2009', Sean Geehan's presentation, http://www.b2bmarketingpost. com/2009/10/20/live-from-summit-on-customer-engagement-2009/.

71 For GE and green managers in China, see A. Aston, 'How GE Became a Green Pioneer in China', 14 May 2009, http://www.business week.com/magazine/content/09_21/b4132043813447.htm; for Russian McDonald's example see K. P. Krishna, *Winning in Emerging Markets: A Road Map For Strategy and Execution*, Harvard Business Press, Boston, MA, 2010.

72 So said Peter Drucker in 'The Next Society: A Survey of the Near Future', *The Economist*, 3 November 2001.

73 'Collaborative Commerce: Compelling Benefits, Significant Obstacles', *Nervewire,* 2002, reported in study from the IBM Institute for Business Value, by J. McKinley, M. Badgett, W. Connor and M. Bowen, 'Building Customer Relationships Through Indirect Channels', 2003.

74 For Lego and Sony co-creation see J. Alabaster, 'Sony and Lego collaborating on toy research', 24 May 2013, http://www.computer-world.com/s/article/9239519/Sony_and_Lego-collaborating_on_toy_research; and for snack habits US see J. McClung, 'Starbucks To Sell Exclusive Danone Greek Yogurt in 2014', 24 July 2013, http://www. digitaljournal.com/article/355086.

75 'Why does Kenya Lead the World in Mobile Money?', 27 May 2013, http://www.economist.com/blogs/economist-explains/2013/05/ economist-explains-18; M. Mbiti and D. Weil, 'Mobile Banking: The Impact of M-PESA in Kenya', working paper 17129, National Bureau of Economic Research, Cambridge, MA, June 2011.

76 More on collaborating and co-inventing with communities and custom-ers to be found in F. Gouillart and D. Billings 'Community Powered Problem Solving', *Harvard Business Review,* 9 April 2013; B. Lee, *The Hidden Wealth Of Customers: Realizing the Untapped Value of your Most Important Asset*, Harvard Business Review Press, Boston, MA, 2012; D. Shiffman, *The Age Of Engage: Reinventing Marketing For Today's Connected, Collaborative, And Hyperinteractive Culture*, Hunt Street Press, CA, 2008.

77 Lego's use of customer communities and crowdsourcing, see Y. Antorini, A. Muniz and T. Askildser, 'Collaborating with Customer Communities: Lessons from the Lego Group', *MIT Sloan Management Review,* Spring 2012, vol 3 (3); J. Surowieckii, *The Wisdom of Crowds: Why the Many Are Smarter Than the Few and How Collective Wisdom Shapes Business, Economies, Societies and Nations,* Knopf Doubleday Publishing Group, 2005; 'Lego Success Built On Open Innovation', 13 June 2013, http://www.ideaconnection.com/open-innovation-success/ Lego-Success-Built-on-Open-Innovation-00258.html.

78 B. Lee, 'Guidelines for Cultivating Customer Altruism', *Harvard Business Review*, 3 May 2013.

79 More on lightning-speed conversions can be found in L. Downes and P. Nunes, 'Big Bang Disruption', *Harvard Business Review*, March 2013.

80 Article and video: L. Kaye, 'Lifebuoy Transforming Hand Washing Habits in India', 6 March 2013, http://www.triplepundit.com/2013/03/ unilever-lifebuoy-handwashing-habits-india/.

81 Statistics on customers turning to friends and family for advice on banks in 'The Customer Takes Control', Ernst and Young Global Consumer Banking Survey, 2012, http://www.ey.com/Publication/ vwLUAssets/Global_Consumer_Banking_Survey_2012_The customer_ takes_control/$FILE/Global_Consumer_Banking_Survey_2012.pdf.

82 For statistics on car buying and online see P. Granger, 'Consumers Desire More Automated Automobiles, According to Cisco Study', 14 May 2013, http://newsroom.cisco.com/press-release-content?articleId= 1184392&type=webcontent; for research on US and global online buying and information-seeking based on research by PricewaterhouseCoopers LLP, see T. Reuter, 'Most Shoppers Go Online to Research Products Before Buying in Stores', 30 March 2012, http://www.internet retailer.com/2012/03/30/most-shoppers-go-online-research-products.

83 I. Mas and A. Ng'weno, 'Three Keys to M-PESA's Success: Branding, Channel Management and Pricing', Bill and Melinda Gates Foundation, March 2012, http://www.gsma.com/mobilefordevelopment/wp-con- tent/uploads/2012/03/keystompesassuccess4jan69.pdf.

84 'IBM Helps City of Stockholm Reduce Road Traffic by 25% in One Month', http://www-03.ibm.com/press/us/en/pressrelease/19300.wss.

85 N. Bilton, 'Disruptions: How Driverless Cars Could Reshape Cities', 7 July 2013, http://bits.blogs.nytimes.com/2013/07/07/disruptions-how- driverless-cars-could-reshape-cities/.

86 Video and statistic on handwashing see: 'Hand-washing Behaviour Change', http://www.unilever.com/sustainable-living/healthandhy- giene/handwashing/handwashingbehaviourchange/index.aspx.

87 Lexis Nexis supplementary data in R. Mitchell, 'How LexisNexis Is Winning on the Web', 19 May 2009, http://www.strategy-business.com/article/li00125?pg=all; 'LexisNexis Customers Enhance Performance Through Smarter Sales Intelligence', May 2010, http://www.lexisnexis.com/bis-user-information/docs/LexisNexis_specific_Aberdeen_Analyst_Insights_report_focused_on_Sales_Intelligence.pdf.

88 N. Davey, 'Lessons from Marks & Spencer: How to Revitalize your Service Experience', 14 March 2013, http://www.mycustomer.com/topic/customer-experience/jo-moran-ms-how-overhaul-service-experience-one-britain-s-biggest-brands/1.

89 For instance, see W. Chan and R. Mauborgne, 'Tipping Point Leadership', *Harvard Business Review*, April 2003.

90 See-feel-change sequence concept is an expression from J. Kotter and D. Cohen, *The Heart of Change*, Harvard Business School Press, Cambridge, MA, 2002.

91 Apple as the largest holder of credit card data in the world, see T. Cook, 'Room to Grow', *Fortune*, 22 July 2013.

92 J. Little, 'GE & Investing in Environmental Technology', http://dailyreckoning.com/ge-investing-in-environmental-technology/.

93 M. Stabingas, 'Building A World Class Customer Experience', *Forrester Consumer Forum Magazine,* September 2003; and the presentation: 'The Evolution of amazon.com', at *Forrester Consumer Forum*, September 2003.

94 Using the Harry Potter series to get more customers onto the Amazon site, see S. Hansell, 'Amazon Reduces its Quarterly Loss', *New York Times,* 23 July 2003.

95 See for example A. Slywotzky and R. Wise, 'The Growth Crisis – And How to Escape It', *Harvard Business Review,* July 2002; and K. Funk, 'Sustainability and Performance', *Sloan Management Review*, Winter 2003.

96 Lev Baruch and Paul Zarowin made this point about accounting for intangibles in 'The Boundaries of Financial Reporting and How to Extend Them', *Journal of Accounting,* vol. 37 (2), Autumn 1999.

97 Amongst others see C. Scott, 'Measuring the Immeasurable: Capturing Intangibles Values', *Conference Keynote, Marketing and Public Relations International Committee of International Council of Museums*, 2011; K. E. Sveiby, 'Methods for Measuring Intangible Assets', 2010, http://www.sveiby.com/articles/IntangibleMethods.htm; J. Daum, *Intangible Assets and Value Creation*, John Wiley & Sons, London, 2003; J. Hand and L. Baruch, *Intangible Assets: Values, Measures, Risks*, Oxford University Press, New York, 2003; J. Ivey, 'Accounting for Knowledge', *Corporate Finance*, March 2002.

98 For interesting thoughts on 'free' pricing see W. D. Eggers and
    P. Macmillan, *The Solution Revolution: How Business, Government,
    and Social Enterprises are Teaming Up to Solve Society's Toughest
    Problems*, Harvard Business Review Press, Boston, MA, 2013.

99 For more on this thought see G. Hamel in *Leading the Revolution,*
    Harvard Business School Press, Cambridge, MA, 2000.

100 GE outcome from equipment, see R. More, 'Creating Profits from
    Integrated Product Service Strategies' May–June 2012 *Ivey Business
    Journal,* http://iveybusinessjournal.com/topics/leadership/creating-
    profits-from-integrated-product-service-strategies#.UiRKA
    OEaJD8\.

101 The Cemex Way, see R. Ramamurti and J. Singh, *Emerging
    Multinationals In Emerging Markets*, Cambridge University Press,
    reprinted 2012.

102 D. Kiron, 'How IBM Builds Vibrant Social Communities', *MIT Sloan
    Management Review*, June 2012.

103 J. Quinn, 'Virgin Money Boss: Free Banking Is a Myth', 25 August
    2012, http://www.telegraph.co.uk/finance/newsbysector/banksandfi-
    nance/9499068/Virgin-Money-boss-free-banking-is-a-myth.html.

104 The relative abundance of financial capital, see C. Christensen,
    'Forget the Mission-Statement: What's Your Mission Question?',
    http://www.fastcodesign.com/1672137/forget-the-mission-statement-
    whats-your-mission-question.

105 Unilever statistic from O. Balch, 'Measuring Social Performance is
    Difficult but Essential', 2 September 2011, http://www.theguardian.
    com/sustainable-business/blog/measuring-companies-social-
    impact-performance.

106 On efforts to adapt financial accounting standards see R. Blaug
    and R. Lekhi, 'Accounting For Intangible: Financial Reporting and
    Value Creation in the Knowledge Economy', The Work Foundation,
    2009; K. P. Jarboe, 'Measuring Intangibles', Alliance for Science
    and Technology Research in America, 2007; J. Daum, *Intangible
    Assets and Value Creation,* John Wiley & Sons, 2003; C. Holtham
    and R. Youngman, 'Measurement and Reporting of Intangibles:
    A European Policy Perspective', paper presented at the January
    2003 Intangibles Conference at McMaster University, Canada;
    OECD, *White Paper: Reporting on Intangible Assets,* Paris, 2002; and
    White Paper: New Measures for the New Economy, Paris, 2002.

107 R&D as a fixed investment and not an expense from: 'Changes to How
    the U.S Economy is Measured' *Department of Commerce Bureau
    of Economic Analysis*, 23 July 2013, http://blog.bea.gov/2013/07/23/
    gdp_changes/.

108 S. Penman, 'Accounting for Intangible Assets: There Is Also an Income Statement', *Occasional Paper Series, Columbia Business School*, May–June 2009.

109 Tangible and intangible components to company value in M. Scott, 'US Companies Urged to Put Natural Capital in Accounts', *Financial Times*, 24 June 2012, http://www.ft.com/cms/s/0/78e36030-b93f-11e1-b4d6-00144feabdc0.html#axzz2dLrXCwX3.

110 J. Blount, 'Top Firms Agree to Natural Capital Accounting', 12 June 2012, http://www.iol.co.za/scitech/science/environment/top-firms-agree-to-natural-capital-accounting-1.1324358.

111 Discussion about the evolving acceptance of the accounting notion of 'natural capital' in, amongst others: Bloomberg, 'Natural Capital Accounting to Change the Way Big Companies Do Business', *Economic Times*, 11 May 2013, http://articles.economictimes.indiatimes.com/2013-05-11/news/39186714_1_coca-cola-co-water-issues-most-water; J. Bonner, A. Grigg, S. Hime, G. Hewitt, R. Jackson and M. Kelley, 'Is Natural Capital a Material Issue?', Executive Summary, KPMG, http://kpmg.com/UK/en/IssuesAndInsights/ArticlesPublications/Documents/PDF/Tax/natural-capital-summary.pdf.

112 Further thoughts on lead and lag indicators in C. McChesney, S. Covey and J. Huling, *The Four Disciplines of Execution: Achieving your Wildly Important Goals*, Simon and Schuster, London, 2012.

113 Bezos quote is attributed to B. Graham, from S. Tibken, 'Amazon's Bezos Defends Heavy Investments in Prime, Kindle', 12 April 2013, http://news.cnet.com/8301-1023_3-57579272-93/amazons-bezos-defends-heavy-investments-in-prime-kindle/.

INDEX

Printed in Great Britain
by Amazon